Amy Tan

BELLA ADAMS

Manchester University Press

Manchester and New York

distributed exclusively in the USA by Palgrave

Published by Manchester University Press
Oxford Road, Manchester M13 9NR, UK
and Room 400, 175 Fifth Avenue, New York, NY 10010, USA
www.manchesteruniversitypress.co.uk

Distributed exclusively in the USA by
Palgrave, 175 Fifth Avenue, New York, NY 10010, USA

Distributed exclusively in Canada by
UBC Press, University of British Columbia, 2029 West Mall,
Vancouver, BC, Canada V6T 1Z2

British Library Cataloguing-in-Publication Data
A catalogue record for this book is available from the British Library

Library of Congress Cataloging-in-Publication Data applied for

ISBN 0 7190 6206 3 *hardback*
EAN 978 0 7190 6206 3
ISBN 0 7190 6207 1 *paperback*
EAN 978 0 7190 6207 0

First published 2005
14 13 12 11 10 09 08 07 06 05   10 9 8 7 6 5 4 3 2 1

Typeset in Aldus
by Koinonia, Manchester
Printed in Great Britain
by Bell & Bain Ltd, Glasgow

Contents

Series editor's foreword

Contemporary World Writers is an innovative series of authoritative introductions to a range of culturally diverse contemporary writers from outside Britain and the United States or from 'minority' backgrounds within Britain or the United States. In addition to providing comprehensive general introductions, books in the series also argue stimulating original theses, often but not always related to contemporary debates in post-colonial studies.

The series locates individual writers within their specific cultural contexts, while recognising that such contexts are themselves invariably a complex mixture of hybridised influences. It aims to counter tendencies to appropriate the writers discussed into the canon of English or American literature or to regard them as 'other'.

Each volume includes a chronology of the writer's life, an introductory section on formative contexts and intertexts, discussion of all the writer's major works, a bibliography of primary and secondary works and an index. Issues of racial, national and cultural identity are explored, as are gender and sexuality. Books in the series also examine writers' use of genre, particularly ways in which Western genres are adapted or subverted and 'traditional' local forms are reworked in a contemporary context.

Contemporary World Writers aims to bring together the theoretical impulse which currently dominates post-colonial studies and closely argued readings of particular authors' works, and by so doing to avoid the danger of appropriating the specifics of particular texts into the hegemony of totalising theories.

Acknowledgements

First of all I would like to thank John Thieme for his conscientious editing and general support during the preparation of this study. I am also indebted to Matthew Frost and his team at Manchester University Press, again for careful editing. As this study was originally part of my PhD thesis, undertaken at the University of Sunderland, I would like to express my appreciation to my Director of Studies, Stuart Sim, as well as to Patricia Waugh, Barry Lewis, Kathleen Kerr, Paul Smith, Tony Purvis and the theory reading group. I am also grateful to the editors and publishers of the following book and journal for their permission to reprint material (in chapters 2 and 3) that had previously appeared in a different form: 'Becoming Chinese? Racial Ambiguity in Amy Tan's *The Joy Luck Club*', in Teresa Hubel and Neil Brooks (eds.) *Literature and Racial Ambiguity* (Amsterdam, Rodopi, 2002); and, 'Representing History in Amy Tan's *The Kitchen God's Wife*', in *MELUS* 28.2 (Summer 2003). This same gratitude also extends to Robert Clark and *www.LitEncyc.com*. Finally, my special thanks as always go to Paul and to my family.

List of abbreviations

BSD	*The Bonesetter's Daughter*
HSS	*The Hundred Secret Senses*
JLC	*The Joy Luck Club*
KGW	*The Kitchen God's Wife*

Chronology

1952	Amy Ruth Tan born (19 February) Oakland, California. Daughter of John (an electrical engineer and a Baptist minister) and Daisy.
1967	Peter Tan, Amy's sixteen-year-old brother, dies of a brain tumour.
1968	John dies of a brain tumour. Daisy leaves California with Amy and her younger brother, John, and boards the SS *Rotterdam* to Holland, taking a train two weeks later to Karlsruhe, Germany. From here the family travel to Montreux, Switzerland.
1969	Graduates from the Institut Monte Rosa Internationale, Montreux, and the family return to the US. Continues her studies at Lichfield College, a Baptist institution in Oregon.
1970–74	Transfers from Lichfield College to San Jose City College and then to San Jose State University where she is awarded BA in English and linguistics and MA in linguistics.
1974	Marries Italian American Louis DeMattei, a tax attorney.
1976	Withdraws from PhD in linguistics at the University of Berkeley, California.
1976–81	Works as a language-development specialist for children with disabilities.
1978	Visits China with Daisy, and meets her three Chinese sisters, Yuhang, Jindo and Lijun, for the first time.
1981–87	Works as a freelance business writer.

1985	In therapy for workaholicism and starts reading and writing fiction. Joins the Squaw Valley Community of Writers. Publishes a short story, 'Endgame', in *FM Magazine* and *Seventeen*. Daisy suffers an apparent heart attack. Having thought her mother was dead, Tan vows to get to know her mother better, to listen to her stories and to write about her life. Sandra Dijkstra agrees to become her agent.
1987	Visits China. Dijkstra negotiates a $50,000 contract for *The Joy Luck Club* with G. P. Putnam's Sons.
1989	Publishes *The Joy Luck Club*, which is nominated for the National Book Award for Fiction, the National Book Critics Circle Award and the *Los Angeles Times* Book Prize. Receives three awards: the Commonwealth Club Award for fiction; the Bay Area Book Reviewers Award for best fiction; and the American Library Association's Best Book for young adults.
1991	Publishes *The Kitchen God's Wife*, which is nominated for Bay Area Book Reviewers Award.
1992	Publishes *The Moon Lady*.
1993	The film version of *The Joy Luck Club* is released.
1994	Publishes *The Chinese Siamese Cat*.
1995	Publishes *The Hundred Secret Senses*. Daisy diagnosed with Alzheimer's.
1996	Visits China with her husband on behalf of an American fundraising group. After a misunderstanding, Tan is banned from travelling to China, although she still contributes financially to various medical, educational and industrial programmes for Chinese and Tibetan groups.
1999	Daisy dies. Tan's editor-mentor-friend, Faith Sale, also dies. Guest editor for *The Best American Short Stories 1999*.
2001	Publishes *The Bonesetter's Daughter*, which is short-listed for the Orange Prize for fiction. Undergoes surgery, a laparoscopy, for a benign tumour on her adrenal gland.

2003   Publishes *The Opposite of Fate*, a collection of pre-
            viously published and unpublished essays. Awarded
            honorary doctorate by Simmons College, Boston.
            Diagnosed as suffering from Lyme disease.

Contexts and intertexts

THE figure of a quilt, 'a torn-up quilt',[1] no less, makes a good starting point for this study of Amy Tan's texts, as well as their contexts and intertexts. 'Quilt' overruns with all sorts of associations, particularly when used as a figure for writing – about other(ed) identities and experiences in, around and beyond North America. References to patchwork quilts and, moreover, to the process of quilt de/construction by women writers especially, often ethnic minority women writers in the US, as well as a good number of post-colonial writers, shift the terms of analysis away from assumptions of autonomy, homogeneity and finality so crucial to dominant American ideologies and by extension a world increasingly dominated by American imperialism. Their differences notwithstanding, these other(ed) texts are instead concerned with communality, heterogeneity and provisionality in forms as 'patchy' as the personal/political identities represented therein.[2] With its emphasis on 'text/tissue/weave',[3] the figure of a quilt, whether patched up or torn up, compels a reading of, in this case, *The Joy Luck Club* (1989), *The Kitchen God's Wife* (1991), *The Hundred Secret Senses* (1995) and *The Bonesetter's Daughter* (2001) responsive to these other(ed) concerns. Threading Tan's texts and others (contexts and intertexts) together, adding to the quilt, not mending it, this study responds to the 'tapestry'[4] of her literary writing vis-à-vis matters related to identity, history, reality and, most crucially, language.

Starting with this quilt figure, and maintaining its 'text/

tissue/weave' associations throughout *Amy Tan*, even in this first chapter, which, in some respects, questions most radically a 'textu-alist' approach by discussing the apparently extra-textual realm of contexts, what biographical material is available on Tan? As it happens, quite a lot, mainly in the form of interviews, as well as biographies compiled, for example, in CliffsNotes and 'in 48,291 websites and growing listed by Google for "Amy Tan"',[5] which is hardly surprising for a literary celebrity whose biography blurs the boundaries between fact and fiction. Aside from the point that biography is a generic category, as is history for that matter, Tan's life story is often regarded as an 'Amazing Adventure', with her 'phenomenal, nearly unimaginable' publishing career resembling a fairy story.[6] Blurring the fact/fiction opposition further, critics also discuss 'The "Luck" of Amy Tan', 'The Joy Luck Lady' and so on. Such blurring does make sense given Tan's tendency for semi-autobiography in both her fiction and non-fiction. Most recently, *The Opposite of Fate* (2003), a(n almost)[7] non-fictional text, usefully illustrates this semi-autobiographical style through its interweaving of personal anecdote, linguistic theory and literary/filmic/cultural criticism.

Born in 1952 in a working-class neighbourhood of Oakland and later moving to and around various Californian suburbs, Tan describes herself as 'the average baby boomer'. She elaborates: 'I have found that everything I do is right at the bulge. ... If I'm buying a VW ... a little dog ... a lot of women and people my age are doing the same thing.'[8] For Tan, the average baby-boomer woman is a consumer, owing to the improving economic conditions of middle-class Americans from the 1950s onwards. The position in this economy of Asian Americans, stereotyped as 'the model minority' somewhere between the race/class hierarchy of black and white, ensures that *some* Asian Americans have access to white middle-class opportunities in terms of education, employment and by implication consumption.[9] Some can buy a car, a dog or whatever, as long as it is the best; they 'expect the best and when [they] get it [they] worry that maybe [they] should have expected more, because it's all diminishing returns after a certain age' (*JLC*, 156). 'Only the usual worries about leaks and calories' (*BSD*, 307), again images connected to consumption, specifically an excessive feminine consumption, seem to concern the baby-boomer woman. How could her worries be anything but 'usual', let alone serious, given that she, like Tan and, indeed, the baby-boomer women in her texts are 'permitted to go to college, permitted to take a stab at a career or two along the way, given "free choice" to marry and have a family, given a "choice" to eventually do both, [making them] ... more or less free'?[10] Such worries do not seem serious, particularly when compared to those of other ethnic minority Americans. As Mitsuye Yamada observes, white Americans '"understood" the anger expressed by the Black and Chicanos and they "empathized" with the frustrations and sorrow expressed by the American Indian. But the Asian Americans??'[11]

Yes, 'the Asian Americans', an umbrella term coined in the late 1960s, the era of the minorities' and women's movements, 'to promote political solidarity and cultural nationalism' in the face of 'ignorance and prejudice. ... An Asian American collectivity' was, as Victor Bascara remarks, 'forged by racism'.[12] At worst, Chinese American history is marked by violation, segregation and, ultimately, exclusion from the US; and, at best, 'seemingly benign stereotypes ... see Chinese people from a limited – and limiting – perspective'.[13] Granted, the '"tradition" – symbolized by railroads [and] immigration exclusion',[14] 'wasn't [Tan's] background',[15] although it is still possible nevertheless to negotiate between a masculine working-class past and a feminine middle-class present. This negotiation is the focus of King-kok Cheung's essay, 'The Woman Warrior versus The Chinaman Pacific: Must a Chinese American Critic Choose between Feminism and Heroism?' Questioning this choice, she seeks 'to reclaim cultural traditions without getting bogged down in the mire of traditional constraints, to attack stereotypes without falling prey to their binary opposites'.[16]

In this respect, then, the Chinese American 'tradition', with its references to various forms of slavery[17] as far back as the nineteenth century, if not before,[18] although not obviously Tan's background, can provide a context for approaching her texts as they, like it, and, indeed, her, are part of a complex history of harmful stereotyping. From the racist 'yellow peril' stereotypes, which emerged from early colonial encounters with China, personified by the British as 'an old, crazy, first-rate Man of War'[19] and, later, by the Americans as 'a great, undifferentiated horde' out to 'conquer the white man's world if left unchecked',[20] reason enough it seems for white America to enslave and emasculate Chinese American men, to the sexist 'Dragon Lady, Susie Wong, and Passive Doll'[21] stereotype, an Orientalist version of the virgin/whore binary opposition: in this context, not one but two question marks about the history of Chinese American oppression is scandalous, to say the least.

Can the same be said about Tan, the average baby boomer left to contemplate the 'usual' feminine middle-class worries such as diminishing returns, leaks and calories? What about her 'Conflicts. Tragedies in life. … Difficulties. A mother who was depressed. A father and a brother who died. Being the only Chinese girl in school. Moving every year. Graduating from a private school in Switzerland among rich people and not being rich'?[22] Added to these difficulties are others: most recently, the death of her mother in 1999, and, following it, the revelation of child abuse,[23] as well as happier experiences, including a successful marriage to Italian American Louis DeMattei and, obviously, the phenomenal success of her fiction. Up to a point, Tan's successes support 'But the Asian Americans??' Beyond it, however, the personal conflicts, tragedies and difficulties she describes do simultaneously relate to a more impersonal history. For instance, the cancer that killed her father and brother, normally considered exterior to impersonal explanations, is, at least to Daisy Tan, an example of bad energy in the home. As Tan recalls, her mother 'called in the geomancers … and turned to ancient Chinese gods for help and protection'.[24]

Aside from Daisy's Chinese beliefs, other beliefs, overtly ideological/political beliefs about 'the Chinese American woman', whether native, immigrant or diasporic, do help to account for Tan's conflicts, tragedies and difficulties. After all, as Amy Ling remarks, the Chinese American woman is 'triply vulnerable …

as a Chinese in a Euro-American world, as a woman in a Chinese man's world, as a Chinese woman in a white man's world'.[25] This vulnerability is intensified by the 'factions' within Asian America(n Studies): 'us-versus-them' or the separatists versus the (so-called) assimilationists, who, if forced to use ethnic descriptors, consider themselves American writers. In writing America, of which Asian America is part, the latter claim the right and, for Tan, the responsibility 'to write whatever [they] want'. As she puts it, 'I claim that freedom', a freedom that other ethnic descriptors, including 'a Chinese-American writer, an ethnic writer, a minority writer, a Third World writer, a writer of color', limit in a context of 'ethnic correctness' that dictates 'what literature must do and mean and say' and, ultimately, 'tell people what to think'. Her 'attitude [is] that American litera-ture, if such a classification exists, should be more democratic than the color of your skin or whether rice or potatoes are served at your fictional dinner table', perhaps an easy attitude for a successful writer such as Tan to have.[26] Whether emphasis is placed on Tan's difficulties or successes, the fact remains, as she suggests here, that her contexts, as well as her texts and intertexts, cannot be understood apart from ideological/political questions.

In this context, then, 'the personal' is, as Shirley Geok-lin Lim argues, 'political … for Asian [and, presumably, Asian American] women'.[27] The fact that they focus on the personal, on relationships and the family, in addition to the usual worries about diminishing returns, leaks and calories, does not neces-sarily make them 'the least political, or the least oppressed, or the most polite'.[28] Again, to quote Lim: 'In the absence of political engagement in the world', an absence that is in itself political, 'they articulate political engagement of their most private encounters with the Male Other' or patriarchal ideology and, moreover, Orientalist ideology in terms of a complex 'colonization' that is at least double, if not triple.[29] Colonization thus understood is complicated further by the generational differences between Asian American women.

In Tan's texts (and contexts), for example, various colonial-isms are depicted, from Japan's imperialist encounters with

China – Suyuan Woo in *The Joy Luck Club* and Winnie Louie in *The Kitchen God's Wife* both flee the invading Japanese army during the Sino-Japanese War (1937–45) – to American neo-colonialism in the form of internal colonization, as it is represented by both generations in all of Tan's texts. The differences between immigrant working-class Chinese mothers and diasporic middle-class American(-born) daughters notwith-standing, both generations frequently describe experiences of displacement. In between cultures, their displacement takes various forms, from a Chinese mother's status as 'a Displaced Person' (*JLC*, 104) to an American-born daughter's concern: 'What if I blend in so well they think I'm one of them? ... What if they don't let me come back to the United States?', a superficial concern when articulated by Waverly Jong, especially as 'she', almost immediately, 'wants to be Chinese. It is so fashionable' (*JLC*, 253). Granted, Waverly's concern seems super-ficial, but it does nevertheless recall past immigration experiences, along with articulating present diasporic experiences.

Up to a point, Tan is like Waverly in as much as she too articulates a complex relationship with the Chinese mother(land). Tan may *now* value the Chinese mother(land), especially after Daisy apparently suffered a heart attack in the late 1980s. About this incident Tan says: 'I have lost her and I don't even know what I am losing. What were her dreams? What did she hope for me? What had she wanted to tell me all these years?'[30] Fortunately, Tan was able to ask Daisy these questions after she recovered, and the responses she received proved fundamental to her literary development.

> I ... decided I should envision a reader for the stories I would write. And the reader I decided upon was my mother. ... So with this reader in mind – and in fact she did read my early drafts – I began to write using all the Englishes I grew up with: the English I spoke to my mother, which for lack of a better term might be described as 'simple'; the English she used with me, which for lack of a better term might be described as 'broken'; my translation of her Chinese, which could certainly be described as 'watered

down'; and what I imagined to be her translation of her Chinese if she could speak in perfect English, her internal language.[31]

Before Daisy's 'heart attack', however, Tan undervalued the Chinese mother(land), a fact also relevant to her proclaimed 'averageness'. This proclamation forms a complex relationship with the ideological/political discourses of assimilationism and, its apparent opposite, tokenism, whereby 'yellow'[32] is assumed identical to and different from white respectively. In a number of interviews, Tan discusses her childhood efforts to assimilate into white America, not easy given that she was frequently the only Chinese girl in school. Average then meant 'whitening' her facial features, albeit unsuccessfully by pegging her nose, along with choosing the most desirable and readily available aspects of mainstream American culture, including convenience food, fashionable clothes and make-up. These choices and others, most crucially for a fiction writer perhaps, changing her undergraduate degree from medicine to English and linguistics, a doubly rebellious choice as both her mother (for economic reasons) and her teachers (for racist reasons) assumed that her 'true abilities lay in math and science',[33] were criticized because they did not strike a balance between 'American circumstances and Chinese character' (*JLC*, 254). It is also worth noting that the Tan household was religious, and the traditional Christian lifestyle promoted by her father, John Tan, a Baptist minister, did not indulge his wife's Chinese beliefs, let alone his daughter's desire for mainstream American culture.

'Averageness' also demanded the teenage Tan ignore, even assault her Chinese cultural background: 'There was shame and self-hate. … [W]hat happens in assimilation is that we deliberately end up choosing the American things – hot dogs and apple pie – and ignoring the Chinese offerings.'[34] In addition to self-shame, Tan was ashamed of her immigrant mother, describing their relationship as 'very rocky',[35] an understatement perhaps given recent revelations or, as Tan puts it, 'Confessions' about Daisy's 'emotional terrorism'.[36] Tan's shame primarily related to Daisy's Chinese behaviour, a point confirmed by her dread concerning 'what her mother would bring to her birthday party at school. Would it be an exotic Chinese dish that the other kids would make fun of?'[37] The fact that 'exotic' means non-convenience food draws attention to the fact that Tan's shame also related to class: 'Fresh vegetables are what poor people eat.'[38] Being almost completely assimilated into a middle-class Euro-American culture compelled Tan to judge her mother from the limited perspective of white classmates, white teachers and white people in general. 'In department stores, at banks, and at restaurants [people] did not take [Daisy] seriously, did not give her good service, pretended not to understand her, or even acted as if they could not hear.' Like them, Tan assumed that her mother's behaviour and 'her English reflected the quality of what she had to say. That is, because she expressed them imperfectly, her thoughts were imperfect.'[39]

Unlike her mother, Tan expressed things perfectly, achieving two degrees in English and linguistics from San Jose State University. She also enrolled on a doctoral programme, again in linguistics, this time at UC Berkeley, although she eventually gave up research after a close friend was murdered. Rather than simply confirming her 'averageness' in terms compatible with assimilationism, Tan's perfect American English gave rise to the apparently opposite effect. When working as a language specialist with children and adults with learning difficulties, Tan was assigned the token role of representative for ethnic minorities by the institutions involved in language development. Tokenism apparently privileges difference, not identity, between, in this case, 'yellow' and white. Compared to assimilationism, an ideology that, although still potent, is presently at issue, if only among liberals, for its none-too-subtle promotion of racist hierarchies, tokenism powerfully informs a multiculturalist ideology that apparently '"respects" the Other's identity'.[40] A 'model' for ethnic minorities in general, Tan was permitted to represent their interests in language development until, that is, she became a freelance business writer instead.

Discussing multiculturalism, Slavoj Žižek highlights its problems, insisting that it is 'a disavowed, inverted, self-referential form of racism, a "racism with a distance" ... the multiculturalist respect for the Other's specificity is the very form of asserting one's own superiority'.[41] Despite the progress in the US after 1960s consciousness raising, which in 'real' terms meant 'the eliminat[ion of] racial discrimination in the electoral process ... in public accommodations, in federally funded programs and activities, and ... in public and private employment' through the Civil Rights Act (1964), the Voting Rights Act (1965) and, crucially for Asian Americans, the Immigration Act (1965), racism persists, albeit more subtly via multiculturalism. In multicultural America, 'what it means to be Asian ... is reduced to mere ornamentation – sushi, Chinatown shops, and the Karate Kid – a series of colorful add-ins to sustain the myth of a pluralist society without fundamentally challenging its categories'.[42] The fact that these categories are fundamentally unchallenged is suggested not only by the persistence of 'chink, gook, chinaman' stereotypes, along with racially-motivated crimes, but also by 'Asian-hate' among white supremacists, 'average' Americans and officialdom.[43] Virtual reality participates too with websites such as 'AmyTanmustdie'.[44]

Not surprisingly, 'AmyTanmustdie' comes not from her being a language specialist and a business writer but a literary celebrity. Fifteen years of successful publishing – the four texts discussed here, as well as her movement into the popular genres of 'kid lit' and 'chick flick' – brings with it fame and fortune. Fame does have its drawbacks, however: dubious websites[45] and, more usually, a loss of privacy, which, recalling Tan's experience as a language specialist, again raises the problem of tokenism. It is worth emphasizing that she does not perform the token role of representative for 'the Chinese American' and 'sometimes all Asian culture'[46] uncritically. Frequently issuing disclaimers – 'I cannot give you much more than personal opinions'[47] and 'I cannot speak for other Chinese Americans, or for their families. Just for myself'[48] – Tan does nevertheless acknowledge her responsibility as a writer, also highlighting the responsibility of the reader vis-à-vis 'quote-unquote *multicultural*'[49] literature. In her words:

Placing on writers the responsibility to represent a culture is an onerous burden. Someone who writes fiction is not necessarily writing a depiction of any generalized group, they're writing a very specific story. There's also a danger in balkanizing literature, as if it should be read as sociology, or politics, or that it should answer questions like, 'What does *The Hundred Secret Senses* have to teach us about Chinese culture?' As opposed to treating it as literature – as a story, language, memory.[50]

The burden of representation, understood not in the aesthetic but the political sense of the term, elsewhere referred to as the 'information retrieval approach',[51] 'does something to literature, not just multicultural literature … turning [it] into very limited rhetoric'[52] by excluding '*literariness* … [that] literature is always also representation, creation, text'.[53] This exclusion is not only problematic for Tan but also for any literary writer, especially in light of the (Russian) formalist assertion that '"literariness" … is what makes a given work a literary work'.[54] Pushing formalism further, in a 'deconstructive' direction, literariness upsets the ideological assumption that a literary text reliably means and references. The fact that 'multicultural' literature is assumed reliable, rarely judged for its aesthetic qualities, only for its 'lessons outside literature, outside the pleasure of reading, outside the whole nature of story',[55] proves significant on an aesthetic and a political level. After all, 'Huck Finn is rarely studied in history classes as a novelistic representation of what life was like in the South before the Civil War'.[56]

So why then are Tan's texts assumed to offer reliable information about 'things Chinese', obscuring in the process their 'Americanness'? Is their representation of the US, including Asian America, obscured for ideologically suspect reasons? Do rigid racial categories prevent mainstream readers from seeing the complexity of Tan's representation of America, Chinese America and China? Complicated not only by memory but also by ideology, her representation of place is invariably mediated. It thus comes as something of a surprise that mainstream readers 'satisfy [their] curiosity about China'[57] when it is either remembered or imagined, with only one narrator in one chapter representing China in the present. Apart from Jing-mei 'June' Woo's 'A Pair of Tickets' (*JLC*), Tan's narrators tell their stories usually from their upmarket homes in the San Francisco Bay Area.

While the Chinese-born characters represent a remembered China, also focusing on the problems of striking a balance between 'American circumstances and Chinese character' (*JLC*, 254), the American-born characters, who are generally critical of 'Chinese character' for its 'wacky' (*HSS*, 17) belief in 'superstitious nonsense' (*BSD*, 40), tend to represent China in terms compatible with Orientalism. Furthermore, Chinese-born characters regard 'American character' in terms compatible with Occidentalism, typically viewing it as 'closed', 'lazy', 'morbid' (*JLC*, 41, 91, 103) and, as it happens, equally 'superstitious' (*HSS*, 218). Granted, 'American circumstances' or a capitalist democracy, *if* combined with 'Chinese character', are viewed in a better light: '*nengkan*, [the] ability to do anything [you] put your mind to' (*JLC*, 121) is consistent with the ideology of the American Dream. Here, then, two belief systems, one Chinese, the other American, both of them 'superstitious', are brought together for the practical purpose of material acquisition in a way that eschews Orientalist binary logic. Such practicality among the Chinese-born characters in particular is also discernible with regard to their spiritual belief systems.

For example, *The Joy Luck Club*'s Rose Hsu Jordan describes how her Chinese immigrant mother utilizes aspects of both Christian and Chinese belief systems in a chapter entitled, appropriately enough, 'Half and Half': 'As proof of her faith', begins Rose, 'my mother used to carry a small leatherette Bible when she went to the First Chinese Baptist Church every Sunday. But later, after my mother lost her faith in God, that leatherette Bible wound up wedged under a too-short table leg, a way for her to correct the imbalances of life. It's been there for over twenty years' (116). An-mei Hsu's apparent (mis)use of the Bible 'embodies the role of religion in the lives of [Tan's] characters as well as their attitude toward Christianity'. Patricia Marby Harrison continues: 'In *The Joy Luck Club* religion is adopted to the extent that it is useful or profitable for the characters. ... Christianity is not actually a *real* issue for these characters'[58] or, it seems, for Tan, whose sermon-writing father mainly influenced her *literary* development.[59] Presumably, 'real' Christianity, as opposed to the 'fake' (?) variety found in *The Joy Luck Club*, has its basis not in materiality but in spirituality. Aside from the fact that the material/spiritual binary opposition is problematized in various religions, including Buddhism (*KGW*, 39), Catholicism and Protestantism, Harrison's reading of Tan's representation of Christianity arguably overlooks An-mei's 'half-and-half' approach to two different belief systems, the point about 'imbalance' relating to geomancy, along with the continuing significance of the Bible in her life: 'My mother pretends the Bible isn't there. ... But I know she sees it. My mother is not the best housekeeper in the world, and after all these years the Bible is still clean white' (116). By using the Bible to correct the imbalance of a table and by extension life, An-mei undoes various binary oppositions, including materiality/spirituality, superstition/modern and China/America, formulating a belief system that exceeds notions of the 'real' and the 'fake'.

Whatever it comprises, a belief system has to be empowering. And, it is here that Tan's characters most obviously divide. This division is not necessarily between Chinese-born believers and American-born non-believers, with the latter looking to the former to show them the way to 'Truth'. If anything, the Chinese-born characters emphasize the importance of hope as a strategy for survival, even in the US where worries are only 'usual'. However it is achieved, a belief in hope is important in all of Tan's texts, from the first page of *The Joy Luck Club*, specifically the vignette about the swan, 'a creature that became more than what was hoped for' (17) to the last pages of *The Kitchen God's Wife*, *The Hundred Secret Senses*, *The Bonesetter's Daughter* and, for that matter, in her last text to date, *The Opposite of Fate*, which in 'A Note to the Reader' discusses 'one all encompassing thing: hope'.[60] Up until the last pages of the literary texts, many of Tan's American-born characters do not believe in hope, often because belief is associated in their minds with 'superstitious nonsense'.

In addition to the 'usual' worries about leaks and calories, Ruth Luyi Young, from *The Bonesetter's Daughter*, worries about which yoga class to attend. Here again is an example of the way in which Tan problematizes the distinction between east and west. While yoga is practised, albeit badly, by Ruth (23), suggesting that it, even in its nude form, is acceptable in multicultural America, along with sushi, Chinatown shops, the Karate Kid and so on, other non-western practices are seen as less acceptable to her and the other American-born characters. This is especially the case when they are practised and, more crucially perhaps, (apparently) believed by the Chinese-born characters. The American-born Ruth may do yoga, but she does not believe in its spiritual possibilities. She needs exercise, even if it is in a 'dangerous' environment where 'torture victim[s] … salut[e] a heathen god', only narrowly avoiding an attack by a 'nude yoga rapist' (24). Preoccupied with everything but spirituality, Ruth makes an interesting contrast to the Chinese-born characters in Tan's texts, all of whom apparently believe in 'superstitious nonsense' as a way of attracting and repelling good and bad fortune.

For instance, Ruth's mother follows an ancestral spirit's advice when deciding which stocks to buy, which films to watch, what food to prepare and so on (*BSD*, 68). Similarly, 'those who have died and now dwell in the World of Yin, ghosts who leave the mists' (3) advise Kwan Li in *The Hundred Secret Senses*. As well as ghosts, the topic of later chapters, astrology, the Five Elements and *feng shui* also affect fortunes. Hence, *The Joy Luck Club*'s Lindo Jong, 'a strong horse', 'born with enough wood, fire, water, and earth, [although] … deficient in metal', adds/removes metal in the form of gold jewellery to affect her fertility, along with the sex of her children (50, 63). Moreover, 'after the gold was removed from [her] body, [s]he felt lighter, more free. They say this is what happens if you lack metal. You begin to think as an independent person' (63). Also in *The Joy Luck Club* is Ying-ying St. Clair's implementation of *feng shui*: 'She whispered something in Chinese about "things not being balanced"', recalls her daughter. 'And then she started to move the larger pieces: the sofa, chairs, end tables, a Chinese scroll of a goldfish' (108).

These sorts of references, to ancestral spirits, Chinese astrology, the Five Elements, *feng shui* and, more generally, the idea that *'nothing* is an accident. ... Everything has a reason' (*KGW*, 29), add to the 'Chineseness' of Tan's texts. The function of Chinese additions such as these is debated by her critics. According to Sinkwan Cheng, for example, Chinese astrology 'caters to the popular racial prejudice that people from non-white cultures operate by animalistic instincts rather than intellect'.[61] Granted, *The Joy Luck Club* reinforces this prejudice when Lindo Jong is described as a Horse, 'destined to be obstinate and frank to the point of tactlessness' (167). What is worth bearing in mind, however, is that this description issues from Waverly Jong, a Rabbit, 'supposedly sensitive, with tendencies toward being thin-skinned and skittery at the first sign of criticism' (167). The 'supposedly' is important because, out of all of Tan's characters in *The Joy Luck Club*, Waverly seems the least sensitive. She could be described as think-skinned, easily dishing out insults, especially to Jing-mei 'June' Woo (204).

Here, then, the insensitive Waverly discusses her supposed instinctual animalistic tendency towards sensitivity, which in turn invites a more complex reading of Chinese astrology. If Chinese astrology does ratify popular racial prejudices, then does it not do so in an ironic way? If irony (and other tropes and figures) is involved, then does Cheng's argument about Tan's neo-racist representation of 'Chineseness' as governed by instinct, as well as larger forces such as the stars, the elements and *ch'i*, indeed, everything but intellect, not become problematic? Arguably, Tan's representation of Chinese beliefs moves in a complex way between literal and figural interpretations, this complexity underpinning the arguments presented throughout this study, with a fuller discussion of the literal/figural debate, specifically in relation to the ghostly 'World of Yin', coming later in the chapters on *The Hundred Secret Senses* and *The Bonesetter's Daughter*.

Another response to the sort of argument advocated by Cheng comes from Patricia L. Hamilton in '*Feng Shui*, Astrology and the Five Elements: Traditional Chinese Belief in Amy Tan's *The Joy Luck Club*'. In this essay, Hamilton argues that Tan's texts draw on these beliefs 'in order to shape character and conflict', and because they offer 'the possibility of choice and action in a world where paralysis is frequently a threat'.[62] While astrology does determine life, its 'complement',[63] the Five Elements, along with *feng shui*, allow determinism to be negotiated, reinforcing the belief, contra Cheng, that 'people have the power to affect their destiny'[64] by adding/removing elements and rearranging furniture. 'Chinese character' thus realized also tallies well with 'American circumstances': 'you could be anything you wanted to be in America' (*JLC*, 132), hardly a statement that assumes a fixed understanding of identity.

More often than not culture, as opposed to nature, 'fixes' Tan's characters. For instance, patriarchal ideology is repeatedly represented as perpetuating fixity, ensuring that women in both China and America are 'like stairs, one step after another, going up and down, but all going the same way' (*JLC*, 215). Images of confinement dominate Tan's texts, from imprisonment and institutionalization in *The Kitchen God's Wife* and *The Hundred Secret Senses* respectively to a general condition of invisibility or marginalization brought about not only by patriarchal ideology but also by war, racism and disease. Although Pearl Louie Brandt's multiple sclerosis is incurable, it is worth noting that her mother formulates this disease in larger terms, not in order to cure her daughter but only to give her hope. *The Kitchen God's Wife* ends with daughter and mother lighting incense to a goddess and an image of movement: 'Of course, it's only superstition, just for fun. But see how fast the smoke rises – oh, even faster when we laugh, lifting our hopes, higher and higher' (415).

Here, as before, superstition lends itself to more than a literal interpretation, reinforcing the point that Tan's representation of Chinese beliefs does not provide 'mere brushstrokes of local colour or authentic detail'.[65] 'Authentic detail' is most obviously compromised when, as two American-born daughters observe, their Chinese mothers formulate their 'own version[s] of organic chemistry', merging 'religion, medicine, and superstition ... with [their] own beliefs', sure in the conviction that '[e]verything has a reason' and, more crucially, '[e]verything could have been prevented' (JLC, 31; KGW, 29). Out of all Tan's Chinese born characters Kwan Li most memorably represents this hybrid approach to various belief systems: 'She bounces from topic to topic. ... Kwan believes in free speech, free association, free car-wash with fill'er up', allowing her not only to distinguish the superstitious from the 'real', (HSS, 18, 218), but also to sustain hope. Whether the things she believes are culturally authentic hardly seems to matter because, to her, 'the world is not a place but the vastness of the soul' (320).

A statement such as this may seem rather trite, particularly as Kwan undergoes electro-shock therapy for her belief in the ghostly 'World of Yin'. Clearly, beliefs do matter; they have repercussions, often harmful repercussions, suggesting that they cannot be divorced from the larger ideological/political context. In '"Sugar Sisterhood": The Amy Tan Phenomenon', Sau-ling Cynthia Wong discusses these repercussions, specifically in relation to Tan's (mis)representation of Chinese myth and Chinese language. According to her, these (mis)representations signal Tan's Orientalism, albeit a 'repackag[ed] Orientalism' that sustains itself through a complex relationship with dominant ideologies – western capitalism and first-world feminism.[66] Along with providing a useful intertext for discussing Tan's negotiation of Orientalist ideology, Wong's essay allows consideration of the ethico-epistemological implications of the Orientalist/counter-Orientalist debate.

The relationship between Tan's texts and dominant ideologies, if not 'downright erroneous'[67] discourses, gives Wong cause for concern, particularly as mainstream readers apparently take these texts as 'Truth'. Wong counters Tan's Orientalist errors systematically, beginning with a discussion of Chinese myth. In *The Joy Luck Club* reference is made to the Moon Festival, an event that involves a performance of the Moon Lady myth as it is remembered almost seventy years later by Ying-ying St. Clair, to which Wong responds:

> burning the Five Evils (68) and eating *zong zi* (73) ... actually belong to the *Duanwu* or 'Dragon-Boat' Festival on the fifth day of the fifth lunar month; the operatic version of the Moon Lady-Hou Yi story witnessed by Ying-ying includes a detail from another legend about another festival – the annual meeting of two star-crossed lovers on the seventh night of the seventh month (80).[68]

Wong is right to argue that *The Joy Luck Club* misrepresents a Chinese myth, with even the most basic details proving unreliable. According to mainstream mythologists, the Moon Lady did not steal a magic peach from the Master Archer, as Ying-ying declares, but 'a magic herb' *and* 'the pill of immortality' *and* 'the elixir of immortality made from the fruit of a tree that only flowered once every one thousand years'.[69]

How to account for such discrepancies? Are they generated by dramatic insertions, socio-political changes, memory lapses and the 'constantly moving turnstile'[70] of (mythical) language? Wong dispenses with these Barthesian interpretative possibilities, privileging in their place an explanation that formulates Tan's misrepresentation of a Chinese myth as Orientalist. Giving little time to artistic licence, that Tan makes things up, not always as carefully as she should,[71] Wong resists the notion that she is 'just writing fiction'.[72] Artistic licence is not even permitted of a fictional character, which is problematic given that Ying-ying's propensity for misrepresentation is openly discussed in *The Joy Luck Club*. Lena St. Clair remarks of her mother's narrative: 'I knew [it] was not true' (105). Misrepresentation is not contingent to Ying-ying, but essential to her development as a character. It concerns her to such an extent that she, in addition to being a repeatedly misrepresented character, serves as a kind of device for theorizing the issue of mythical misrepresentation.

More precisely, again to quote Lena: 'I knew my mother made up anything to warn me, to help me avoid some unknown danger' (105). Arguably, then, Ying-ying's dramatic insertions involve an ethical dimension, also possibly explaining her misrepresentation of a Chinese myth. Making a similar point, albeit with reference to politics, the mythologist Tao Tao Liu observes that '[s]hortly after the Communist Party took power they issued a new version of the Monkey story. ... It was interpreted as the rebellion of the humble and the weak against the powers of the establishment.'[73] Clearly, socio-political changes within China, along with the changes brought about by Chinese diaspora, feature significantly in the production of the Monkey story and by implication the Moon Lady myth. Liu also points out that the latter was mentioned 'in sources from ... the BC era'.[74] This ancient history, together with the fact that for Ying-ying the Moon Festival might as well be ancient history, occurring as it did almost seventy years earlier when she was just four years old, generates a further explanation for the erroneous rendering of the Moon Lady myth. However, a lapse in time does not adequately account for misrepresentation in Wong's opinion, particularly as '[i]n the minds of many older people, recollections of remote childhood events often surpass, in clarity and specificity, those of more proximate occurrences.'[75] As it happens, *The Joy Luck Club* does lend support to Wong on this point: 'But now that I [Ying-ying] am old, moving every year closer to the end of my life, I also feel closer to the beginning. And I remember everything that happened that day' (83).

At once reliable and unreliable regarding the Moon Lady myth and its accompanying festivities, *The Joy Luck Club* 'ceaselessly deconstructs is own narrative authority. ... Its governing rhetorical trope is the palinode, or the taking back of what is said'.[76] With rhetoric moving in this contradictory way, the decision about whether a myth is 'real' or 'fake' is made difficult, if not impossible. For this reason, a discrepancy of the fruit-herb-pill-elixir type is inevitable, particularly as 'the mythical concept ... has at its disposal an unlimited mass of signifiers'.[77] To discredit Tan for misrepresenting a Chinese myth is to overlook, whether explicitly or implicitly, 'the open character of the [mythical] concept; it is not at all an abstract, purified essence; it is a formless, unstable, nebulous condensation'.[78] Yet, Wong does precisely this when she overlooks the movement of a myth, not to mention 'The Moon Lady' and *The Joy Luck Club*, by making Tan a functionary for Orientalist ideology.

The fact that a discussion of myth inevitably involves a discussion of language provides Wong with a second reason for criticizing Tan: 'egregious mistranslation'[79] is especially problematic because mainstream readers apparently accept Tan's glossing as truth, with other linguistic mechanisms, including epideixis, italicized words and pidginized Chinese English, also serving to generate what Wong calls 'The Oriental Effect'. An effect of this kind uses 'broken' English gratuitously, developing neither plot nor character, but functioning instead to offer 'a reassuring affinity between the given work and American preconceptions about what the Orient is/should be'. Wong continues: this affinity happens 'in a discursive rather than referential dimension'.[80] This emphasis on the discursive is important because it underlines the point that Orientalist ideology has its basis in language, as opposed to nature. While Wong highlights the ways in which Tan's texts linguistically effect 'Chineseness', she seems unwilling to acknowledge how such an effect also de-naturalizes and, ultimately, undermines this ideological category.

Further, Wong observes that 'the same narrative detail may yield widely divergent readings – Orientalist, culturalist, essentialist, and ahistorical on the one hand, and counter-Orientalist, anticulturalist, constructionist, and historicist on the other'.[81] Following this insight about divergent readings, it proves difficult to make the claim that Tan's texts *are* Orientalist, unless, of course, as Wong claims, they are 'epistemologically unproblematized – in [her] view, [their] narrative modality is "declarative"'.[82] What she means by this is that they refrain from questioning the epistemological reliability of, in this case, the Chinese mother(land), effectively delineating the latter as 'locus of truth'.[83]

On one level, Tan's texts do concede that the Chinese 'mother [is] right' (JLC, 267), particularly when it comes to 'Genes, Generation, and Geospiritual (Be)Longings',[84] with both the setting and the timing of this concession by an American-born daughter, The Joy Luck Club's Jing-mei 'June' Woo, reinforcing the notion that the Chinese mother(land) is epistemologically reliable. In China and (almost) at the end of The Joy Luck Club, Jing-mei has a 'bloody' epiphany, as her mother rightly predicted: 'And now I also see what part of me is Chinese. It is so obvious. It is my family. It is in our blood. After all these years, it can finally be let go' (288). For Jing-mei, as for her mother, 'Chineseness' has its basis in blood. It seems, then, that 'Once you are born Chinese, you cannot help but feel and think Chinese' (267), apparently regardless of 'personal experience, political history, or place of residence'.[85] A similar pattern, whereby 'truths', often genealogical truths, are 'finally let go', is discernible in Tan's other texts. The endings of The Kitchen God's Wife (400) and The Bonesetter's Daughter (305) see two American-born daughters learning the truth from their Chinese mothers about their ancestral origins. In The Hundred Secret Senses an American-born relative, a half-sister this time, acknowledging that 'truth lies not in logic' (319), articulates a belief in the ghostly 'World of Yin'.

It is worth considering at this point for whom these 'truths' are true. Granted, Tan's characters typically formulate their identities in essentialist terms, most obviously when they proclaim that 'Chineseness' is in their 'blood' (JLC, 288) and 'bones' (JLC, 40; BSD, 304). However, proclamations such as these are not necessarily endorsed by the texts themselves, particularly because the latter complicate essentialism by repeatedly raising the issue of representation. A fuller discussion of this complication occurs in the chapters that follow, although, for now, three questions should hopefully suffice. First, how 'bloody' or 'bony' is a character's 'Chineseness' if it relies on textual forms, including photographs, to make it obvious (JLC and

IISS)? Second, how reliable are photographs, along with news-reels and eyewitness reports, when the events they depict are regarded, in some contexts, as heterogeneous to historical reality (*KGW*)? Third, what does 'It's in your bones' mean given that '*gu*', the Chinese word for 'bone', can also mean '"old," "gorge," … "thigh," "blind," "grain," "merchant" … [and] "character"' (*BSD*, 304)?

Formulated in response to Tan's texts, particularly the preoccupation therein with linguistic movement, these questions gesture towards an alternative reading of Tan's texts that does not regard them as epistemologically unproblematized. On one level, the Chinese mother(land) is represented as 'a locus of truth', if only for Tan's characters, who, at times, overvalue/ overdetermine its ability to 'right' their emotional, epistemolo-gical and ethico-political problems. At other times, however, this overvaluation/overdetermination of the Chinese mother(land) is ironically achieved, as some of Tan's American-born characters acknowledge. 'My big spiritual epiphany', which, significantly, happens in China, is, as Oliva Yee observes, 'a joke on me. And I can't even laugh about. How stupid I feel' (*HSS*, 264). On another level, then, the Chinese mother(land) as 'a locus of truth', although naturalized via references to 'blood' and 'bones', is linguistically and ideologically effected, and, as such, is liable to a de-naturalization.

As insightful as Wong is with respect to the part played by language in effecting 'Chineseness', an insightfulness that also seems to take into account divergent readings, she nevertheless approaches Tan's texts in terms of an inside/outside model of ideology critique. This critique makes possible reliable distinc-tions between representation and misrepresentation, translation and mistranslation, 'what is Chinese [and] what is not Chinese' (*JLC*, 203). These distinctions come into play when Wong argues that the removal of a veil *during* a Chinese wedding in *The Joy Luck Cub* is 'a suspiciously Western practice'.[86] Neither international alliances nor national variances, both of which could perhaps explain the untimely removal of the veil, are sufficient to problematize a final decision on Wong's part about the non-Chinese nature of this Chinese wedding. However, the issue here is less with *what* and more with *how* Wong decides Chinese/non-Chinese. By focusing on how a final decision is reached about veil lifting, if not Tan's texts in general, the ideological underpinnings of (Wong's) counter-Orientalist critique are made available.

Counter-Orientalism exploits 'the power of dichotomization as an epistemological weapon' by bringing about a reversal of the Orientalist hierarchy.[87] While not ineffective as a critique of ideology, this reversal demands analysis because it inadvertently reinforces the ideological categories that are most in need of questioning. For instance, Orientalist ideology perpetrates a binary opposition between east and west. This same opposition is taken on board when counter-Orientalists, many of whom are Chinese and Chinese American, proclaim their exteriority with respect to western(ized) Orientalism: 'Asian American critics are busily engaged in defining a canon dissociated as much as possible from Orientalist concerns'.[88] However qualified it is, dissociation from such concerns is not just impossible but uncritical too because it leaves unchallenged the Orientalist distinction that empowers these Asian American critics. Indeed, it hardly seems to matter whether 'the Orientalist ... makes the Orient speak' or the counter-Orientalist makes the Orientalist speak because in both cases the possibility of exteriority is taken for granted. Moreover, exteriority enables Orientalist and counter-Orientalist alike to 'render ... mysteries plain'.[89] The similarities between such seemingly asymmetrical ideological positions ensure that Orientalism persists even in confrontation with counter-Orientalism, making the latter an ultimately self-defeating project.

Counter-Orientalism is also problematic because it puts a stop to debate by uncritically essentializing identity and de-historicizing experience. Experience is de-historicized because self-critique on the part of western(ized) thinkers and, for that matter, counter-Orientalists is prohibited. In short, both groups are born into structure, one that is assumed impervious to historical (ideological) reality. Similarly, as Rey Chow comments, 'the moralistic charge of ... being "too Westernized" is devastating; it signals an attempt on the part of those who are specialists in ["her"] culture to demolish the only premises on which [she] can speak'.[90] Critical of all 'things western', these counter-Orientalists claim an ethico-epistemological privilege in order to marginalize western(ized) thinkers irrespective of what they have to say. The difficulties involved in making decisions about 'Chineseness' (and 'Americanness') are in this way marginalized without adequate attention to the fact that these difficulties need preserving because they ensure that a debate about ethnic essences has a future, as opposed to ending with stereotypical statements about 'the Chinese', 'the Chinese American' and 'the American'.

What is being proposed here, then, is not indecision, which is both elitist and impossible, but vigilance with respect to *how* decisions about ethnic essences are effected. Vigilance concerning how involves acknowledging both the inescapability and the instability of dominant ideological categories. The theorist often criticized for articulating the inescapability of Orientalism in particular is Edward W. Said: 'the Orient was not (and is not) a free subject of thought or action'.[91] Gayatri Chakravorty Spivak and Lisa Lowe also articulate, albeit in terms of deconstruction, the inescapability *and* the instability of dominant ideologies. All three theorists analyze 'representations *as representations*, not as "natural" depictions of the Orient. ... The things to look at are style, figures of speech, setting, narrative devices, ... *not* the correctness of the presentation nor its fidelity to some great original.'[92] What distinguishes Spivak and Lowe from Said is the fact that their respective analyses highlight the instability of style, figures of speech and narrative devices, of how representation involves a 'double session' that at once ratifies and resists ideological categories.[93]

Summarizing Spivak's argument about the double session or the two ways of representing, via proxy (*Vertretung*) and portrait (*Darstellung*), Donna Landry and Gerald MacLean note that 'mistaking the aesthetic or theatrical sense of representation – as re-staging or portraiture – for an actual being-in-the-other's-shoes ... leads to the fundamentalist mistake: assuming that always and imagined constituencies based on unstable identifications have literal referents: "the workers," "the women," "the word"' and, presumably, 'the Chinese' and 'the Chinese American'. 'But there is no *Vertretung* without *Darstellung*, without dissimulation', continue Landry and MacLean; 'the two terms are locked into complicity with one another',[94] with *Darstellung* ratifying *Vertretung* even as it resists it. From this perspective, an essence has to be strategic, as Lowe acknowledges in relation to 'Asian American':

> The concept of 'strategic essentialism' suggests that it is possible to utilize specific signifiers of ethnic identity, such as Asian American, for the purpose of contesting and disrupting discourses that exclude Asian Americans, while simultaneously revealing the internal contradictions and slippages of Asian American so as to insure that such essentialism will not be produced and proliferated by the very apparatuses we seek to disempower.[95]

In this respect, Said, Lowe and Spivak move away from what has typically occurred in Asian American studies: Orientalism versus counter-Orientalism, which all too easily degenerates into uncritical arguments about the 'real' versus the 'fake'. Binary oppositions like these characterize identity politics. Although identity politics is powerful, the essences produced in its name overlook difference, ultimately rendering 'the other' identical to 'the one'. A politics of difference, as Spivak and Lowe argue, utilizes essences strategically. It acknowledges that essences *have to* be formulated in relation to identity, but the fact that they have to be *formulated* at all ensures that these essences are liable to a deconstructive questioning. Deconstruction articulates a concern with difference, as well as unmasking the linguistic and ideological bases of identity. Arguably, Tan's texts participate in this unmasking because they problematize identification and discrimination that authoritatively appeal to nature and to essentialized notions of ethnicity and gender, including 'Chineseness' and 'the Chinese American woman'.

Following this argument, Tan's texts negotiate Orientalist

ideology in more complex ways than her counter-Orientalist critics are willing to admit. Granted, Tan's texts do promote a range of stereotypes, although they simultaneously unmask the linguistic and ideological underpinnings of these stereotypes. In short, they take back what is said, making 'saying' altogether more complex, if not ironic. As soon as Tan's characters say something essentialist, whether through an appeal to nature ('blood' and 'bones') or 'super-nature' (astrology, the Five Elements and *feng shui*), the texts take back what is said or, at least, draw attention to *how* it is said from a position that is not outside ideology. They are inside ideology, and inescapably so, although this does not mean that the ideologically suspect remarks therein are invulnerable to criticism. Rather than asserting that Tan's texts are Orientalist or, for that matter, counter-Orientalist because these apparently asymmetrical assertions both adhere to the inside/outside model of ideology critique, the former assuming Tan's critics are 'non-duped',[96] the latter, Tan's texts/ characters, the emphasis here is on negotiating Orientalist ideology critically by raising the issue of representation. A critique that responds to 'representations *as representations*, not as "natural" depictions of the Orient',[97] involves analyzing the contradictory movement of tropes and figures as they at once ratify and resist this naturalization.

The 'ethnic issues' that this chapter has heretofore discussed, if not privileged, are, as Tan puts it, 'just part of the tapestry. What I believe my books are about is relationships and family. I've had women come up to me and say they've felt the same way about their mothers, and they weren't immigrants.'[98] Commenting on this 'ethnic' privileging, she observes:

> The main issue seems to be the ethnic identity, and not the gender ones – and not even literary issues so much. ... I rarely get asked about my literary aspirations – what I intend to do with language, for example. I think that every writer who's serious has strong feelings about language – voice or story or the importance of narrative versus characterization. This is never asked of me.[99]

She may not be asked about gender, although many of her critics focus on the womanist/feminist issues in her texts, most obviously the mother–daughter relationship as it is affected by dominant ideologies, including patriarchal ideology, in both China and America. It is these issues that help to account for the popularity of her writing, and, '[e]ven if there had been no white buyers for *The Joy Luck Club* and *The Kitchen God's Wife'*, remarks Wong, 'there would still have been a readership for these books among Asian American women, many of whom are hungry for validation of their own experiences as daughters of immigrant mothers'.[100]

More about the gender issues and, with them, the literary issues, specifically Tan's literary influences,[101] which, as it happens, come together through the figure of Maxine Hong Kingston, as well as other 'multicultural' women writers including Isabel Allende, Louise Erdrich, Jamaica Kincaid, Toni Morrison and Alice Walker: 'When I think about the books that I started reading in 1985, when I was becoming interested in writing fiction', Tan recalls, an interest also pursued for therapeutic reasons, her psychiatrist inadvertently (?) reinforcing her depression, 'the authors I chose ... had really come out with different voices, and those voices were of different cultures often times.'[102] Dovetailing gender and ethnic issues here, Tan discusses how Erdrich's writing 'held particular resonance'. She was 'amazed by her [Erdrich's] voice. It was different and yet it seemed I could identify with the powerful images, the beautiful language and such moving stories.'[103] With Erdrich's complex interweaving of fact/fiction and realism/magic, an interweaving also achieved by Allende, Kincaid, Morrison and Walker, as they too negotiate a violent 'neocolonial' history,[104] typically as it affects women, Tan identified a model for her own writing.

As influential as this diverse group of writers is on Tan, it is with Kingston that she is usually compared, whether favourably or unfavourably. Similar in terms of ethnicity, gender and religion,[105] both Kingston and Tan created, in Ling's words, 'a furor[e] on the literary scene' with the publication of their first novels. Ling goes on to add that *The Joy Luck Club* is 'in parts an echo and a response and in parts a continuation and expansion' of *The Woman Warrior* (1976).[106] Indeed, it also coheres with the Chinese tradition of 'talk-story'[107]: 'Here is a story my mother told me, not when I was young, but recently, when I told her I also am a story-talker. The Beginning is hers, the ending, mine.'[108] For the Chinese mothers and the American-born daughters in both Kingston's and Tan's texts, and, arguably for Tan herself,[109] talk-story is 'a unique kind of semiotic system exemplifying different levels of female existence. These levels complement and contrast with one another to form a vigorous dialogic process of moulding femininity.'[110] Talk-story is not just intergenerational, but intertextual too, at least as it is understood here, 'beginning' with *The Woman Warrior* and 'ending' with *The Joy Luck Club*, if not *The Bonesetter's Daughter* in its echo, response, continuation and expansion of a mute(d) 'No Name Woman'[111] who communicates via 'hand-talk, face-talk, chalk-talk' and 'sand-writing' (4, 67), even after she commits suicide.

The reason why 'No Name Women' commit suicide in both Kingston's and Tan's texts (and contexts)[112] has much to do with an oppressive Chinese patriarchal culture, specifically the patriarchal institution of marriage, historically viewed in the west as 'a form of slavery'.[113] Out of all Tan's texts, *The Kitchen God's Wife* adheres most consistently to this view. Written in part as a response to Daisy's assertion to '[t]ell the world'[114] about her Chinese marriage to 'that bad man',[115] *The Kitchen God's Wife* represents Chinese marriage as a form of physical and psychological enslavement for women, whether mythical (the Kitchen God's wife), fictional (Winnie Louie) or, indeed, factual (Daisy). Aside from Winnie's husband, the monstrous Wen Fu, Tan's male characters generally function more marginally. For this and, more importantly, for her critique of patriarchy, in both China and America, Tan is situated in an Asian American feminist tradition that is critical of both Asian American literary studies and mainstream American feminism for their respective tendencies to marginalize gender and ethnicity issues. This marginalization ensures the continuing construction of Asian American women as, among other things, 'those little dolls sold in Chinatown tourist shops, heads bobbing up and down in complacent agreement to anything said!'[116]

With its emphasis on objectification and commodification, this particular stereotype can be traced back to the nineteenth century when the relatively small numbers of Chinese women permitted into the US were exoticized and/or eroticized as 'the exhibit'[117] and 'the prostitute'.[118] These different yet related figures of Chinese femininity circulated in popular and official discourses alike,[119] 'even' dominating twentieth-century Asian American Studies, which, as Sylvia Yanagisako argues, privileges a masculine working-class past that, if it takes Chinese women into account at all, focuses on 'the prostitutes who were the complement to the "bachelor society"', along with adhering to 'the ethnocentric definition of "family" as the "natural unit" of the conjugal (nuclear) family composed of husband, wife, and unmarried children who live under the same roof'.[120] Yanagisako instead 'transnationalizes' the family and, with it, Chinese American history, thereby allowing for the recovery of a diverse range of nineteenth-century 'ancestresses' (and ancestors), from prostitutes (and bachelors) to wives, mothers and sisters. Many of the latter facilitated the advent of the twentieth-century 'new woman',[121] a figure who more closely resembles the ancestresses in Tan's texts (and contexts).

Strictly speaking, the 'new woman' predates Tan's textual ancestresses, most of them, like Daisy, immigrating to the US just before the Communist takeover in 1949. This said they do exhibit 'new' traits. All work(ed) and, crucially, as far as their American-born daughters are concerned, all are powerful, so powerful in fact that the Chinese mothers in *The Joy Luck Club* especially are represented as a '*Mysterious Malignant Maternal Force*'.[122] Most notoriously, Waverly Jong says: 'I don't know if it's explicitly stated in the law, but you can't *ever* tell a Chinese mother to shut up. You could be charged as an accessory to your own murder' (173), hardly surprising for Lindo Jong, a Horse (167). Another Chinese mother, Ying-ying St. Clair, also discusses astrological empowerment. To her daughter, she is 'a small old lady. That is because she sees only with her outside eyes. She has no *chuming*, no inside knowing of things. If she had *chuming*, she would see a tiger lady. And she would have careful fear' (248). This 'fearful' relationship between Chinese mothers and American-born daughters preoccupies *The Joy Luck Club* and *The Bonesetter's Daughter*. In the interim, intergenerational/ intercultural relationships marked not so much by 'anger and cynicism' but 'careful ... polite[ness]' (*KGW*, 45, 82) and in *The Hundred Secret Senses* humour, constitute Tan's preoccupations. These differences aside, all four texts describe powerful Chinese mothers (and, in the case of *The Hundred Secret Senses*, a powerful Chinese mother substitute, as well as a powerful 'all-American' mother), reinforcing the argument that they '"wear the pants" at home'[123] and, sometimes, at work too.

It is worth noting that 'pant wearing' is not a transnational phenomenon, a point reinforced by the experiences of Tan's own ancestresses. Both her grandmother and her mother entered arranged marriages in keeping with Chinese feudal tradition. Tan's widowed grandmother, Gu Jingmei, was forced into concubinage by a rapist, eventually committing suicide presumably because, as *The Joy Luck Club*'s An-mei Hsu comments, her own mother having suffered a similar experience, 'That was China. That was what people did back then. They had no choice. They could not speak up. They could not run away. That was their fate. But now', she continues, 'they can do something else. ... I know this because I read this news in a magazine from China' (241). Tan's adulterous mother did something else, albeit the then criminal act of running away from her violent husband without a divorce certificate. 'Daisy was captured, raped and thrown into jail – her trial ... was covered in the Shanghai tabloids – before she ... was able to escape to California' where she married John, Tan's father, with whom she had a relationship while he was working for the US information services in China.[124] Running away to the US in 1949, just prior to the closure of the 'bamboo curtain', meant that Daisy lost contact with her three Chinese daughters, about whom Tan knew nothing until her teens when her father was dying in hospital. Daisy and all her daughters finally met up in China in 1978.

Although lost family members, including daughters (Wang Chwun Yu and Wang Chwun Hwa), sisters (Kwan Li) and mothers (Precious Auntie and, to some extent, LuLing Young) feature in all of Tan's texts, *The Kitchen God's Wife* covers Daisy's Chinese losses most closely.

The history that Tan recovers and represents in her texts lends support to the argument that Chinese marriage typically functioned to oppress women, often in ways that were compatible with slavery. Not even upper-class Chinese women like Jingmei and Daisy were in a position to articulate oppression apart from suicide and running away. It is this history of oppression and silence, represented by the figure of the passive doll, now in a Chinatown shop, that Tan inherits and, most significantly, resists through her texts. In so doing, she participates in a feminist rewriting of Chinese, Chinese American and American histories, transforming a legacy of silence and oppression into 'a legacy of strength'[125] by offering a challenge to ethnic and gender stereotypes enough to disrupt the pattern powerfully described in *The Joy Luck Club*: 'I was raised the Chinese way', recalls An-mei Hsu.

> I was taught to desire nothing, to swallow other people's misery, to eat my own bitterness. And even though I taught my daughter the opposite, still she came out the same way! Maybe because she was born to me and born a girl. And I was born to my mother and I was born a girl. All of us like stairs, one step after another, going up and down, but all going the same way. (215)

A description such as this is not without its critics, the most notorious being Frank Chin. Tan stands accused of 'male bashing' and, along with Kingston, of representing Chinese culture in stereotypical terms. According to him, both women represent 'misogyny [as] the only unifying moral imperative in ... Chinese civilization. All women are victims. America and Christianity represent freedom from Chinese civilization. In the Christian yin/yang of the dual personality/identity, Chinese evil and perversity is male. And the Americanized honorary white Chinese American is female.'[126] Combining gender, ethnic and religious ideologies here, Chin insists that they 'fake' all aspects of Chinese culture, including history, myth, literature, language and, most crucially for him, masculinity. Moreover, the popularity and by implication the profitability of their 'Ornamental Orientalia'[127] indicates to him that Kingston and by implication Tan are 'in bed with the white literary establishment … pander[ing] to the white tastes for feminist writing [and] … put[ting] out exotic visions, images, because whites find it romantic'.[128] For Chin, their relationships to white America(n racism) contributes to 'cultural extinction and behaviour modification',[129] a point apparently confirmed by their 'out-marriages'.

Chin claims to resist the genocidal logic of exoticized, romanticized and Orientalized misrepresentations of Chinese civilization generically via 'raging satires, polemic and slapstick comedies'. For him, (semi-)autobiography, the form employed by both Kingston and Tan, is passive, whereas satires and comedies are active, if not aggressive: 'the fighter writer uses literary forms as weapons of war'.[130] Genres that rage enable a representation of Chinese masculinity/culture – the two terms are synonymous for Chin – that is not feminine but heroic, exhibiting 'aggressiveness, creativity, individuality, just being taken seriously'.[131] As critical as Chin is of the 'fake' Kingston and Tan, he does not occupy a 'real' position outside dominant ideologies because his hero is at once sexist and heterosexist: 'the homophobia … is intimately bound up with the misogyny, for by disparaging the feminine, [Chin] denigrate[s] not only women but also men who are in some way "feminine"'.[132]

Along with advancing a limited politics, Chin understands aesthetics in limited terms. Genres are not liable to his rigid ideological/political categorization. Indeed, how radical are his satires and comedies given that they objectify Chinese women as sex, animal, object and, indeed, anything that renders them less than human?[133] Similarly, how reactionary is autobiography, 'the form of perpetual self-contempt and … self-hatred', to continue quoting Chin, with its 'oozings of viscous putrescence and luminous radiant guilt'[134] given that '[f]or women of Chinese ancestry … writing is not only an act of self-assertion but an act of defiance against the weight of historical and societal injunctions'?[135] Moreover, Chin's proclamation about autobiographical writing passively reproducing identity, while relevant to 'older notions of autobiography as a genre constrained by truth and history, one that is a process of simple transcription, the faithful replication of a "self" presumed to exist prior to writing',[136] overlooks more recent insights about autobiographical writing actively producing identity. Whether assertive, defiant or productive, the writing/written 'self' complicates Chin's active/passive binary opposition.

With respect to 'Kingston's autobiographical act, far from betokening submission, as Chin believes, [it] turns the self into a "heroine" and is in a sense an act of "revenge" ... against both the Chinese and the white cultures that undermine her self-esteem'.[137] The apparently opposite dilemma affects Tan's semi-autobiographical act because she is often over-esteemed via a tokenism that calls on her to become a representative for Chinese America, if not for all ethnic minority groups in the US. Tan's references to the personal potentially resist an assimilationism by which all others are rendered identical. For both writers, then, semi-autobiography enables a questioning of stereotypical representations of Chinese American women, as perpetuated by Chinese, Chinese American and American cultures.

The insight that representation is ultimately unreliable regarding meaning and reference is a main preoccupation for both Kingston and Tan. In their critical texts, for example, they blatantly resist efforts by mainstream readers to imagine 'multicultural' literature only in terms of 'information retrieval' or ethnography. This information is judged reliable and by implication real if it adheres to the fantasy of the 'exotic-inscrutable-mysterious-oriental'.[138] Kingston makes explicit her response to mis-readings of *The Woman Warrior* by resisting the fantastic ideology of Orientalism, as well as the realist ideology of ethnography: 'No. No. No. Don't you hear the American slang? ... I am not writing history or sociology.'[139] Tan is also critical of mainstream readers who approach 'multicultural' literature purely for 'role models, cultural explanation, historical point of view'.[140] By itself, a realist ideology leaves unacknowledged the literary dimension of her texts, effectively rewriting figure as ethnographic fact in keeping with dominant ideologies.

Any response to 'multicultural' literature that takes for granted the possibility of reliability regarding meaning and reference, including ethnography and, for that matter, Orientalism, is further problematized by Kingston and Tan's literary texts, which use 'postmodern techniques ... such as deconstruction, mimicry, and parody'.[141] These techniques are not inherently meaningful, owing to the fact that postmodernism responds to the aporetic condition of postmodernity. Such a condition resists all efforts at reconciliation, not least because totalizing narratives made in the name of 'Truth' generate 'terror. ... We have paid a high enough price for the nostalgia of the whole and the one, for the reconciliation of the concept and the sensible, of the transparent and the communicable experience',[142] as ethnic minority Americans understand only too well. No less 'fascistic' than this 'nostalgia of the one' is the apparently asymmetrical 'nostalgia of the other', or, as Tan calls it, 'ethnic correctness' whereby 'ethnic authority [is] invoked ... as a new and more insidious form of censorship', involving all sorts of prohibitions with regard to both aesthetic and political representation.[143]

Apart from generating ethico-political problems, the assumption of a reliable meaning is epistemologically problematic. To overlook the way in which literature resists such an assumption even as it ratifies it, and, moreover, to announce that it means this or that, is to adhere to an ideological understanding of literary language. For Tan, this ideologization is antithetical to literature, effectively reducing its questions to answers, if not the final answer consistent with propaganda that 'tells you how to think', as opposed to 'mak[ing] you think'.[144] The finality of this answer, as opposed to the answers themselves, as they are strictly speaking unavoidable, engenders difficulties not only for Tan's texts and intertexts but also for a radical critique of dominant ideologies.

Given that Tan's contexts and intertexts are so bound up with language – she grew up with different Englishes; studied English and linguistics; worked with language in various careers; loves[145] and worries[146] about language; writes about language; identifies with writers with different voices; and, includes in her list of favourite books 'any unabridged dictionary'[147] – and her literary texts promote insights about the linguistic and ideological underpinnings of identity, history and reality, make it difficult to overlook language-related issues when reading *The Joy Luck Club*, *The Kitchen God's Wife* and *The Hundred Secret Senses*. Even when reading *The Bonesetter's Daughter*, 'her most autobiographical novel to date',[148] it proves difficult to overlook the fact that this text represents different theories of writing via an array of characters, all of whom are connected to writing in one way or another.

Clearly, then, language is a crucial theme in these texts. For these reasons, the following chapters all privilege the 'text/tissue/weave' of Tan's writing. By responding to the way in which tropes and figures complicate the representation of identity, history, reality and, for that matter, Tan's texts themselves, this study treats the latter 'as literature – as a story, language, memory', not presuming to offer answers to questions like, 'What do [Tan's texts] teach us about Chinese culture?'[149] If they do teach us anything at all, they teach us about writing and reading, specifically about how literary language holds few guarantees with regard to meaning and reference apart from ideology. Throughout this study, then, the emphasis is on *how*, as opposed to what: how is culture represented and, moreover, how is this represented culture read?

The Joy Luck Club

A phenomenally successful text that can just as easily be found at an American airport news-stand as at a Hong Kong university bookshop, *The Joy Luck Club* (1989) invites a whole host of readings, some emotive, others critical. While its gender-specific content makes it popular among women, particularly baby-boomer women, as well as their daughters, 'men', in general, 'can't get on with it'[1] because of its apparent 'sweet[ness]',[2] all the talk of female relationships and feminist/womanist issues. Placing Amy Tan alongside Charlotte Brontë, the British writer Nicci Gerrard argues that *The Joy Luck Club*, like one of Tan's favourite books, *Jane Eyre*, 'a masterclass in what women want from fiction', also has 'everything', from 'empathy', with the first-person narratives by three Chinese mothers and four American-born daughters 'draw[ing] us in close', to 'a narrative that takes us from loss to gain, desire to fulfilment, loneliness to community. ... It has a happy sad ending, the kind of sweet melancholy ever after we want and can't get from real life.'[3]

As fairy tale, 'family romance' and 'chick lit', the latter postfeminist genre necessitating the representation of the mother, not the father, and, in a 'multicultural' turn, the Chinese mother(land), *The Joy Luck Club* does come across as a fairly formulaic text. The vignettes introducing each of the text's four parts affirm a narrative that moves from language-induced 'loneliness' between Mandarin-speaking 'Swan-Feather Mothers' and English-speaking 'Coca-Cola Daughters',[4] to 'community', whereby these two generations of women form through 'translation' better relationships consistent with 'joy luck'.[5] It is no coincidence that the last two vignettes see Chinese mothers teaching their American-born daughters about how to *multiply [their] peach-blossom luck'* and *'to lose [their] innocence, but not hope. How to laugh forever'* (147, 213). Tan's text thus seems 'to end … on a happy note' (25) despite all the earlier generational disputes over language and culture. Presumably, it is for this reason that *The Joy Luck Club* invokes 'a strong sense of personal connection'[6] among women in the UK, the US, Hong Kong and, presumably, in the twenty or so countries it appears in translation.

While the emotional draw of *The Joy Luck Club* is powerful, the text does nevertheless draw us in critically through its promotion of a 'Nabokovian' reading. For Tan, Vladimir Nabokov's *Lolita*, its language, imagery, wit, allusions, parody, prosody and so on, constitutes 'the clichéd litmus test of literature'. His 'Nabokovian revenge' on certain readers also receives Tan's approval.[7] Resistant to romanticized readings of literary language, Nabokov emphasized its formal dimension, responding with more than Tan's 'Hmm'[8] to those intent on reading for 'the infantile purpose of identifying oneself with the characters, and … for the adolescent purpose of indulging generalization'.[9] Similarly, Tan's 'Hmm' invites a reading of *The Joy Luck Club* that does not envisage it wholly as a 'sweet' recognition novel about the 'happy sad' relationships between Chinese mothers and American-born daughters. This 'sweetness' is further undermined by Tan's general 'pragmatism' with regard to so-called romantic/symbolic 'authentic details', particularly of Chinese food: 'The way I figure it, if I order prawns and sablefish and sesame-seed dumplings in a restaurant and the next day I write about these dishes, that food bill becomes tax-deductible as necessary research.'[10]

Problematizing generic, never mind ideological/political categories, the novel (or, more precisely, 'the short story cycle', a 'hybrid'[11] of both forms), is closer to difficult, even 'dark',[12] than to 'sweet', attributes arguably associated with postmodernism. Most obviously, *The Joy Luck Club*'s multiple micronarratives from seven narrators who between them tell sixteen different stories that upset traditional temporal, spatial and formal categories make it postmodern. More upsetting still *perhaps* are the postmodern insights it affords about the de/constructed nature of identity and the impossibility of becoming one with the (m)other(land). Whether it is between one/other, daughter/ mother, American/China, life/death, image/referent or reader/ text, difference is necessarily preserved and no amount of romantic ideologizing on the part of the narrators therein and, indeed, Tan's readers, can conceal this 'dark' condition of postmodernity. And, how could it given that *The Joy Luck Club* negotiates the issue of representation, both political and aesthetic?

This question draws attention to a main preoccupation of this chapter: representation by, for and about the other. Not only do the narrators understand themselves and each other in representation, negotiating dominant ethnic/gender representations with varying degrees of self-reflexivity, which, in turn, allows a different slant on the much discussed topic of matrilineality. For example, Chinese mothers and American-born daughters (mis)represent each other throughout *The Joy Luck Club*, often in accordance with dominant ideologies, a situation not helped by English questions, Chinese answers and confusions of the Taiyuan-Taiwan type (34, 183). It is also the case that *The Joy Luck Club* promotes insights about 'subaltern representation'. By having so many traditionally subalternized women speak for themselves and, in speaking, contest harmful stereotypes of 'the Chinese American woman', the text acknowledges the benefits of 'subaltern representation'. On this count, then, it seems to endorse 'an essentialist, utopian politics' that 'restore[s]', in Gayatri Chakravorty Spivak's words, 'the category of the sovereign subject within the theory that seems most to question it'.[13] But is this what happens in *The Joy Luck Club* when it *also* articulates two related reservations about 'subaltern representation'? Both are usefully articulated by Spivak: 'it is not a solution, the idea of the disenfranchised speaking for themselves'[14] because simply changing speakers, although empowering up to a point, ultimately constitutes an asymmetric exchange since the disenfranchized merely appropriate the category of the sovereign subject apparently relinquished by the Self. This 'persistent constitution of Other as the Self's shadow', she insists, 'will, in the long run, cohere with the work of imperialist subject-constitution, mingling epistemic violence with the advancement of leaning and civilization. And the subaltern woman will be as mute as ever.'[15]

The Joy Luck Club draws attention to the complexity of 'subaltern representation', along with strategically negotiating, in Spivak's terms, 'the double session of representation'[16] or the two ways of representing via proxy (*Vertretung*) and portrait (*Darstellung*). Out of all of Tan's narrators, Jing-mei 'June' Woo engages this double session most profoundly, acknowledging what speaking for and about the other, in this case, her recently deceased Chinese mother, involves: 'how [can] someone like me take my mother's place[?]; and, 'What will I say? What can I tell them about my mother? I don't know anything. She was my mother' (27, 40). *The Joy Luck Club*'s response to these questions gestures towards a reciprocal relationship not only between the Woos but also between reader/text and, more generally still, one/other. A reciprocal relationship compels an affirmation of difference in terms other than a mere appropriation, as Jing-mei's narrative in particular highlights.

Perhaps this constitutes a 'sweet' reading of *The Joy Luck Club*, but it is worth bearing in mind the 'darker side' of those readings that understand the text wholly in terms of reconciliation. The latter marginalize the not so sweet side of the text, all the ideologically suspect remarks made by the narrators and, more importantly, the Woos' situation, which, more dramatically than the other mother–daughter relationships, highlights what Tan refers to as the 'double jeopardy' of this relationship, of how the two generations 'could both help … and hurt' each other.[17] They also marginalize the text's complexity regarding the issue of representation, of how essences *have to* be represented, but the fact that they have to be *represented* at all ensures that these essences are liable to a deconstructive questioning.

Before discussing the 'margins', it would be useful to analyze the aspects of *The Joy Luck Club* that have generated the most debate, albeit by relating them to the issue of 'subaltern representation': at the level of content, the mother–daughter relationships and, at the level of form, the multiple micro-narratives, as well as dialogue and dialogism. By bringing these two debates together, this chapter considers whether the dialogues and by extension the relationships in and around the text are dialogic, a Bakhtinian figure emphasizing the ideological struggle in 'a hybrid construction ... that contains mixed within it two utterances, two speech manners, two styles, two "languages," two semantic and axiological belief systems'.[18] Uttered by a single speaker, in *The Joy Luck Club*, seven speakers, a hybrid construction, whether a single word, sentence or text, 'can ... simply mean double-talk, the necessary obliqueness of any persecuted speech that cannot, at the risk of survival, openly say what it means to say'.[19] This 'simple' meaning is relevant to *The Joy Luck Club*, the older generation in particular relying on double-talk in their respective struggles with dominant ideologies. However, double-talk as an 'answering back' can risk what is most radical in dialogism, that is, an openness proscribed by a dialectical system of question/answer: 'the function of dialogism is to sustain and think through the radical exteriority or heterogeneity of one voice with regard to any other'.[20] Dialogism thus sustains or preserves difference, if permitted to function deconstructively.

From the outset, Tan's narrators view the mother–daughter relationship as anything but dialogic, frequently commenting on the monologism of their cultures and, indeed, of each other. For instance, both generations criticize patriarchal ideology and its perpetration of 'the Chinese American woman', a 'shadowy' figure who is 'unseen and not seeing, unheard and not hearing, unknown by others' (67). Clearly, subalternity is bad, becoming even more so when perpetrated by women: the grandmother in 'Scar', the mother-in-law in 'The Red Candle', the 'lady' in 'The Moon Lady', the Second Wife in 'Magpies' and, moving to the American present, both generations of women as they stereotype each other respectively. Inescapably *in* patriarchal ideology, along with other dominant ideologies to do with age, class and ethnicity, it is hardly surprising that the women in *The Joy Luck Club* are unable to see/hear/know each other, a situation not *resolved* by 'subaltern representation'.

Granted, 'subaltern representation' does have its benefits: Ying-ying and Lena St. Clair resist their 'displace[ment]' (104) via speaking; Lindo and Waverly Jong utilize 'the art of invisible strength' or 'sneak[y]'[21] speech in order to 'get what [they] want' (89, 266); and, An-mei Hsu and her daughter, Rose Hsu Jordan, understand that the effectiveness of their speech depends on the listener. While the first four narrators endorse the utopian view of 'subaltern representation', the last two narrators question this view, if only temporarily, by emphasizing that 'speaking *and* hearing complete the speech act'.[22] For these narrators, and for a number of Tan's critics, 'subaltern speech acts' do seem to be successful, nowhere more so than in their intergenerational/intercultural relationships: 'through the act of storytelling – by means of the narrative itself – the intercultural gap between mothers and daughters is narrowed',[23] if not closed. Indeed, 'reconciliation',[24] 'whole[ness]',[25] 'one[ness]'[26] and other terms to do with closure are commonly used by Tan's critics to describe *The Joy Luck Club* and the relationships therein.

'Subaltern representation' thus (mis)understood raises a number of problems. First, the St. Clairs, the Jongs and the Hsus all highlight its *personal* benefits, thereby 'domesticating' it in a way that potentially depoliticizes the disenfranchized speaking for themselves. As David Leiwei Li puts it, arguably reconfiguring the dominant nationalist/feminist debate in Asian American studies, '*The Joy Luck Club*'s treatment of female familial experiences exemplifies Tan's active participation in the dominant privatization [and naturalization] of social problems'[27] by neoconservatives and feminists, not just white feminists. However, Li's masculinist/nationalist criticism marginalizes the complexity of 'the nation' both inside and outside *The Joy Luck Club* via an adherence to the personal/political or, in his terms, the 'club/

country' binary opposition. Is it really the case that 'the filiality of the "club" rather than the consent of the "country" is an amazing act of narrative "privatization"'[28] when both clubs, one in Kweilin, the other in San Francisco, are formed in response to political crises, specifically war and immigration? Whether the result of China's external or internal politics, 'unspeakable tragedies', including 'lost generations', 'lost homes' and lost 'arms and legs hanging from telephone wires and starving dogs running down the streets with half-chewed hands dangling from the jaws', 'cast … long shadows' into the lives of Chinese immigrants and their American-born children, necessitating the formation of both clubs. 'What was worse', asks the clubs' founder, 'to sit and wait for our own deaths with proper somber faces? Or to choose our own happiness?' (20–5). In the context of war, immigration and, moreover, diaspora, the Chinese mothers in particular drawing attention to 'the insidious links between their pasts and present struggles in America and between their pasts and their daughters present lives',[29] the personal/political binary opposition inadequately responds to the complexity of either *The Joy Luck Club* or, indeed, the nation. If anything, the family is the exact opposite of conservative, being matriarchal, extended and transnational: the Chinese mothers, also known as 'aunties', wear the trousers at home, if only from their daughters' perspectives; and, Suyuan Woo has children living in both China and America.

To continue with the personal *benefits* of 'subaltern representation', albeit in the context of two further problems: *The Joy Luck Club* questions the view that the disenfranchized speaking for themselves resolves social problems. And, related to this, it questions the possibility and the desirability of resolution, along with other terms endorsing closure as they apply not only to intergenerational/intercultural relationships but also to identity. The ultimate impossibility/undesirability of a 'closed' or, in Spivak's terms, a 'sovereign' and 'undivided' identity, the latter relying on 'a network, a weave – you can put names on it – politico-psycho-sexual-socio'[30] and, here, the mother–daughter relationship, to de/construct it, is represented positively not only by Spivak but also by *The Joy Luck Club*. In short, the transforming of negative into positive, or, more properly, 'conditions of impossibility into possibility', is a 'gift'.[31] Among the many gifts exchanged in *The Joy Luck Club*, from swan feathers to jade pendants, arguably the greatest gift it offers is a complex negotiation of 'subaltern representation'.

For example, the St. Clairs, Jongs and Hsus may speak for themselves, but their narratives repeatedly highlight the ideological limitations of 'subaltern representation' and its 'cohere[nce] with the work of imperialist subject-constitution'.[32] These limitations suggest that '[t]he subaltern cannot speak', a suggestion dramatically reinforced by the properly subalternized figure of Jing-mei's Chinese mother. This notion of 'proper' subalternization brought about, in this case, by Suyuan's death contrasts with the way in which 'subaltern representation' has heretofore been (mis)used in relation to *The Joy Luck Club*'s other characters, who, as *narrators*, come closer to 'token subalterns'.[33] Following Spivak's point that 'there is ... something of a not-speakingness in the very notion of subalternity', which she develops from the Subaltern Studies group's 'redoing of Gramsci's notion of the subaltern' as heterogeneous 'space', rather than an identity and a consciousness, 'cut off from the lines of mobility in a colonized country', *only* Suyuan inhabits this space.[34] Her death (from a cerebral aneurysm) arguably functions as a kind of figure, admittedly, an extreme figure since she literally cannot talk,[35] for those outside these lines of mobility, as she, like them, 'cannot represent [herself]; [she] must be represented'[36] by Jing-mei, whose narrative focuses on the emotional, theoretical and political implications of speaking for and about the (m)other.

So, the subaltern cannot speak. How is Spivak's controversial assertion reinforced in *The Joy Luck Club*? And, moreover, how does it impact on the Chinese mothers and the American-born daughters? Starting with the St. Clairs: 'A girl can never ask, only listen' (70), says Ying-ying's nursemaid on the morning of the Chinese Moon Lady Festival. Chinese patriarchy is not alone in subalternizing women. As Ying-ying remarks about herself and her daughter, and the relationship between them: 'For all these years I kept my mouth closed. ... And because I remained quiet for so long my daughter does not hear me ... [or] see me. She sees lists of things to buy. ... And I want to tell her this: We are lost, she and I, unseen and not seeing, unheard and not hearing, unknown by others' (67), 'even' in the US. Given that American patriarchy renders both the immigrant Ying-ying and the diasporic Lena shadowy or ghostly 'yin people', a subalternization also advanced by other dominant ideologies, the masculinist assertion about Tan's representation of a China dominated by misogyny not present in America proves questionable. Perhaps, at a push, as a number of feminist critics have argued, 'misogyny is [represented as] the ... unifying moral imperative in ... Chinese [*and* American] civilization[s]'.[37]

In her chapter, 'The Moon Lady', Ying-ying traces her general displacement back to the Moon Lady Festival. Perhaps this is a surprising outcome of a festival that not only has a (Moon) 'lady' at its centre but also grants Chinese women the privilege of speaking for themselves: 'today is the only day [they] can ... have a secret wish fulfilled' (70). Following Mikhail Bakhtin's insights about carnival and the carnivalesque, this 'liberation from the prevailing truth and from the established order ... the suspension of all hierarchical rank, privileges, norms and prohibitions' is only 'temporary'[38] and, ultimately, illusory, with a variety of limitations being imposed by a middle-class Chinese patriarchy before and during the Moon Lady Festival.

For example, Ying-ying is instructed by her nursemaid to 'behave, follow [her] mother's example' (69). Exemplariness is attributed to this woman because she understands masculinity and femininity in conventional terms: 'A boy can run and chase dragonflies, because that is in his nature. ... But a girl should stand still. If you are still for a very long time, a dragonfly will no longer see you. Then it will come to you and hide in the comfort of your shadow.' Although passivity eventually benefits the girl – she gets the dragonfly or, rather, it gets her – this representation of femininity fails to correspond with Ying-

ying's 'restless nature' (72) that leads to nightmarish encounters
with a cleaver-wielding man, two rough-looking boys fishing
with a ringed bird and a sullen-faced woman cutting up dead
animals. Spattered with blood after this last encounter, Ying-
ying tries to resolve the problem by following the advice meted
out by her mother in the dragonfly story: 'I quickly dipped my
hands in the bowl of turtle's blood and smeared this on ... all my
clothes ... and I stood perfectly still [so that] no one would
notice this change' (76). But they do, and Ying-ying is punished
by being stripped and isolated from the family, accidentally
reinforcing her isolation by falling into the lake, nearly
drowning and, understandably confused, suffering a case of
mistaken identity when another girl cries: 'That's not me! ...
I'm here. I didn't fall in the water' (79).

Ying-ying's nightmare continues, however, as do the
bloody, shadowy and slimy images, when, on the lakeshore, she
observes 'a shadow play' of crime and punishment: the Moon
Lady is condemned to eternal exile on the moon after stealing
the magic peach of everlasting life from her husband, the Master
Archer (80–1). At the end of the play, the Moon Lady consents
to grant secret wishes. Ying-ying ventures forwards: 'I have a
wish! I have one!' only to discover the 'shrunken cheeks, a
broad oily nose, large glaring teeth, and red-stained eyes ... [of]
a man' (82). The Moon Lady's maleness is significant not
because Ying-ying 'will become a non-woman. She will *act* like
a man' by having an abortion, 'a twisted life-destroying deed'
that, to continue quoting Chris Boldt, 'den[ies] the primary
motivation of womanhood – the protection of her off-spring'.[39]
Dubious on so many fronts, for men, women and, most
crucially, the debate about abortion, Boldt's definition of femininity as productive/protective womb also overlooks Ying-ying's
protection of Lena (105), the only one of two actual offspring to
survive. Contra Boldt, a man acts a woman because 'her'
femininity is ultimately determined by patriarchal ideology, the
'ugliness' of the Moon Lady's face also 'disclosing the ugliness
of women's victimization and crystallizing the insidious "secret"
behind the making of the myth' that 'subjugate[s] women and

turn[s] them into sexed subjects' through gendered binary oppositions.[40] As the Moon Lady laments, 'For woman is yin … the darkness within, where untempered passions lie. And man is yang, bright truth lightening our minds' (81).

In addition to the fact the secret wishes are told to a man at a one-day event that excludes 'poor-looking people' (74), who continue working during the festivities, secret wishes cost money. At the mention of 'a small monetary donation … the crowd laughed and groaned, then began to disperse' (82). Secret wishes are only available to wealthy Chinese women, and then not radically so because money is traditionally managed by male family members in accordance with the 'Three Obediences'.[41] Patriarchal control over the Moon Lady Festival is further ensured because wealthy Chinese women speak without speaking: 'a secret wish … is what you want but cannot ask. … [I]f you ask … it is no longer a wish but a selfish desire' (70). Through a powerful combination of denigration (a *selfish* desire) and transformation (a *secret* wish), Chinese patriarchy effectively displaces femininity, a displacement continued in America when officials declare Ying-ying 'a Displaced Person, lost in the sea of immigration categories'. Her sense of loss is reinforced when her American husband gives her the wrong history, the wrong name, the wrong birthyear and the wrong astrological sign (104).

Whether in China or America, in a lake or a swimming pool, the St. Clair women confront, albeit differently, the fact the subaltern cannot speak. While class hierarchies in China, alongside class/race hierarchies in America, ensure that Ying-ying and Lena are 'more or less free',[42] it is worth analysing the nature of this freedom in more detail. Yes, Ying-ying is permitted a secret wish; and, yes, Lena is 'permitted to go to college, permitted to take a stab at a career or two along the way, given "free choice" to marry'[43] the 'clear-skinned' and 'wiry' (156) Harold Livotny, a man, who, like her Irish American father, Clifford St. Clair, 'put[s] words in [his wife's] mouth' (106). As figures of patriarchal authority, both husbands subalternize their wives by speaking on their behalf. Perhaps this is a strong claim to make about Clifford and Harold, especially as they, like many of Tan's male characters, seem fairly innocuous. After all, both love their wives, albeit on *their* terms, Clifford as 'the angel of light' and Harold as 'the big, important husband' (250, 67). Here, then, the subaltern woman speaks without speaking, and, in Lena's case, eats without eating.

Lena's eating disorder, her bulimia, which Harold misrepresents as dieting, makes her so thin that '[s]he like a ghost, disappear' (163). On reading the '*Lena* [and] *HAROLD*' list (160) of shared household expenses, Ying-ying notices a $4.50 tub of ice cream: '"This you do not share!" exclaims my mother in an astonished voice. ... My mother must remember the incident on the fire escape landing, where she found me, shivering and exhausted, sitting next to [a] container of regurgitated ice cream. I could never stand the stuff after that.' Typically, a ghost's actions go unseen and unheard, this time, to Lena's astonishment: 'Harold has never noticed that I don't eat any of the ice cream he brings home every Friday evening.' She confronts her husband, supported by Ying-ying: 'I've hated ice cream almost all my life' and, to reinforce her point, Lena removes 'ice cream' from the list (161–2). At first he is 'amused', then 'exasperated', especially when she starts crying. Feeling 'uncomfortable, angry [and] manipulat[ed]', Harold issues a subtle threat: 'Well I know our marriage is based on a lot more than a balance sheet. A lot more. And if you don't then I think you should think about what else you want, before you change things' (164–5). But things do need changing, particularly when Harold is more equal than Lena, not just at home but at work too. As the boss and 'the concept man' (159) of Livotny & Associates, a thematic restaurant business, started by him, but inspired by her, Harold pays himself seven times more than Lena, also having 'the deciding vote on how the house should look. It is sleek, spare, and what he calls "fluid," nothing to disrupt the line, meaning none of my cluttered look' (161). Here, then, Lena is 'equal, except' (159) if she does not conform to the 'soft and squishy and lovable' woman Harold married for an 'extraordinar[iness]' that can be exotic, but preferably not other, let alone Chinese (155, 163).

Ying-ying and Lena eventually assume responsibility for speaking, a responsibility that influences their identities and their mother–daughter relationship. Indeed, 'subaltern representation' apparently serves to liberate them from 'the Chinese American woman': telling Lena about her past enables Ying-ying to find herself, and arguing with Harold brings mother and daughter closer, as well as allowing Lena to plan a future free of 'ice cream'. Not all is this straightforward, however, because a departure from the 'ghostly' identity bestowed on both mother and daughter by patriarchal ideologies has its limitations. In Lena's words: 'None of it seems right. Nothing makes sense. I can admit to nothing and I am in complete despair' (164–5). This despair is made all the more intense because the ideological underpinnings of 'subaltern representation' undermine the radicalism of Ying-ying asking for a secret wish, of Lena erasing 'ice cream' from a list and by implication the disenfranchized speaking for themselves.

While the St. Clairs' narratives are, in some respects, the most straightforward, charting the progress from silence to speech, *almost* suggesting that it is a solution, the idea of the disenfranchized speaking for themselves, the Jongs narratives offer a more complex negotiation of 'subaltern representation'. According to Lindo, silence is not necessarily disempowering, particularly if it is linked to air imagery – the wind and the breath. Silence or, more properly, 'the art of invisible strength ... was a strategy for winning arguments, respect from others. ... "Bite back your tongue. ... Wise guy, he not go against wind. In Chinese we say, Come from the South, blow with wind – poom! – North will follow. Strongest wind cannot be seen"' (89). In 'The CliffsNotes Version of My Life' from *The Opposite of Fate*, Tan admits to borrowing the phrase 'invisible strength' from her mother. 'She'd say, "*Fang pi bu-cho, cho pi bu-fang,*" which ... translates approximately to: "There's more power in silence."' 'The strict linguist', Tan continues, 'might want to note that the literal translation of that Chinese phrase runs along these noble lines: "Loud farts don't smell, the really smelly ones are deadly silent."[44] Putting this point about 'double-talk' less crudely and less idiomatically, Amy Ling argues that 'victory over hostile forces ... may be achieved not through direct confrontation but by apparent accommodation and giving in'.[45]

In her chapter, 'The Red Candle', Lindo, keen to avoid dishonour, the usual outcome for 'direct' Chinese women, apparently accommodates hostile forces, represented by the Huangs, the family she is betrothed to as a baby. Lindo is 'seal[ed] forever with [her] husband and his family, no excuses' (59) by marriage, specifically by the red candle marriage ritual. All looks hopeless for Lindo, until, that is, she acknowledges the art of invisible strength: 'I saw the red candle flickering just a little in the breeze ... and the flame bent down low, but still both ends burned strong. My throat filled with so much hope that it finally burst and blew out my husband's end of the candle' (60). Rather than invalidating the marriage straightaway, Lindo bites back her tongue and tries to love a man who is more like a younger brother than a husband. Their childlessness, the result of a sexless marriage, is blamed on Lindo, whose gold jewellery has apparently affected her fertility. The metal is removed, making her lighter and, in her terms, independent. Only now can Lindo exploit the art of invisible strength, 'double-talking' her way out of a bad marriage by appropriating Chinese super-stition about the red candle ritual and ancestral spirits without dishonouring either herself or her family. She eventually flies to the US with the Huangs' consent and money.

Lindo assumes that the art of invisible strength will also benefit her American-born daughter, which it does, up to a point. Waverly is a chess champion, 'the Great American hope, a child prodigy and a girl to boot' (97), and, commenting on her game, she says: 'I found out about all the whys. ... I also found out why I should never reveal "why" to others. A little knowledge withheld is a great advantage one should store for future use' (94–5). In short, then, chess empowers Waverly, the 'two-faced' tactics underpinning it especially. As she remarks to Lindo, 'we're looking one way, while following the other. We're for one side and also the other. We mean what we say but our intentions are different. ... [W]e're two-faced. ... This is good if you get what you want' (266). But Waverly only wants a poor quality mink coat and the best crab on the plate, demonstrating, at least to Lindo, that 'she is all-American made. ... Only that kind of thinking stuck' (254). 'Chinese thinking' is displaced or, rather, Americanized, being affirmed by Waverly merely as a fashion statement: 'Chinese ... is so fashionable' (253), a 'colorful add-in ... that work[s] to sustain the myth of a pluralist society without fundamentally challenging its categories'.[46] Her empowerment, in short, depends on an adherence to the assimilationist stereotype of the 'model minority'.

Along with affording the insight that 'subaltern representation' is really already determined by dominant ethnic/gender assumptions, *The Joy Luck Club* further problematizes the possibility of Chinese and Chinese American women speaking for themselves by raising the issue of the listener. Spivak also notes that 'the question "Who should speak?" is less crucial than "Who will listen?"',[47] as the Hsus understand only too well. In Rose's words: 'I had been talking to too many people, my friends, everybody. ... To each person I told a different story. ... And so I didn't know what to think anymore' (188–9). Neither her heart nor, for that matter, one of the most 'heartfelt' discourses of all, American psychiatry or 'psycheatricks' (188), deliver Rose self-understanding about her failing marriage to Ted Jordan. Criticizing her daughter's tendency to talk to everybody, except Ted, An-mei says: 'She lies down on a psychiatrist couch, squeezing tears out about this shame. ... [S]he will lie there until there is nothing more to fall, nothing left to cry about, everything dry' (215).

The turtle story told to An-mei as a child illustrates the importance of speaking to the right type of listener. Generations of Hsu women have cried tears into a pond, which a turtle consumes: 'I have eaten your tears, and this is why I know your misery. But I must warn you. If you cry, your life will always be sad.' After conveying this message, the turtle opens its beak and seven eggs pour out. The eggs break to reveal seven laughing and singing magpies. '"Now you see," said the turtle, "why it is useless to cry. Your tears do not wash away your sorrows. They feed someone else's joy. And that is why you must learn to swallow your own tears"' (217). Similarly, 'a psychiatrist does not want you to wake up. He tells you to dream some more, to find the pond and pour more tears into it. And really he is just another bird drinking from your misery' (241). Benevolent as these three listeners – turtle, bird and psychiatrist – seem to be, they do nothing to better the Hsu women's circumstances. Without a listener that matters, Rose might as well remain silent. Hence she informs *Ted*: '"You can't just pull me out of your life and throw me away." I saw what I wanted: his eyes, confused, then scared. He was *hulihudu* ["confused"]. The power of my words was strong' (196).

The St. Clairs, Jongs and Hsus articulate, albeit differently, the benefits of 'subaltern representation', not least when they contest ethnic/gender stereotypes and, in the process, form better matrilineal relationships. From opponents to allies, albeit uneasy allies since a violent rhetoric of fighting tigers and women armed with kitchen utensils (252, 183–4) is still in evidence contra the mainstream claim that 'if mothers and daughters … talk long enough, share their stories, go back far enough into their past suffering to unearth and expose the causes, then mothers and daughters will reconcile, the psychic barriers and wounds created by generations of male and social domination will fall away, and they will find peace, under-standing, comfort, union, and wholeness'.[48] The causes of ethnic/gender oppression are not so easily resolved by 'subaltern representation', particularly as the St. Clairs, Jongs and Hsus continue to (mis)represent themselves and each other in terms compatible with dominant ideologies, most obviously 'the Chinese American woman' and the 'model minority'. And, it is for the persistence of ethnic stereotyping that *The Joy Luck Club* is considered neoconservative, if not neo-Orientalist and neo-racist by Tan's more critical commentators, both masculinist and feminist.

Interestingly, the dominant nationalism/feminism debate,

as Lisa Lowe notes, 'not only organizes the cultural debates of Asian American discourse but figures *in* Asian American literature, as well',[49] often in terms of generational conflict: an immigrant/nativist generation versus a diasporic/assimilationist generation, which *The Joy Luck Club* represents via the disputes between Chinese mothers and American-born daughters, the two generations frequently representing the other in Occidentalist and Orientalist terms respectively. For this reason, the 'neo' readings of the text make sense, especially as 'American-born minds' are described as 'closed' (41), only too preoccupied with consuming Coca Cola, a description that, as it turns out, also suggests that 'Chinese-born minds' are closed. En-closed in different yet related ideologies, namely, Occidentalism and Orientalism, it is hardly surprising that stereotyping occurs in the text.

However, it is more for the Orientalism than the Occidentalism that *The Joy Luck Club* is criticized, particularly its reductive representation of the Chinese mother(land) as 'bad', 'good' and 'true'. The 'bad' Chinese mother is discussed by Waverly and Lena respectively, bad because she is either too strong or too weak: 'you can't *ever* tell a Chinese mother to shut up. You could be charged as an accessory to your own murder'; and, 'my father said he saved her from a terrible life' in a poor Chinese village (173, 104). Jing-mei confronts a similar binary opposition, wondering whether she should represent Suyuan as either monstrous or angelic in keeping with the 'malignant' (87) and 'fairy' (81) Chinese mothers in the vignettes introducing 'The Twenty-Six Malignant Gates' and 'Queen Mother of the Western Skies'. Countering patriarchal/Orientalist binary logic, the American-born daughters concede towards the end of their narratives that the Chinese 'mother was right' (267), making her, according to Sau-ling Cynthia Wong, 'a locus of truth' in terms compatible with neo-Orientalism.[50] The younger generation are in a no-win situation and so, apparently, is *The Joy Luck Club*.

For Tan's more critical commentators, not only Wong but also Sinkwan Cheng, *The Joy Luck Club* homogenizes 'Chineseness', and so is 'darkly' complicit with dominant ideologies. As different as their critiques are, both feminist critics propose that because and not in spite of its heterogeneity – the heterogeneous representation of the Chinese mother(land) as bad, good and true, and, more generally, the heterogeneous form – a heterogeneity that sells, *The Joy Luck Club* is neo-Orientalist and neo-racist. Cheng elaborates this apparent contradiction between heterogeneous form and homogenous meaning: 'Tan's voice, and the voice of late-capitalism in general, are double in that they can be discriminatory even as they make claim to universal acceptance. They recolonize other voices as they pretend to be championing diversity and humanity and the suppression of imperial hierarchies'.[51] This 'recolonization' is only too apparent in the text: from Waverly's, 'he *is* gay. … He could have AIDS' (204), and Rose's, 'I was victim to his [white] hero' (118), to An-mei's assumption that M & M's and sweatshirts 'would make her brother very rich and happy by communist standards' (36), never mind the Orientalist/Occidentalist stereotyping.

Here, 'double-talk' undergoes a kind of reversal in so far as persecuted speech serves rather than subverts dominant ideologies, making *The Joy Luck Club* monologic, not dialogic, in the opinion of its more critical commentators. But is this criticism misdirected given that dialogism as 'double-talk' *inevitably* reaffirms dominant ideologies? There is no getting away from the fact that the American-born daughters, as well as the Chinese mothers, are embroiled *in* ideological structures, in ageism, classism, homophobia, racism and sexism. Answering dominant ideologies back does not resolve the problem of embroilment, far from it, since this would effectively explain away the suspect remarks made by Tan's narrators potentially in terms compatible with 'The Native [as] the Non-Duped'.[52] And, anyway, 'non-dupedness' or the assumption of an outside to ideology is the ideological effect *par excellence*. Rather than pursing an inside/outside model of ideology critique, which constructs 'the native' as either duped or (non-)duped, *The Joy Luck Club* arguably offers a more complex and strategic negotiation of ideology in keeping with Spivak's 'double session' of representation, which is where the Woos finally come in.

Subalternized via death, Suyuan cannot represent herself. Hence Jing-mei speaks both for and about her in the text and, crucially, to her Chinese sisters, who were separated from their mother by war, immigration and, now, death. The two senses of representation – proxy and portrait – are at issue in Jing-mei's narrative, with much depending on how they are negotiated, not least her own identity and her relationships with Suyuan, Wang Chwun Yu and Wang Chwun Hwa. Under pressure to tell 'everything' (41) about Suyuan, Jing-mei assumes realism is most appropriate to this task, after discounting the monster/ angel binary opposition. This pressure comes from various sources, some external, others internal. A realistic portrait of Suyuan, 'The mother they did not know, they must now know' (40), should be presented to Chwun Yu and Chwun Hwa, especially as they only have a photograph and a 'spirit ghost' (286) fantasy of Suyuan. Moreover, Jing-mei's 'aunties' demand such a portrait, as she realizes at a meeting of the Joy Luck Club. To Jing-mei's questions, 'What will I say? What can I tell them about my mother? I don't know anything. She was my mother', her aunties respond with disbelief and fear: they 'are looking at me as if I had become crazy right before their eyes. ... "Imagine, a daughter not knowing her own mother!"' 'In me', comments Jing-mei, 'they see their own daughters, just as ignorant, just as unmindful of all the truths and hopes they have brought to America. They see daughters who grow impatient when their mothers talk in Chinese, who think they are stupid when they explain things in fractured English. ... They see daughters who will bear grandchildren born without any connecting hope passed from generation to generation' (40–1).

With so much at stake, it is hardly surprising that Jing-mei considers a realistic portrait of the (m)other, her 'objective' being 'to preserve various consciousnesses from doubt' by 'stabiliz[ing] the referent', in this case, Suyuan, 'arrang[ing] it according to a point of view which endows it with a recognizable meaning, ... reproduc[ing] the syntax and vocabulary which enable the addressee to decipher images and sequences quickly, and so ... arriv[ing] easily at the consciousness of [her] own identity as well as the approval which [she] receives from others'.[53] With text/referent thus stabilized, Suyuan's identity is transparently reflected as though through the window of Jing-mei's words, to the satisfaction of all parties. Or, so it seems. In a position of power, over her mother, sisters and language, the latter because realism appears to coincide reliably with the referent, which, in this case *'is'* Suyuan, how can Jing-mei relate reciprocally, let alone dialogically to others? Moreover, realism generates a problem for Jing-mei, as is suggested by the advice she receives from one of her 'aunties': 'her mind ... has ... [to] become your mind' (40). Two minds are brought together, as are the two senses of representation in that a realistic portrait of Suyuan depends on Jing-mei replacing her mother at the club, on the China trip and in *The Joy Luck Club*. But, as Jing-mei asks: 'How can I be my mother at Joy Luck?' (27), and, in so asking, she problematizes the possibility of intergenerational (and intragenerational) interchangeability celebrated by so many of Tan's critics.[54]

Granted, interchangeability is represented in *The Joy Luck Club*. But is it celebrated? Does the 'los[ing] track of the individual women's voices' constitute 'a triumph'?[55] On one level, yes. The narrators do highlight the emotional benefits of intergenerational similarity, albeit as a way of averting the 'irritat[ion]', 'upset', 'silence' and 'paralysis' (183, 186) engendered when the daughters defy maternal expectations with their 'new thoughts, willful thoughts, or rather thoughts filled with lots of won'ts' (134). For example, Waverly's defiance leaves her 'othered': '"We no concerning this girl. This girl not have concerning for us." Nobody looked at me ... and I was alone' (100–1). Similarly Lena, Rose and Jing-mei comment on the 'unbearable ... pain of not being seen' (115) by mothers who appear to be on and for the other side. Apparently unseen by their mothers, and not seeing their mothers, as the latter painfully realize when steamed dumplings, 'swan-feather' gifts and criticism do not signify maternal affection, the American-born daughters seem unable/unwilling to see that 'Chinese mothers never pay a direct compliment but, instead, express their support and love indirectly'.⁵⁶ This direct/indirect opposition is vividly reconfigured as skin/bone or surface/depth in An-mei's 'Scar' (48). Not magical enough to cure the grandmother, the soup made from the mother's flesh does nevertheless work its magic on An-mei and, for that matter, the critics who celebrate interchangeability: 'Your mother is in your bones!' (40), an emotionally powerful assertion that represents femininity triumphing over life/death, as well as mother/daughter, Chinese/American and so on.

For some feminist critics, the 'oneness' represented by the steaming pot (of soup) is worth celebrating, although it does become more problematic for post-colonial critics vis-à-vis the melting pot. In Rose's chapter, 'Half and Half', interchange-ability is criticized via the white character of Mrs Jordan, who offers a warm handshake, 'but never seemed to look at [Rose]. ... "I'm so glad to meet you *finally*," Mrs Jordan said. ... "I think it's nice that you and Ted are having such a lot of fun together"' (118). 'Oriental sex'⁵⁷ is 'nice', but Rose would be judged differently if she and Ted decided to legitimate their relationship in marriage:

> She assured me she had nothing against minorities; she and her husband, who owned a chain of office-supply stores, personally knew many fine people who were Oriental, Spanish, and even black. But Ted was going to be in one of those professions where he would be judged by a different standard, by patients and doctors who might not be as understanding as the Jordans were. She said it was so unfortunate the way the rest of the world was, how unpopular the Vietnam War was.
>
> 'Mrs. Jordan, I am not Vietnamese,' I said softly, even though I was on the verge of shouting. (118)

Mrs Jordan's multiculturalist 'understanding' of minorities, brought about by close encounters with 'many fine people' not privy, presumably, to a middle-class profession, differentiates her from the rest of the world. This said, she asserts her own class/race superiority by generalizing not only about 'Oriental',

Spanish and black people but also the world in terms compatible with American imperialism. To Mrs Jordan, then, minorities are all alike, 'Orientals', in this case, Chinese and Vietnamese especially, although their interchangeability is not based on the fact that they are Americans. Rose's 'I'm American' (117), admittedly articulated to her mother, not her mother-in-law, would in all likelihood be wasted on Mrs Jordan.

In Jing-mei's chapter, 'The Joy Luck Club', interchange-ability is again criticized for a political reason, as well as more formal reasons. At the club's first meeting since Suyuan's death, the Jongs hand out 'nondescript picture[s]' of their recent China trip. 'There is nothing in this picture', Jing-mei observes, 'that shows it was taken in China rather than San Francisco, or any other city for that matter' (27). Indistinguishable cities in nondescript pictures, along with dispensable calendars, free from the Bank of Canton, potentially function as figures for a general indifference not only to Suyuan but also to Jing-mei, and, for that matter, to the difference between them: 'what's the Chinese word that means indifferent because you can't *see* any differences?' (27). In view of this question, how can Jing-mei replace Suyuan when they are two different women, one too emotionally weak, the other too emotionally strong, a difference emphasized to Jing-mei as a child. 'A friend once told me that my mother and I were alike. ... When I shyly told my mother this, she seemed insulted and said, "You don't even know little percent of me! How can you be me?" And she's right. How can I be my mother at Joy Luck?' (27). But, then again, why would she want to be the *late* Suyuan? Perhaps Jing-mei's references to things such as cities, pictures and calendars also convey the idea that to replace Suyuan involves a deadening objectification. From this perspective, then, interchangeability is harmful because it obliterates identity, objectifying and essentializing women to such an extent that they become things, if not 'those little dolls sold in Chinatown tourist shops, heads bobbing up and down in complacent agreement to anything said!'[58]

In addition to being politically problematic, interchange-ability is literally impossible, as is suggested by the Woos' life/

death opposition that arguably serves as a reminder of the difference between all the mothers and the daughters. This difference is insurmountable and nothing, not even 'the same wispy hand gestures, the same girlish laugh and sideways look' (27), can render Suyuan and Jing-mei 'indifferent'. Another formal problem with interchangeability is that inhibits the intergenerational/intercultural dialogue so fundamental to *The Joy Luck Club*, and, crucially, its critical and strategic negotiation of essentialism. Depending on at least two speakers, dialogue and conversation facilitate better matrilineal relationships, although not always in a way that is obvious to the narrators: Suyuan only asks Jing-mei to be her best. 'For you sake. You think I want you be genius? Hnnh! What for? Who ask you?' (136); Lindo asks why Waverly thinks bad things about her. 'So you think your mother is this bad. You think I have secret meaning. But it is you who has this meaning' (181); An-mei does not tell Rose to save her marriage. 'I only say you should speak up' (193); and, Ying-ying speaks with 'pride' about Lena's move to Woodside. 'Of course, it's not best house in neighborhood, not million-dollar house, not yet. But it's good investment' (38). Here, then, the figure of the 'malignant' Chinese mother is questioned through conversation, a questioning further reinforced by the older generations' recognition of their daughters' 'best qualities'.

More than conversation, talk-story 'challenges the denial of Asian American women's voices and identities – denials not only by male-dominated Chinese society and a Eurocentric American society but also by their very own daughters'.[59] This Chinese oral tradition involves the older generation speaking in Chinese and im/perfect American English to their American-born daughters and by extension to non-Chinese readers, although not necessarily successfully as their addressees are apparently too full of Coca-Cola to reciprocate talk-story. Crucial to understanding the ideological/political implications of *The Joy Luck Club*, particularly Orientalism, this mother/daughter/reader relationship generates various interpretative possibilities. Generally speaking, critics view this relationship as hierarchical, with some arguing that the Chinese mother is privileged, others, the American-born daughter/reader. This division is itself significant because the text arguably *promotes* such a contradictory interpretation, both thematically and formally.

Form is privileged here, albeit as a kind of content, because the multiple micronarratives, all in the first person, alongside other issues to do with form, structure and language, complicate what the narrators and, ultimately, *The Joy Luck Club* say. In short, 'how' complicates 'what'. A number of Tan's critics acknowledge this complication *almost*, arguing that 'the narrative's structure', its sandwich effect, 'invites the reader to apprehend the daughter against the backdrop of mothers, giv[ing] the mothers the upper hand'.[60] Yet, this argument ignores the fact that Jing-mei opens, closes and generally dominates the text, thereby giving the daughters the upper hand. Is this reversal not reversed and reversed again by the 'swan-feather' mother's vignette and the 'Coca-Cola' daughter's epigraph? All these reversals put into question the intergenerational/intercultural hierarchy, as does the fact that the Chinese mothers in particular use 'part English, part Chinese, part standardized, part free invention, and part a hybrid combination'.[61] How these parts are negotiated – as a hierarchy or a hybrid – gives a sense of the intercultural/intergenerational relationships in *The Joy Luck Club*, along with having a bearing on the nationalist/assimilationist debate in Asian American literary studies.

In the opening vignette, the Chinese mother raises the issue of language, specifically *'perfect American English'* (17) and the impact it has on the intergenerational/intercultural relationship. This mother, who, to her monoglossic, 'Coca-Cola daughter' speaks 'imperfect' American English and Chinese, describes how she *'waited, year after year, for the day she could tell her daughter ... in perfect American English'* about the feather from a creature representing change, hope and good intentions. The swan feather is an interesting gift for a mother to bequeath to a daughter because 'in traditional Chinese stories, swans symbolize married, heterosexual love'.[62] Not only does the vignette disrupt this symbol of Chinese patriarchy but it also disrupts symbolism per se. The swan is forcibly removed from the mother at American immigration, leaving her not with a symbol but a synecdoche or, alternatively, not with a whole but a part, which, crucially, eschews the notion of a beginning and an end, and, by extension, the nationalist/masculinist fixation with an originary 'Chineseness' unaffected by immigration and diaspora: the swan-feather mother *'forgot why she had come and what she had left behind'*; and, *'she waited, year after year'* (17).

Approximately twenty-five pages later, the wait seems to be over as An-mei, Lindo and Ying-ying tell stories in perfect American English about what they left behind in China. Or do they? After all, their daughters still hear 'imperfect' American English, also keeping actual communication with their Chinese mothers to a minimum. For these reasons, the mothers 'speak into a void', a technique that suggests they are still waiting *à la* the swan-feather mother, and, as Stephen Souris argues, makes the reader, not the daughters, 'the agent and site of the dialogicity'.[63] Much depends on how the reader responds to this role. Granted, some readers respond passively and uncritically, 'borne along as if in a dream', the exotic and romantic representations of 'old China' confirming their ideological assumptions.[64] Orientalism functions so powerfully here that resistance is impossible. And, why should it be resisted given that the Chinese mother(land) is 'a locus of truth', offering, in an apparent reversal of the Orientalist binary opposition, the American-born daughter/reader happiness in relation to a literary text that is postmodern and dialogic? But, then again, is it not the case that 'truth' and, with it, a hierarchical relationship between mother/daughter/reader, are problematized by 'postmodern' and 'dialogic', never mind 'literary'? Following the logic of this question, other readers respond to the dialogic dimension of *The Joy Luck Club*, particularly to the 'hybrid combination' of the Chinese mothers' language. For instance, 'imperfect' American English empowers the older generation to criticize American culture indirectly/dialogically: 'psyche-atricks', 'Fukien landlady' and 'so-so security' (188, 200, 243).[65] The fact that they speak perfectly in their chapters further empowers them vis-à-vis a language/culture that has historically considered them 'imperfect'.[66]

The Chinese mothers' use of Chinese, as well as Chinese-sounding sentences, often 'short and choppy'[67] sentences accompanied by 'Aii-ya!', 'pah!' and so on, arguably works in a more complex way than their use of Englishes. Their romanized Chinese words printed in italics can convey a sense of cultural specificity, also undermining the presumed authority of American Orientalists. For example, Ying-ying uses Chinese when talking to Lena, thereby 'express[ing] her resentment against an American husband who persistently puts English words in her mouth',[68] embarrassingly badly as he speaks 'only a few canned Chinese expressions' (106). Chinese(-sounding) utterances are used to express anger, with 'Aii-ya!', for example, arguably like 'AIIIEEEEE!', the latter expression being re-appropriated by Asian American critics, signifying 'more than a whine, shout, or scream. It is fifty years of our whole voice.'[69] Chinese is also used at intimate moments, 'as when [Suyuan] … mak[es] her daughter a gift of a jade pendant' (208).[70] Chinese(-sounding) words/sentences function powerfully here, resisting Orientalist/patriarchal stereotypes and improving the mother–daughter relationship. However, they can also convey a stereotypical sense of cultural specificity, particularly in light of the fact that the American-born daughters (mis)translate Chinese.

One example should suffice as the same pattern of translation is used throughout *The Joy Luck Club*: '"Nala, nala" – Take it, take it – she said' (208). Note the punctuation, which is, according to Steven P. Sondrup, 'so carefully crafted that the non-Chinese-speaking reader may not realize the translation is a[n American-born daughter's, not a Chinese mother's] translation'.[71] Is this another instance of the subaltern cannot speak, with the American-born daughter putting English words in her Chinese mother's mouth, often badly/idiosyncratically? Mistranslation is particularly problematic given, as Wong notes, non-Chinese-speaking readers assume that the un/translated

Chinese functions reliably/ethnographically. The odd romanized Chinese word/sentence printed in italics, she continues, is 'minimally warranted by the immediate narrative context … providing occasion for elucidating an exotic Chinese culture'.[72] To Wong, the mother/daughter/reader relationship is hierarchical, the older generation providing Chinese linguistic exotica, conveniently (mis)translated by the younger generation, to placate the American-born reader and by extension to popularize *The Joy Luck Club*.

Wong's criticism is certainly powerful, although it does encounter at least two problems. First, the American-born daughters make no secret of their 'imperfect' Chinese. In Jing-mei's first chapter, for example, after confusing *chabudwo/butong*, she admits to 'never remember[ing] things [she] didn't understand in the first place', a point reinforced a few pages later: 'My mother and I never really understood one another. We translated each other's meanings', albeit in 'circular' fashion. 'I seemed to hear less than what was said, while my mother heard more' (37–8). This linguistic/cultural problem is apparently resolved in the final chapter when Jing-mei urges her father to tell her about her mother's Kweilin story in Chinese. Heretofore monoglossic for the most part, she becomes bilingual, a miraculous achievement for somebody who only a few lines earlier asked: 'what does "Jing-mei" mean?' (280). More suited to a child than a women in her late thirties, this question supports Lindo's point about Waverly's Chinese: *'sh-sh, houche, chr fan,* and *gwan deng shweijyau'*, words meaning 'pee-pee, choo-choo train, eat, close light sleep' (253–4). No experts in Chinese, the American-born daughters are clearly not reliable translators.

Second, translation, regardless of its reliability, runs the risk of sanctioning a violent hierarchy because, as Tan observes, almost repeating Wong's criticism, '[o]ne language [English] … is used as the standard, the benchmark for a logical form of expression. And so the other language [Chinese] is in danger of being judged by comparison deficient or superfluous, simplistic or unnecessarily complex, melodious or cacophonous.'[73] Translation thus understood is hierarchical, and arguably fails to

represent the intergenerational/intercultural/interlinguistic relationships in *The Joy Luck Club*, the Chinese oral tradition of
talk-story and, indeed, translation itself, all of which 'ultimately
serve the purpose ... of expressing the central reciprocal
relationship between languages', reciprocal because translation
functions 'ironically'.[74] Following Walter Benjamin's argument,
a translation simultaneously de/canonizes an original. It comes
after and continues the 'life' of the original via a popularization
that, ironically, kills it. As 'afterlife', translation is 'derivative'
and destined to fail, not because it badly reproduces the (stable)
original in terms compatible with mimesis, but because the
original is really already unstable.[75] Benjamin's 'fragments are
the broken parts of a vessel' passage, often (mis)translated
according to a totalizing logic of translation/original and part/
whole, actually articulates the reciprocal relationship between
languages: 'the translation is the fragment of a fragment, is
breaking the fragment – so the vessel keeps breaking, constantly
– and never reconstitutes it'.[76]

Moving from Benjamin to Tan, from theory to literature,
and from translation to talk-story: this 'breaking vessel' gestures
towards a reciprocal relationship between generations, cultures
and languages: 'The beginning is hers, the ending, mine.'[77]
Similarly, *The Joy Luck Club*'s pattern of translation represents
talk-story, albeit on a smaller scale, the beginning, '*Nala, nala*',
coming from the Chinese mother, the ending, 'Take it, take it',
from the American-born daughter (208). Not hierarchical, but
reciprocal, *The Joy Luck Club*'s negotiation of languages, *part*
English, *part* Chinese, *part* standardized, *part* free invention and
part a hybrid combination, never reconstitute a whole because
the latter depends on linguistic and ideological effects or, more
precisely, an ideologized understanding of literary language for
its de/construction. And, it is precisely this ideologization that
Tan puts into question, both inside and outside *The Joy Luck
Club*, most directly when she identifies with Nabokov's hatred of
symbolism[78] and, in so doing, criticizes the 'monologic' assumption that 'green', for example, means 'growth and regeneration'.
This assumption marginalizes the difference between symbol

and symbolized and, with it, different interpretative possibilities: green means decay/degeneration; and, green means green, nothing more.

In *The Joy Luck Club*, Jing-mei contemplates the meaning of 'life's importance', a green jade pendant given to her by Suyuan, also coming up with different interpretative possibilities, none of which are final:

> What if ... this curving line branching into three oval shapes is a pomegranate tree and that my mother was ... wishing me fertility and posterity? What if my mother really meant the carvings were a branch of pears to give me purity and honesty? Or ten-thousand-year droplets from the magic mountain, giving me my life's direction and a thousand years of fame and immortality? (197–8)

Significantly, Jing-mei's questions go unanswered, even though she wears the pendant close to her skin like Suyuan wore it close to hers, this closeness obviously not being close enough to finalize the meaning of the pendant and by implication the Chinese mother (208). The fact that green can mean regeneration/ degeneration and something/nothing, alongside Jing-mei's ideas/'no idea' (198) about the green jade pendant, reveals something not about green but about meaning, about *how* green means. By focusing on how meaning is de/constructed linguisti- cally and ideologically, the dialogicity marginalized by the hierarchical and totalizing logic of symbolism is 'returned'. This return of dialogism in its more radical sense of sustaining or preserving difference not permitted in a dialectical system of question/answer is crucial to understanding Jing-mei's 'return' to China in 'A Pair of Tickets' and by extension the ideological/ political implications of *The Joy Luck Club* vis-à-vis the debate about essentialism.

Already, Jing-mei's narrative has highlighted the undesir- ability and impossibility of intergenerational/intercultural reconciliation and, in the process, the 'dark' side of those readings that represent *The Joy Luck Club* wholly in terms of reconciliation. Even as Suyuan's representative at the Joy Luck Club and on the trip to China, she cannot be her mother. They

are two different women, a difference 'darkly' reinforced by the
life/death opposition so central to the text and the mother–
daughter relationships therein. But *The Joy Luck Club* cannot
stop here, however, in silence, death and a situation where the
(m)other is unpresentable even to her own daughter. It has to
negotiate the difference between life/death, daughter/mother
and one/other. This pressure comes from the narrative itself in
the sense that Suyuan's 'unfinished business' (19), the family
reunion planned by her for forty years, compels Jing-mei to
speak for and about the (m)other. This pressure is not only
emotional and historical but also linguistic. Indeed, a fundamental
assumption about language, that it has to mean, although not
necessarily reliably, compels Jing-mei to represent Suyuan via
proxy and portrait. This assumption is negatively articulated
several times in the text, most obviously when Jing-mei's
'aunties' accord a meaning to her claim that she does not know
and therefore cannot say anything about Suyuan. Whether
brought about by death, not knowing and not speaking, it is
impossible *not* to make silence meaningful. And, it is with this
insight about the impossibility of stopping at the 'dark'
condition of postmodernity that *The Joy Luck Club* ends.

'A Pair of Tickets' has Jing-mei negotiate the difference of
her late Chinese mother on a trip to the Chinese motherland. In
China, Jing-mei apparently re-establishes contact with Suyuan
through Chwun Yu and Chwun Hwa. As she puts it in her
penultimate sentence: 'Together we look like our mother' (288),
a togetherness repeatedly asserted in terms compatible with
essentialism. Her various epiphanies – 'becoming Chinese' (267),
discovering China and, most controversially, discovering a
blood-based 'Chineseness' – seem closer to modern than postmodern. Whether celebrated or criticized, these epiphanies are
typically assumed to function symbolically by Tan's critics. Most
read 'A Pair of Tickets' as simply endorsing 'togetherness' or,
alternatively, thematic and formal closure, insisting that it
reveals the telos of the whole text: 'The unique structure of *The
Joy Luck Club* allows the unconnected fragments of life ... to
unfold into a meaningful continuous whole', a 'whole' that,

while celebrated by some, is criticized by others for uncritically reducing culture to nature in keeping with essentialism, if not neo-Orientalism and neo-racism.

However, a symbolic reading of Jing-mei's epiphanies is at odds with Tan's 'Nabokovian' privileging of image over symbol and, authorial remarks aside, the logic of *The Joy Luck Club* itself. '[A]s literature – as a story, language',[79] the text functions unreliably, ratifying a reading it simultaneously resists by 'build[ing] up the romantic concept of cultural origins and lost ethnic essence only in order to radically undermine and reconfigure the notion of ethnic essence'.[80] Arguably, what Jing-mei says about 'Chineseness' is undermined and reconfigured, often to ironic effect, by *how* it is said. The difference between what/ how is difficult to marginalize not only because Jing-mei 'could never pass for true Chinese ... [e]ven without makeup' (272), but also because the text persistently highlights the cultural forms used to naturalize a 'true' ethnic essence. 'Retuning the native' less with a modern truthfulness and more with a postmodern playfulness, Tan's text, like that of Kingston's and, further back still, Ralph Ellison's, 'operates within the tradition of ... *jaw jieh* (catching pigs), "a time-honored practice of bullshitting white people"'[81] by using 'the face Americans think is Chinese' (255) in order to 'de-face' stereotypical assumptions.

So what then does Jing-mei say in 'A Pair of Tickets' about 'Chineseness', specifically on the train journey, in the hotel shower and on meeting her sisters for the first time, and is it possible to read her comments as operating within the tradition of *jaw jieh*? To begin with the train journey: 'The minute our train leaves the Hong Kong border and enters Shenzhen, China, I feel different. ... And I think, My mother was right. I am becoming Chinese' (267). Jing-mei's experience of becoming Chinese certainly seems to assume an essentialism based on 'returning the native to [a] natural habitat'[82] that is 'faithful to the geopolitical borders of the sovereign and colonial China, and more so to the conceptual and symbolic boundaries of East and West[.] Tan does not consider the then British colony of Hong Kong to be the true China', argues Li in 'Genes, Generation, and

Geospiritual (Be)longings'. He continues: 'The miracle island of capitalist and technological savvy is a principally Western conservatory of Chinese impurity, while the People's Republic is the real good earth of ancient tradition and magical wisdom.'[83]

Li's is a fair point, although it does raise a number of questions with respect to China versus Hong Kong, natural versus cultural and secular versus magical. If 'Chineseness' is essential, *in* the (mother)land, if not *in* the natural 'real good earth', why does Jing-mei mention cultural borders? Should 'Chineseness' not simply be there, presumably like the 'be' in Li's '(Be)longing'? But Jing-mei uses neither the infinitive nor the present simple, only the present progressive, suggesting that ethnic essence is a cultural process, a point reinforced by the werewolf simile. Countering Suyuan's 'science' with myth, not a myth specific to the 'magical' east, Jing-mei, crucially, a younger assimilationist Jing-mei, melodramatically likens 'becoming Chinese' to 'transforming like a werewolf, a mutant tag of DNA suddenly triggered, replicating insidiously into a *syndrome*, a cluster of telltale Chinese behaviours, all those things my mother did to embarrass me' (267). Now, twenty-one years later, she concedes: 'today I realize I've never really known what it means to be Chinese' (268). Science/myth, past/ present and east/west combine in such a way as to complicate the presumed essentialism of Jing-mei's opening lines.

Jing-mei continues her train journey, describing the Chinese countryside in 'mistyfying' terms. She openly admits to having 'misty eyes' as she mystifies her travelling companion, as well as the countryside. Of her aged father, she says: 'all he is seeing … is a sectioned field of yellow, green, and brown, a narrow canal flanking the tracks, low rising hills, and three people in blue jackets riding an ox-driven cart on this early October morning' (268). Such a description would not be out of place in a guidebook, which, as it turns out, is Jing-mei's next point of departure. Rural fixity is displaced by change that is more than urban: 'It seems all the cities I have heard of, except Shanghai, have changed their spellings. I think they are saying China has changed in other ways as well' (268). Only through misty, guidebook eyes or 'popular representations'[84] can Jing-mei generate 'Chineseness', albeit momentarily because of the similarity between Guangzhou and San Francisco (272). Urbanization and, for that matter, invasion undermine 'Chineseness' so much so that not 'even' the Chinese know China. For example, Great Auntie Aiyi is 'astonished' (279) by the news that Japanese soldiers invaded Kweilin during the Sino-Japanese War (1937–45). Once again, then, essentialism is undermined and reconfigured via an open 'mistyfication' that is not absolute in its affect on Jing-mei.

Eventually arriving at the hotel, apparently too grand for 'communist China' (276–7), Jing-mei takes a shower: 'The hotel has provided little packets of shampoo which, upon opening, I discover is the consistency and color of hoisin sauce. This is more like it, I think. This is China. And I rub some in my damp hair' (278). Arguably, this comment of Jing-mei's is essentialist in that 'Chineseness' is discoverable in a packet of shampoo. She also seems duped by the advertising industry in her belief that she can 'Wash and Go' to China.[85] Many advertisements openly and ironically overdetermine the capabilities of their products, appealing to a 'sophisticated' consumer who needs more than the usual '*Three* benefits, *three* needs, *three* reasons to buy. ... Satisfaction *guaranteed* ... for today's and tomorrow's tax needs' (205–6). Given the advertising industry's tendency for overdetermination or 'bullshitting', perhaps 'Wash and Go' to China also functions ironically.

From hair roots to cultural roots: Jing-mei finally meets her Chinese sisters, a poignant moment marked by the taking of a Polaroid photograph. The photograph promotes a sense of unity not only between siblings but also between them and their dead mother: 'Together we look like our mother' (288). 'This composite image', remarks Bonnie TuSmith, 'reflects the novel's communal subtext, which works as a counterpoint to the textual surface of individualistic strife'. Reinforcing these hierarchies of surface/depth and individuality/communality, TuSmith proclaims that 'underneath the skin, we (mother/daughter, Chinese/American, etc.) are all one'.[86] This hierarchy is reinforced by Jing-mei: 'And now I also see what part of me is Chinese. It is so obvious. It is my family. It is in our blood. After all these years, it can finally be let go' (288). While 'it' generates some ambiguity, it does harp back to a comment made by Suyuan about being born Chinese and feeling/thinking Chinese: '"Someday you will see," said my mother. "It is in your blood waiting to be let go"' (267). Jing-mei's use of such powerful words as 'family' and 'blood' does seem to lend support to the argument about one-ness underneath the skin or, more formally, togetherness reflected in the photograph.

However, this reflection is put into question by the last two paragraphs of *The Joy Luck Club*. Even before this, Jing-mei problematizes the privileging of the communal when on looking at her sisters' faces she 'see[s] no trace of [her] mother in them' (287). Her inability to trace her mother is quickly passed over via the reference to family and blood. Next come the photograph paragraphs: 'The flash of the Polaroid goes off and my father hands me the snapshot. My sisters and I watch quietly together, eager to see what develops'. Significantly, oneness develops in terms of a representation: 'The gray-green surface changes to the bright colors of our three images, sharpening and deepening all at once' (288). That the images *in*, or, more properly, *on* the photograph develop all at once, and that they do so *before* Jing-mei's unspoken proclamation of togetherness outside the photo-graph, would seem to suggest that the textual surface effects the communal subtext. TuSmith's hierarchy is thus reversed: an analogy on the textual surface unites image and referent, and, crucially, it is this apparent unity that effects, rather than reflects, Jing-mei's sense of togetherness.

As with all literary structures, the analogy functions unreliably. It performs a contradiction by uniting *different* phenomena: inside/outside, image/referent and, less formally speaking, Jing-mei and others. To marginalize this contradiction and, with it, the literariness of *The Joy Luck Club* is to read the latter as functioning reliably/ethnographically. Such a reading turns literature, not just 'multicultural' literature, as Tan remarks, 'into very limited rhetoric'[87] by privileging proxy over portrait, *Vertretung* over *Darstellung*, the implications of which are highlighted by Spivak in her discussion of the double session of representation: 'The relationship between the two kinds of representation brings in, also, the use of essentialism because no representation can take place – no *Vertretung*, representation – can take place without essentialism. What it has to take into account is that the "essence" that is being represented is a representation of the other kind, *Darstellung*.'[88]

To apply this format to *The Joy Luck Club*, specifically to what Jing-mei says in 'A Pair of Tickets': she represents her identity, her family and China in terms of an essential 'Chineseness'. Clearly, then, the notion of ethnic essence circulates in the text, and it is to this apparently unproblematic formulation of 'Chineseness' that Tan's more critical commentators direct their critiques. But what is also clear is the fact that Jing-mei's representation of self and others has its basis in a photograph. Similarly, becoming Chinese and discovering China depend on a myth, a guidebook and a shampoo. This emphasis on the cultural underpinnings of 'Chineseness' and *how* Jing-mei says what she says suggests a critical, if not a strategic negotiation of essentialism. By moving from 'blood' to a photograph and, more crucially, by focusing on the photograph's formal dimension – 'the gray-green surface', 'the bright colors' and 'three images sharpening and deepening all at once' – questions emerge about the nature of Jing-mei's 'bloody' epiphany. If 'Chineseness' is 'so obvious[ly] … in [Jing-mei's] blood' (288), why refer to a photograph at all? Indeed, what *kind* of ethnic essence depends on a myth, a guidebook, a shampoo and a photograph to make it obvious?

It is with this less than 'bloody' ending that this chapter ends, although not in some 'sweet' or fairy-tale way. From the opening vignette and the Kweilin story to the final chapter, *The Joy Luck Club* focuses on change, movement and difference. Crucially, its different parts, functioning synecdochically, not symbolically, resist reconciliation and other terms endorsing closure, wholeness and oneness. Difference proves fundamental to *The Joy Luck Club*; indeed, without it neither dialogues nor relationships/identities would be possible. Rather than envisaging difference wholly in negative terms, as that which generates upset, irritation and silence between the two generations of women, can it not also be understood more positively, especially given that a final reconciliation is both undesirable and impossible? For Jing-mei, it implies death and, less dramatically, as is the case for the other daughters, a loss of self. Hence reconciliation is understood in terms of fighting tigers and women armed with kitchen utensils and knitting needles (252, 183–4), preserving difference between Chinese mothers and American-born daughters to their mutual benefit.

This preservation of difference also provides the basis for a politics of representation. Seven subaltern women speak for themselves in *The Joy Luck Club*, with the narratives by the St. Clairs, Jongs and Hsus highlighting its political/personal benefits, albeit in ideological conditions that really already determine 'subaltern representation'. Jing-mei's negotiation of representation is more critical than that of these six narrators because she has to speak for and about the subalternized Suyuan. Her realization that she cannot be/know Suyuan – limitations that function positively by allowing an affirmation of the (m)other's heterogeneity – marks the beginning of a reciprocal and dialogic relationship between Jing-mei and others. *The Joy Luck Club* thus offers different negotiations of representation through its seven narrators, acknowledging that 'subaltern representation' is empowering but not to the extent that it *resolves* disenfranchizement.

In problematizing the idea that it is a solution the disenfranchized speaking for themselves, the text allows for a complex analysis of ideology. When subaltern women speak for/about themselves and each other, such activities necessarily involve essentialism: 'the Chinese mother' and 'the American-born daughter'. By drawing attention to the linguistic bases of these stereotypes, of *how* they are de/constructed in representation, *Darstellung* ratifying and resisting *Vertretung* simultaneously, *The Joy Luck Club* does not uncritically reproduce dominant ideologies, far from it, since 'how' radicalizes the text's negotiation of essences in keeping with strategic essentialism. Gender/ ethnic essences, so necessary for the formulation of identities and relationships in the context of the family and the nation, and, moreover, 'double-talk', depend on language, not nature, a point most obviously reinforced at the end of the text when Jing-mei's narrative moves from blood to a photograph. This movement is crucial to *The Joy Luck Club* because it ensures that the gender/ethnic essences therein are open to debate and questioning in terms compatible with dialogism. Overall, then, this movement towards the 'text/tissue/weave' of personal/ familial identities is regarded as beneficial, although, 'outside' the Joy Luck Club and, indeed, *The Joy Luck Club*, as the next chapter on *The Kitchen God's Wife* highlights, this movement demands careful negotiation, nowhere more so than in a theoretico-political context that assumes a 'textualist' approach, in this case, to history effectively marginalizes and, worse, denies the suffering of the Chinese, in particular Chinese women.

The Kitchen God's Wife

'PERTURBED at having to tell friends she wasn't the mothers of *The Joy Luck Club*', Daisy Tan said, 'next book, tell my true story',[1] even giving her daughter a videotaped account that would provide the material – images, language, voice, rhythm – for the Chinese mother's lengthy monologue in *The Kitchen God's Wife* (1991). Such an unequivocal request did not come easily, however, all sorts of reasons, some personal, others political, pushing Daisy towards silence, not speech. 'That was China. It's past. You must accept it, why tell it?' But she said: 'Why should I accept? I will never accept what happened to me. Tell the world.'[2] Amy Tan obliges with a story about the subalternized figure of the Kitchen God's wife, also examining the production of subalternity in the 'text/tissue/weave'[3] of a history that effectively renders 'acceptable' a range of patriarchal and/or imperialist abuses as they happened to her semi-biographical 'eponymous' narrator, Winnie Louie, formerly Jiang Weili.

Much of Winnie's narrative represents the Sino-Japanese War (1937–45), specifically the experience of '*taonan*' as it relates to the Japanese military and a Chinese military-husband, both of them breathing down her neck as she struggles to '"Escape! Escape!" – nothing else, day and night. And … you are running and stumbling, running and stumbling.'[4] By concentrating the bulk of *The Kitchen God's Wife* on the violent experiences of one Chinese mother – Winnie's twenty-two chapters greatly outnumber her American-born daughter's chapters, of which there are only three, arguably in response to the very different assaults on their bodies by an unscrupulous husband and an incurable disease respectively – Tan once again risks domesticating or privatizing political problems potentially in keeping with American neoconservatism. On one level, Winnie does represent a personal 'herstory' about family relationships marked by matrilineal conflict and matrimonial violence, although, on another level, 'Winnie' represents the subalternized woman, her identity and experiences moving from the semi-biographical to the mythical and the historical. *The Kitchen God's Wife* promotes this movement analogically: Winnie 'is' the mythical Guo 'is' the Chinese women in Nanking during the Sino-Japanese War, all of them suffering under patriarchy and/or imperialism, and without 'safe structures ... to express their grievances',[5] let alone assign blame to those responsible for a range of abuses from infidelity to rape.

Guo's unfaithful husband, Zhang, and Winnie's rapist husband, Wen Fu, are effectively rewarded with immortality and longevity respectively, their bad behaviour toward their wives officially forgotten. Officially forgotten also is Japan's atrocious behaviour during the war, including its assaults on Shanghai, Nanking and 'safe place[s] ... almost to the edge of China' (220). For the historian Iris Chang, Japan's six-week Rape of Nanking, beginning in December 1937, constitutes a holocaust exceeding other mass exterminations in World War Two, including Dresden, Hiroshima and Nagasaki, 'not only for the number of people slaughtered but for the cruel manner in which many met their deaths'. The torture and murder of more than 300,000 Chinese civilians, an estimated 20,000–80,000 of them raped, shocked even the Nazis in the city, 'one proclaiming the massacre to be the work of "bestial machinery"'.[6] For deliberately forgetting this war crime, Chang charges Japan with 'A Second Rape',[7] also implicating the west and the Chinese in this holocaust denial.[8]

Why and, indeed, how can rape happen once, let alone twice? Can anything be done about violence that is at once sexual and textual? Both questions are crucial to *The Kitchen God's Wife*, the analogies it sets up between mythical, literary and historical Chinese women going some ways towards understanding a typically feminine form of oppression. Objectified in patriarchal stories, their skin compared to 'white jade' and 'summer peach' and their bodies to 'chamber pot[s]' (101, 158), it is no coincidence that Chinese women were used as 'public toilets' and, in some cases, cannibalized during the Sino-Japanese War.[9] *The Kitchen God's Wife* implies that rape, the first rape, cannot be understood apart from a *his*tory of ideological encoding, reinforcing this emphasis on textuality and, more generally, the postmodern condition in its negotiation of the second rape. Granted, this emphasis could inadvertently perpetrate the forgetting of war/sex crimes in terms compatible with Japan's holocaust denial.[10] As one critic troubled by the postmodern condition points out, albeit in relation to nuclear holocaust:

> It seems to me that given the overwhelming and great, grand traumatic nature of what we face, we need modes of thought which are equal to those threats. And ... mak[ing] the whole world into a text ... seems to banish any comprehension beyond the texts. ... What troubles me is the seeming self-exclusion of the world, the absorption of everything in the world into the world of discourse, the world of words, the world of texts, and the lack of concern for those problems of human suffering.[11]

The Kitchen God's Wife sets up an intergenerational/intercultural 'dialogue' between Winnie and her daughter, Pearl Louie Brandt, as well as an intragenerational/intracultural 'dialogue' between Winnie and her friend, Helen Kwong, formerly Long Hulan, as a rejoinder to this 'dark' condition of postmodernity so effectively exploited by Japan and, in the text, by Wen Fu. Following the logic of 'anything goes' or, more precisely, 'anything they say goes' in an appropriation of postmodernism that preserves ethnic/gender hierarchies, Japan and Wen Fu proclaim that their war/sex crimes are stories and lies, a proclamation apparently supported by Helen's happy memories of wartime China, particularly of Nanking, a city seemingly remembered for fancy furniture and fine food (218), as opposed to mass extermination and rape. In her 'dialogue' with Helen,

Winnie questions this holocaust denial via a strategy of de-sanitization and deconstruction, also questioning in her 'dialogue' with Pearl the assumption that such a strategy destroys all narratives, if not the possibility of narrativization per se.

While all narratives may ultimately be 'sham' (34) or, to put it less emotively than Pearl, fictional, 'this does not mean that [they] are not part of the world and of reality; their impact on the world may well be all too strong for comfort'.[12] Those Japan raped suffer the impact of a fictional narrative, as does Winnie when she is arrested and imprisoned on the basis of Wen Fu's 'lies' (373) towards the end of her story. By addressing this 'textual violence',[13] and its complex relationship to sexual violence, *The Kitchen God's Wife* helps to ensure that experiences other to and, for that matter, 'othered' by official narratives, are brought into history, no easy task given that dominant ideologies operating in China, Japan and America work hard to appropriate such experiences. While Chinese patriarchy attempts to render the fact of Winnie's rape a fiction, as does Japanese ultranationalism with respect to the Rape of Nanking, American multiculturalism attempts to render fiction a fact in line with the 'information retrieval approach' to 'multicultural' literature.[14] And, it is these apparently asymmetrical acts of appropriation that Tan's text needs to resist if it is to tell the world a true story of ethnic/gender oppression, as requested by Daisy, without relinquishing its status 'as literature – as a story, language, memory'.[15]

At the beginning of *The Kitchen God's Wife*, Pearl and Winnie describe how they heretofore assumed the position of the subaltern woman, confined to 'limbo land[s]' (28) somewhere between the past and the future, a 'betweeness' that also extends to the post-colonial condition, if not to the postmodern condition. While immigration and diaspora render them neither 'Chinese' nor 'American', the unpresentability of their experiences cuts them off from the official narratives in these cultures governing acceptable behaviour, as well as from narrative per se. How can Pearl represent the disease that afflicts her body when multiple sclerosis is officially '"without known etiology," "extremely variable," "unpredictable," and "without specific treatment"' (27), and how can Winnie represent the sexual violence that afflicted her body (and 20,000–80,000 Chinese women's bodies) when rape is officially denied? Both narrators are thus displaced from language and by extension from history; it is as if they were 'already in the middle of an argument' (11), an argument profoundly indifferent to the subaltern woman. This indifference is analogically represented in terms of the diseased/raped body: no matter what they say their words cannot change, let alone resolve the brute fact of suffering. 'No prognosis' (26) seems available to either narrator, not to Winnie because she cannot be un-raped, and not to Pearl because she cannot be cured.

In this context of denial and indifference, it is hardly surprising that Winnie's first sentence includes the phrase, 'no choice' (11), a view (almost) repeated later by Pearl: 'the whole issue of individual choice became tricky, a burden to keep up, until it fell away' (15). The brute fact of suffering that resists easy telling, a whole variety of reasons, some personal, others political, pushing them towards silence, not speech, seems to put a stop to everything, particularly to the capacity of both mother and daughter to choose, and to interact meaningfully with the cultures and the people around them. Focusing on this latter problem, Winnie says: 'That is how she is. That is how I am. Always careful to be polite, always trying not to bump into each other, just like strangers' (82). Pearl also comments on mother–daughter 'estrangement': 'I feel as lonely as I imagine her to be. I think of the enormous distance that separates us and makes us unable to share the most important matters of our life' (34).

While the determination of both narrators to keep their 'sick' experiences secret for years, if not decades, contributes to the rigid division between mother and daughter, a rigidity represented more generally – temporally, spatially, politically – it does nevertheless make for 'a smoother life' (16). After all, 'the past is gone, nothing to be done, just forget it' (109), a forgetting seemingly made easier by Winnie's immigration to the US in 1949: 'China turned off the light, closed the door, told everyone to be quiet. All those people there became like ghosts. We could not see them. We could not hear them. So I thought I really could forget everything. Nobody could get out to remind me' (72), especially not during the Cold War. Although the geographical distance is considerably shorter, only fifty miles, Pearl similarly assumes that forgetting is made easier by not seeing/hearing Winnie. She rarely telephones her mother in San Francisco, particularly not for 'no reason' (76), and is normally harangued into attending the occasional family event: 'Pearl-ah, have to go, no choice' (11). As it stands, this 'long, long distance' (76) is better than no relationship at all. In Winnie's words to Pearl: 'I didn't tell you about my past', which includes, not necessarily through fault of her own, abortion, child abuse and infanticide, 'and still you thought I was a bad mother. If I had told you – then it would be even worse!' (398).

For personal reasons, then, Winnie and Pearl keep their 'sick' experiences secret from each other. Yet, here, as elsewhere in Tan's fiction, the personal is political, a feminist argument supported most obviously by the analogical relationship *The Kitchen God's Wife* sets up between the Japanese military and a Chinese military-husband, both rendering the rape of '"hsiao ren" (inferior or small human beings)'[16] 'acceptable' in war[17] and marriage. Even before 1937, when the relationship between China/Japan and Winnie/Wen Fu escalated into violence not resolved by the end of war/marriage in 1945 and 1949 respectively, Winnie's Chinese past was marked by upheaval that was at once personal and political: 'That's how everything was in China then. Too busy fighting each other. ... The old revolutionaries, the new revolutionaries, the Kuomintang, the Communists, the warlords, the bandits, and the students – gwah! gwah! gwah! – everybody squabbling like old roosters claiming the same sunrise.' Continuing with this image, Winnie says that 'the rest of us – women and children, old people and poor people – we were like scared hens, letting everyone chase us from one corner to another' (166).

In 'Ten Thousand Things', Winnie describes infighting in the Chinese home and the impact it has on women and children.

One of her earliest memories is of her parents arguing, unusual in a feudal family regulated by the 'Three Obediences and Four Virtues', a first-century behavioural code that 'remained continually effective, helping to maintain patriarchal power, until the early twentieth century'.[18] Winnie elaborates this code: 'The girl's eyes should never be used for reading, only for sewing. The girl's ears should never be used for listening to ideas, only to orders. The girl's lips should be small, rarely used, except to express appreciation or to ask for approval' (102). Although Winnie's mother is educated against this code, she is married off to a feudal family out of personal/political necessity. Chased from one corner to another, from circumstances that are modern but poor to those that are wealthy but traditional, Winnie's mother eventually takes the inauspicious place of Jiang Sao-yen's late second wife. Chased still further, firstly, into the (attic?) room above those of her fellow concubines, possibly for her modern or 'upside-down thinking' (103), and, finally, to her death, she mysteriously disappears when her daughter is six years old.

This pattern of 'crime' and punishment is repeated when Winnie is 'chased' from her father's house in Shanghai to her uncle's house on Tsungming Island, 'learn[ing] to expect nothing' from either family (112), and only too glad to escape at eighteen when she was married off to Wen Fu who violently exploits the 'Three Obediences and Four Virtues' to such an extent she 'become[s] like a chicken in a cage, mindless, never dreaming of freedom' (313). Their Chinese children similarly suffer, all three dying from (un)natural causes: Mochou is stillborn (242); the battered Yiku dies from dysentery (265); and, Danru, the son, dies from a disease carried by Japanese-raised rats (370). Indifferent to the deaths of his two daughters – 'At least it was not a boy' and 'If she dies, I wouldn't care' (242, 265–6) – Wen Fu's attitude seems altogether different when his son dies: 'The judge told me what my crime was. I was being sued', says Winnie, 'for stealing my son and letting him die' (373). She is also sued for defying the other two Obediences, to her father('s valuables) and to her husband, 'all because [she] was crazy for American sex' (375), at least as Wen Fu tells it at his wife's trial. While these charges are dropped, perhaps unwillingly given the ideological returns for convicting the revolutionary wife of a 'Kuomintang hero' (375), Winnie does nevertheless incur a two-year prison sentence for leaving her husband without a divorce certificate, as was the law then.

Wen Fu's reference to 'American sex' appeals to a powerful combination of dominant ideologies, to Chinese patriarchal, nationalist and reactionary ideologies vis-à-vis American imperialism. The west's hierarchical relationship to the east, the latter invariably being femininized in an imperial romance or, more explicitly, a 'white ... racial wetdream'[19] in which Chinese men and women are lovable for their accommodation to 'things American', arguably underpins Wen Fu's exposé of a revolutionary wife whose desire for a Chinese American GI, Jimmy Louie, threatens the patriarchal family/nation.

Caught between patriarchy and nationalism in China, Winnie may as well be invisible, an invisibility also perpetuated in America where she is caught between patriarchy and imperialism. Apart from the fact that the dominant American ideology of multiculturalism stereotypes immigrant/diasporic Chinese as a 'model minority', a seemingly benign stereotype that demands invisibility from 'the least political, or the least oppressed, or the most polite'[20] of America's ethnic minorities, an invisibility also perpetuated by immigrant Chinese in relation to a history of exclusion (79), Winnie is pushed towards silence, not speech, because her story puts into question the west's representation of the 1930s and 1940s. It is difficult for Winnie to speak about events in China because '*American* history' gives 1941 as the start date of World War Two, long after it began in Europe, not to mention China (172), a difficulty made all the more intense because her story implicates 'the West in ... the very historical catastrophes from which [she] so gladly escape[s]':[21] Britain's closure of the Burma Road, which prevented war supplies reaching the Chinese; and, America's 'big business with the Japanese, selling them gasoline and metal for airplanes – the same ones that were dropping bombs all over China' (283).

Just as Winnie's secrecy about rape has its basis in ideology/

politics, so too does Pearl's secrecy about MS in relation to a medical system dominated by 'the Western man of reason and science' of which Dr Phil Brandt is an example, if not 'the epitome'.[22] Out of all the husbands in the text, specifically the two Kitchen Gods, Zhang and Wen Fu, Phil comes across as the most reasonable, not inclined to infidelity, let alone rape. This said, his reason(ableness) does function oppressively: 'He takes arrogant pride in his "rational," "scientific," objective mind. He feels superior to his "ignorant" Chinese immigrant mother-in-law, whom he perceives as silly because she is superstitious. He includes his wife in his sneers whenever Pearl inclines so much as a minute fraction of an inch in her mother's direction.' To Phillipa Kafka, Dr Phil, resembling the supposedly benign Dr John in *The Yellow Wallpaper*, endorses 'the Western white phallocentric system' through a violent ethnic/gender hierarchy.[23] Not even Pearl's MS compromises this hierarchy, Phil still managing, somewhat selfishly, to privilege his response to her medical condition. 'Phil would read his old textbooks and every medical article he could find on the subject. And then he would become depressed that his own medical training offered no better understanding of [her] disease' (27).

With the 'smooth' family/national life of both Winnie and Pearl at stake, it is not surprising that they embark on a process of deliberate forgetting and secrecy. Such a deliberate act is bound to fail, however, because secrecy exceeds the binary opposition between concealment and revelation. Winnie may conceal the past, if not 'Chineseness' generally, but her act of concealment is revelatory. Pearl's comments about her mother and herself are useful here: 'She was always trying to suppress certain beliefs ... but sometimes they popped out anyway' (41–2); and, 'I wanted what had become impossible; I wanted to forget' (41–2, 26). Forgetting and secrecy are impossible because they necessarily reveal themselves, their form, more so perhaps than a conscious choice by Winnie and Pearl, many other things, including a casserole, a one-storey house, a 'relative' from China, the 'estranged' mother–daughter relationship and, more generally, an ethico-political need to represent those 'raped' in/

by history, compelling them to remember and, moreover, to reveal their 'sick' secrets to each other.

Getting out of China in 1953, sponsored by Winnie, who misinforms US immigration officials that her friend is family, Helen, now suffering from a (phoney) brain tumour, most obviously sets revelation in motion. She adheres to a relatively straightforward model of history, whereby experiences are easily told/resolved: 'We should sweep all the lies out of our life. Tell everyone our true situation. ... I want to correct everything before it's too late. No more secrets. No more lying', especially in view of her imminent death. To Winnie she says: 'Why should I go to my grave with all those lies? That I am your sister-in-law, married to your half-brother, a man I never met. And by birthdate is wrong. ... Now when I die, my life is cut short one year early' (79). And, besides, 'Hard life in China, that's very popular now, nothing shameful in that' (80). Helen uses a similar tactic on Pearl: 'How can I fly to heaven when this is weighing me down? No, you must tell your mother ... about your multiple neurosis [*sic*]' (36).

With Helen threatening 'to let all [their] secrets out' (73), alongside the fact that concealment is necessarily revelatory, Winnie and Pearl cannot *not* tell each other (and the world) about their raped and diseased bodies only to confront the fact that 'memory narrative does not represent a perfect equivalent of the events it purports to describe'.[24] The problem of memory is repeatedly addressed in *The Kitchen God's Wife*, a problem that analogically relates to the larger domain of public memory and Japan's insistence that photographs and newsreels of the Rape of Nanking are not perfectly equivalent to war crime. For instance, Pearl's 'private memories' of her late 'Daddy' 'are just images from photos' (46), the qualifier suggesting that image and referent are not perfectly equivalent. Similarly, Winnie's 'private memories' of her late mother 'are confusing. ... [She] would try to make one whole story. But then each part would contradict the next, until no part made sense' (88, 100). Gossip, dreams and her imagination add to this confusion, so much so that she 'no longer know[s] which story is the truth. ... They are all the same, all true, all false' (109). Winnie's inability to distinguish true from false is arguably a response to her mother's mysterious disappearance, the first of a series of traumatic experiences that 'shocks [her] out of [her] assumed categories of thinking'.[25]

The Kitchen God's Wife repeatedly highlights the limitations of assumed categories of thinking vis-à-vis military/domestic violence against the Chinese mother(land). This violence is excessive on so many counts. At one point, Winnie refers to 'the war as if [it] were an epidemic, spreading around sickness' (283), an analogy particularly relevant to the Japanese military in its assault on targets in excess of the conventions governing warfare. The movement of Winnie's narrative from Shanghai and Nanking to Kunming via *'taonan'* that affects 'everyone' – soldiers and civilians, adults and children, men and women (207) – suggests a military indiscriminate about its target. Continuing with the sickness analogy, Winnie refers to the impossibility of a post-war situation: 'the war was like a bad illness, and when it was over, it did not mean everybody suddenly became healthy again' (343), *The Kitchen God's Wife* in and of itself also articulating the impossibility of a post-war return to 'health' when such excessive violence makes impossible 'smart thoughts' (295), if not categorization per se.

For example, 'The Four Gates' describes a Japanese bombing raid on Kunming's busy marketplace, a raid so shocking that all Winnie's 'smart thoughts' relating to categories such as space, time and reality undergo crisis:

> I did not know whether I had fallen or whether the explosion had pushed me down, whether one second had passed, or one day. ... I thought maybe I was dreaming, because people were walking slowly, as if they were still dreaming too. Or perhaps we were dead and now waiting to go to the next world. ... And lying on the rooftops and in the road were all the things that ... I did not want to recognize. (295–6)

This unwillingness, if not inability, to conceptualize shock is also acknowledged in connection to the Rape of Nanking. In slightly more than one page, 'we learn … the news about Nanking' (233) from a passing Chinese soldier:

> Raped old women, married women, and little girls, taking turns with them, over and over again. Sliced them open with a sword when they were all used up. Cut off their fingers to take their rings. Shot all the little sons, no more generations. Raped ten thousand, chopped down twenty or thirty thousand, a number that is no longer a number, no longer people. (234)

Such economy with words and numbers, the latter being decreased tenfold, seems problematic considering that 'the Rape of Nanking represents one of the worst instances of mass extermination'.[26]

Here, *The Kitchen God's Wife* could be charged with minimizing Chinese suffering in keeping with revisionist histories determined to marginalize and/or melodramatize the violence of this event so as not to discomfort Japanese ultranationalists keen to forget this suffering, even if it is aestheticized or 'glamorize[d]' in a way that potentially titillates western Orientalists.[27] From this perspective, then, a one-page account of the Rape of Nanking certainly seems to minimize Chinese suffering, although Winnie offers a different explanation: 'What happened in Nanking, I couldn't claim that as my tragedy. I was not affected. I was not killed' (295). Almost directly quoted from Daisy, this statement was for Tan 'a remarkable revelation about the difference between her own perspective and her mother's. … "[T]he shock of that difference"' arguably explains Winnie's seemingly 'passing' reference to the Rape of Nanking.[28]

Related to this shocking difference of perspective is a problem that preoccupies Winnie from the beginning of *The Kitchen God's Wife* – namely, *how* to tell her story to Pearl (and the world) when violence 'infects' nations, families, individuals and, crucially, the assumed categories of thinking deemed necessary for representing past experiences. Not only is 'History' affected by war, the violence exceeding a system of representation that assumes time 'flow[s] forward like a river from the beginning to the end, everything connected, the lake to the sea'

(62), but it also *effects* war through its violent hierarchies and structures. Apart from the fact that '*History*' privileges certain experiences over others, history, any history, Winnie's included, is 'more or less violent in [its] necessary constitutive exclusions'.[29] As she comments, albeit in a different context: 'You are not just choosing one thing over another. You are choosing what you want. And you are also choosing what somebody else does not want, and all the consequences that follow. You can tell yourself that's not my problem, but those words do not wash the trouble away' (360). Alike in so far as 'History' and 'herstory' both involve choices that are necessarily violent, the latter differentiates itself from the former in that it affirms rather than denies the 'trouble' involved in 'choosing' one date over another, one document over another and so on.

Indeed, dates and documents prove particularly 'troublesome' in *The Kitchen God's Wife*: is 4638, a Horse year, 1929, 1930 or 1931, and is Winnie's birthdate 1918 and/or 1919? What about her divorce? It is 'officially valid when Wen Fu holds a gun to her head and makes her sign the paper, but it can be made invalid by her ex-husband's tearing up the paper. What is a divorce and ... [w]hen does a divorce ... begin or end?'[30] Moreover, Winnie's story does not move 'from the beginning to the end, everything connected' (62) for a reason arguably to do with the politics of representation. Tan's critics are divided about this politics, a division that is analogically addressed in *The Kitchen God's Wife* via the intragenerational/intracultural 'dialogue' between Winnie and Helen. Actually, it is not so much a dialogue because of their unequal roles, Winnie, the narrator, and Helen, a character. Their inequality is emphasized on numerous occasions, most blatantly when Winnie says of Helen: 'Sometimes I do not even enjoy her company. I do not agree with her opinions. I do not admire her character' (72–3). 'Find[ing] Helen coarse and vulgar, especially about her bodily functions[, Winnie] feels superior to her. She is convinced that she has nothing in common with her but accidental propinquity, an elitist attitude she retains to some degree all of her life, although she always sympathizes with the lower classes philosophically.'[31]

Pearl is similarly elitist about a working-class 'Chineseness' that she ascribes to the Kwongs *and* Winnie: at a family engagement party, the couple toasted with ginger ale in a plastic glass by a buffoonish uncle, Pearl observes Helen and Winnie, both poorly dressed in pastel-coloured synthetic dresses (32–3). Her middle-class American sensibilities are similarly offended at Grand Auntie Du's Buddhist funeral, complete with burning incense, farewell provisions and hired mourners. 'I can't believe it: Uncle Henry is standing in the middle of the aisle – videotaping the funeral!' (39), catching on camera the chaos that ensues in response to the open casket and a ten-foot funeral banner falling on 'Grand Auntie's chest like a beauty pageant banner' (43).

Helen (and her family) give *The Kitchen God's Wife* a darkly comic dimension, her 'coarse' and 'vulgar' character anticipating *The Hundred Secret Senses'* Kwan Li, who is similarly criticized by a middle-class narrator for a working-class 'Chineseness'. But Helen is not merely Winnie's comic foil. Indeed, she apparently assumes an altogether 'darker' function in the text as an uncritical purveyor of dominant opinion. For instance, she jokes about the military build-up to the Rape of Nanking, also describing Winnie's final encounter with Wen Fu 'as if it were only a funny story', complete with a Hollywood ending: 'the next morning, you were on an airplane [to America]. Lucky for you' (394). Gone is the violence; no mention is made of 'the city gone mad' (216) and a woman raped. 'Isn't this strange?' observes Winnie. 'We were at the same place, at the same time. For me, this was one of the worst moments of my life' (218). More than 'strange', Helen's sanitized history is seriously troubling. By marginalizing the violence of Japanese imperialism and Chinese patriarchy respectively via 'dark' comedy, she potentially makes 'the enormity of Chinese suffering ... safe for literary consumption'.[32]

In addition to applying the Hollywood format to wartime relationships between Japan/China and Wen Fu/Winnie, Helen applies it to the mother–daughter relationship when she assumes that the disclosure of their 'sick' secrets will bring about closure for/between Winnie and Pearl. Here, Helen adheres to a dominant 'motif in women's fiction' and, moreover, to the dominant reading of Tan's fiction:

> if mothers and daughters … talk long enough, share their stories, go back far enough into their past suffering to unearth and expose the causes, then mothers and daughters will reconcile, the psychic barriers created by generations of male and social domination will fall away, and they will find peace, understanding, comfort, union, and wholeness.[33]

For character and critic(s) alike, Chinese talk-story is a cure for intergenerational/intercultural 'estrangement'. In Helen's words: 'And now you are closer, mother and daughter, I can already see this' (408).

'Chineseness' is thus represented as curative, a point further reinforced by Helen's story about a Chinese magic spring, '"able to cure anything"' (232–3), including, presumably, a '"B Nine"' brain tumour and '"multiple neurosis."' This story adheres to '"the psychospiritual plantation system"' so popular in Holly-wood(ized) narratives from the Reagan era, all of them featuring 'Third World Healers' capable of curing 'multiple neuroses' brought on by America's 'shallow, acquisitive, image-conscious (read "middle- and upper-middle-class white") world of wealth and institutional power'.[34] According to Sau-ling Cynthia Wong, the wealthy Americanized daughter(s) in Tan's text(s), resembling her Hollywood counterparts in films such as Bruce Beresford's *Driving Miss Daisy* (1989), Woody Allen's *Alice* (1990) and Jerry Zucker's *Ghost* (1990), are cared for, if not magically cured by 'Africanness/Chineseness'. But does the 'Third World', in this case, the Chinese mother(land), actually offer a cure for Pearl's multiple sclerosis? Yes, *if* Helen's 'Hollywoodized' view is read as representative. All Pearl needs to do, Helen informs her, is 'return' to 'the real good earth of ancient tradition and magical wisdom'[35] and drink the 'the real good water' of the Chinese magic spring and she will be cured of her multiple neurosis and preferably her multiple sclerosis consistent with the Hollywood ending. For once, Winnie agrees with her friend: 'Everything inside you is peaceful, no worries, no sorrows' (410). Significantly, however, Winnie's agreement is founded on a lie: 'I don't really have a brain tumour. ... I made it up', Helen informs Pearl. 'Of course, when we go to China, you must pretend it was the magic spring that cured me, the same one that can cure you' (408).

Here, then, the Chinese mother(land) merely offers a *pretend* cure for an incurable disease, a fact or, more properly, a fiction that situates Tan's text less in the 'Hollywood(ized)' tradition of '"the psychospiritual plantation system"' and more in 'the Chinese American tradition of *jaw jieh* (catching pigs), "a time-honored practice of bullshitting white people into buying up ... junk"', including 'abalone shells, "beggars chicken," tour guides, cookbooks and all the rest, both in the name of economic survival *and* revenge'.[36] Although Tan does not use the term *jaw jieh*, a number of her characters practise it, often 'dishonorabl[y]' (156). For example, the Wen family 'bullshit' people from America and England into buying '*Chinese* garbage', bought for 'a few coppers' from poor Chinese people whose survival depends on such asymmetrical economic exchanges (156). Also considered 'dishonorable' is Helen's 'bullshitting', at least until the end of *The Kitchen God's Wife* when it is revealed that she lied in the name of loyalty and friendship, her apparent 'blind[ness]' and 'deaf[ness]' (260) to Wen Fu's violence functioning as a survival strategy. As Kafka argues, 'Helen's primary concern all along was that Winnie's husband never realize that she did know about all his evil doings. If so, she brilliantly reasoned, he would have deprived Winnie of her proximity, of whatever small comfort she could be to her.'[37] 'This revelation', Kafka continues, 'is amazing in its profundity. It is profound that a woman who seems so insensitive and so self-absorbed as Helen should all the time have known and cared and have had her friend's best interests at heart. ... She is not the collaborationist she appears to be, but a saboteur. She fights guerrilla warfare, with maximum safety for herself and her allies.'[38]

Helen's movement from a collaborationist to a saboteur thus compels a re-reading of her character, a re-reading suggested in Winnie's first chapter, 'When Fish are Three Days Old'. This chapter describes how Helen, defying logic or, better, adhering to a contradictory logic, makes a good meal out of an old fish, whereas Winnie makes a bad meal out of a fresh fish. Their difference of culinary opinion prompts a discussion of luck and, after it, truth: 'If something is false, she thinks it is true. If something is true, she thinks it is false' (137). Helen's contradictory logic arguably facilitates the 'vengeful' use of *jaw jieh*: in the role of 'pig catcher' and devil's advocate, she collaborates with dominant ideologies – multiculturalism and revisionism – in order to sabotage them. Thus understood, Helen's sanitization of military/domestic violence via stories, often comic stories, that end happily ever after with 'some sort of hero popping up and marrying an ugly animal who then turned out to be a kind and beautiful princess' (230), his love, presumably, miraculously returning her to humanity in much the same way as the Chinese mother(land) miraculously returns the American-born daughter and, with her, the American-born reader to a condition apparently 'cured' of multiple sclerosis/ neurosis, proves, in Judith Caesar's satirical words, 'as true as the printed leaflets the Japanese drop on Nanjing [Nanking] explaining that civilians will not be harmed'.[39] Helen's complex negotiation of the true/false binary opposition empowers a de-sanitization of Chinese history by playing up to the apparently asymmetrical dominant ideologies of multiculturalism and revisionism without playing into the hands of either. In this way, then, *The Kitchen God's Wife* practises *jaw jieh* as a form of 'revenge' on the multiculturalist indifference to the *fiction* of a curative 'Chineseness' and on the revisionist indifference to the *fact* of rape in Chinese history.

After all the lies and 'bullshit', then, Helen finally affirms Winnie's 'herstory' of ethnic/gender oppression. But, as Winnie asks, '"how could you ... know at not say anything?" And Helen patted [her] arm. "Eh, little person, who are you to ask such a question"' (412), especially given Winnie's fifty-year silence? Another example of their one-up(wo)manship perhaps, although it could also reinforce Kafka's point that Helen knew all along the enormity of her friend's subalternization. As the victim of sexual *and* textual violence, Winnie should understand only too well the unreliable relationship between seeing/telling. So effectively exploited by Wen Fu, this unreliability is the focus of two central chapters, 'Bad Eye' and 'A Flea on a Tiger's Head', but, even before this, Winnie's narrative highlighted the unreliable relationship between signifier/signified and sign/referent, specifically in relation to two paintings. Although realistic, both paintings resist one meaning/referent, even generating contradictory meanings: 'You could not tell if the lady playing the lute was singing a happy or a sad song. You could not tell if the woman carrying the heavy load was beginning her journey or ending it' (144); and, 'I wanted to believe this painting was my mother, because that was all I had left. ... But her face always looked in another direction, never at me. She showed no thoughts. I could not tell what she was thinking. ... I could not ask her ... questions' (88). Winnie tries to render signifier/signified and sign/referent perfectly equivalent, even washing (and destroying) the latter painting after it develops mould as if washing (and destroying) her mother, but both paintings remain profoundly indifferent to her gaze and questions.

Winnie's inability 'to tell' is confined neither to these paintings nor to the aesthetic domain. Indeed, it preoccupies her narrative, if not *The Kitchen God's Wife* per se, also moving into the political domain when eyewitnesses to Wen Fu's increasingly violent behaviour towards his wife, daughter and, indeed, any woman who comes into contact with him, seem profoundly indifferent to his violence and their suffering. Of these eyewitnesses, Winnie remarks: 'They watched and did nothing.' 'They said nothing.' 'They did not protest.' And, 'I was thinking, Why doesn't anyone help me? Why do they stand there, as if I were truly wrong?' (252–3). This same scenario is repeated *ad nauseam* in *The Kitchen God's Wife*, and in every case eyewitnesses seem unable to tell that Wen Fu is 'a monster' despite his monstrous appearance. After a car accident, which leaves his mistress dead and his face disfigured, 'His eye was big and dark in the middle, yellow and bloody all around. It seemed to be looking out with so much anger, no good feelings behind it. He looked like a monster' (248). Tan's tendency to depict Chinese men as 'ugly', the Moon Lady in *The Joy Luck Club* and, here, Winnie's husband, as well as her father, Jiang Sao-yen, whose face is also 'divided in half, a different expression on each side' (326), after he suffers a stroke arguably brought on by his collaboration with the Japanese during the war, could be interpreted as anti-male and anti-Chinese,[40] were it not for that fact that Tan's monstrous men analogically represent the 'ugliness'[41] of 'gender asymmetry'.[42]

Rather than 'merely' holding an individual Chinese man responsible for various crimes against Chinese women, 'Bad Eye' and 'A Flea on a Tiger's Head' address the relationship between sexual violence and textual violence, most dramatically when Wen Fu beats Winnie in front of eyewitnesses apparently indifferent to her domestic situation. Their apparent indifference leaves Winnie with little alternative but to address why/how it is that her suffering repeatedly fails to signify as such, at least in patriarchal China (and ultranationalist Japan). Apart from their own fear of Wen Fu, generated by his 'laughing-scaring game' (180), a playful form of bullying, Winnie's eyewitnesses, most of whom are men, live in a culture that 'never ... criticize[s] men or the society they ruled, or Confucius, that awful man who made society' (257). Chinese patriarchy is so powerful in its affect that there is no structure, no language even, for criticizing men. As Kafka observes, 'women had difficulty in complaining about that for which no language existed'.[43] She continues: 'Gender asymmetry ... was such that the language discourse contained no female gender referentiality. Gender was erased, [as were] ... safe structures for women to express their grievances.'[44] Unable to use words like 'nuisance' and 'rape' in relation to Wen Fu, Winnie can 'only blame other women' for her suffering (256–9), even though it inadvertently reinforces gender asymmetry.

The critique of gender asymmetry is thus cut short, leaving 'the Chinese woman' in 'a limbo land' (28). This confinement is 'even' experienced by the powerful Chinese mother-in-law, her power depending on tokenization achieved via fearful complicity with Chinese patriarchy (257). Thus confined, it is hardly surprising that Chinese women resort to using their bodies as a form of criticism. Hence the emphasis in Tan's fiction on female suicide: at times, it can function as 'a weapon' (*JLC*, 239), although, at others, it is 'wrong … that [Chinese women] could find no other way [and] no one to help [them]' (354). While contemplating death as a means of liberation, not self-empowerment, Winnie resists suicide because it would mean abandoning her only surviving child, Danru, as she herself was abandoned: 'I could never do what my mother did to me.' And, besides: 'How foolish I was! To think my body was my own, something to protect or lose only for myself' (308) when it is raped twice, sexually and textually.

For this reason, the raped body of the Chinese mother and, for that matter, the diseased body of the American-born daughter, do not constitute a reliable point of reference. The female body is *not* 'a locus of truth'[45] or a 'constant'; it is *not* one those 'things [Winnie and Pearl] could isolate and control in a life of unknown variables' (28), a point graphically made when Wen Fu not only manipulates his wife's body physically, using it 'as if [it] were – what? – a machine!' (312), but also linguistically and semiotically so as to ensure that he is victor *and* victim. In this context, then, it would be 'foolish' of Winnie and, indeed, *The Kitchen God's Wife* to assume that the fact of rape is easily told via an appeal to the body and experientiality when revisionist histories pre-determine that rape is not perfectly equivalent to sex/war crime. Hence *The Kitchen God's Wife* moves from sexual violence to textual violence, from the 'im-mediate'[46] body to the mediated body. In addition to putting into question the assumed essentialism of Tan's text(s), this movement empowers a critique of the second rape, which in turn brings the first rape into history.

In a text preoccupied with (other) texts, 'The Kitchen God' most obviously,[47] it is hardly surprising that its 'eponymous' narrator focuses on the part played by language, particularly the rhetorical dimension of language, in perpetrating Chinese women's oppression. In particular, romantic stories and sexy stories describe these women as 'white jade', 'summer peach' and, more explicitly, 'a chamber pot' (101, 158). Of their impact, Winnie says: 'Why did stories always describe women that way, making us believe we had to be that way too?' (101), an impact that is felt by her (and 20,000–80,000 Chinese women) when she suffers sexual/textual violence. These stories serve patriarchal/ imperialist ideologies via the analogies they set up between Chinese women and various objects – precious stones, soft fruits and public toilets. At the same time, however, the fact that objectification is not natural, 'only' ideological and rhetorical, and that analogies are used to bring *different* entities together, subverts patriarchal/imperialist ideologies. This difference is crucial to both Winnie and to *The Kitchen God's Wife*, particularly as the debate about Tan's text(s) turns on the analogical relationships it sets up between the personal and the political, in this case, Wen Fu/Japan and Winnie/China, as well as between imperialism/patriarchy and Winnie/Pearl.

Of the analogy between imperialism and patriarchy, for instance, Caesar argues that 'Weili's suffering is that of a middle-class woman married to a bully. An American reader can identify with this, at least to some degree; and, once one has done this, one can begin to get a sense of the type of suffering that Tan suggests only metaphorically or seemingly incidentally – the Nanjing [Nanking] massacre, for instance.'[48] The analogy between 'the horrors that befell Winnie and the disease that has befallen her daughter' is for Robb Forman Dew more problematic because it invites parallels between two experiences that are 'simply not equally horrific'.[49] Both critics understand Tan's analogies in terms of identity and equality, justifiably so given that *The Kitchen God's Wife* highlights the part played by analogies in the objectification of Chinese women, although Caesar also preserves the difference underpinning the analogy, as does Winnie when she notes that classical stories are 'only stories' (340). The 'only' is uttered here in a way that neither underestimates nor overestimates the power of official stories.

More precisely, Winnie, like Pearl, is incredulous of official stories, although, unlike her daughter, whose 'American mind' (313) vacillates between binary oppositions so much so that 'everything feels like a sham' (34), Winnie proclaims that 'everything [is] always in between – without hope, yet without despair; without resistance, but without acceptance. So you see, weak and strong' (313). Following Winnie's in-between logic, a logic marked by simultaneity, as opposed to either/or, the 'only' in 'only stories' acknowledges that their strength is also their weakness and vice versa. This logic enables Winnie to perform 'a linguistic and semiotic subversion'[50] made possible by the difference between signifier/signified and sign/referent, the same difference so effectively exploited by Wen Fu to subalternize his wife.

For example, Winnie subverts 'a sex story about newly-weds' (158). On hearing how the wife kills her husband during sex by draining him of his *yang* (male essence), she unmasks the subjective and ideological limitations of this story as it passes from a treacherous friend to a slow-minded uncle and a foolish cousin. 'Why do people say these things?' Winnie asks. 'How does anyone know who you are supposed to believe? And why do we always believe the bad things first?' (162). Determined not to believe bad things about the wife/widow with too much *yin* (female essence), Winnie makes her a happily married émigré. She also insists: 'Of course it's a true story', at least as she 'dream[s] and 'imagin[es]' it (162–3). Winnie's (imaginative) appeal to truth and to experientiality – 'I saw [the *yin* woman] myself' – when reinforced by 'insignificant stretches' of the 'three bedrooms, two baths' (163) sort, announces *'we are the real'*.[51] Moreover, this announcement *has to* be a 'reality effect',[52] first, because the yin-woman liaison is dreamt/imagined, and, second, because the problem of reference is raised throughout *The Kitchen God's Wife*.

Winnie's 'herstory' also relies on reality effects. In addition to her position as the 'eponymous' narrator, Winnie's American nationality empowers 'herstory', a point wryly made by Caesar: 'the personal emotional crisis of an American is the only suffering interesting enough to write about'.[53] Given American interest in 'Hard life in China' (80), an interest Rey Chow describes as 'China watching'[54] whereby western systems of representation adhere to the Orientalist binary opposition of an uncivilized/inhuman China versus a civilized/human America, the fact that Winnie was Weili also empowers 'herstory', albeit as 'spectacle, entertainment, and spiritual enrichment for the 'First World'.[55] Both forms of empowerment, the first dependent on Winnie's American identity, the second, on Weili's Chinese identity, are, above all, strategies in that the essentialist identities they presuppose are complicated by the narrator's 'two identities, two voices, two cultures, and even two names'.[56] Specifically with respect to the second form of empowerment, the fact it is the often-criticized Helen who proclaims 'Hard life in China, that's very popular now' (80) arguably bolsters the case for *The Kitchen God's Wife*'s strategic use of 'China watching'. Indeed, 'China watching' is 'something [the text] must adopt in order to produce a critique'[57] of dominant ideologies that render the rape of '"*hsiao ren*" (inferior or small human beings)'[58] 'acceptable' in war/marriage, all the time remembering the ideological/political limitations of such a strategy.

When used strategically, 'China watching' problematizes a number of dominant ideologies, most obviously Chinese patriarchy and Japanese ultranationalism as they attempt to deny Winnie's 'herstory' and Chinese history, reducing both to lies, stories and 'sham' (34), but also American multiculturalism in its attempt to affirm 'multicultural' literature as 'Truth' and other similarly capitalized concepts such as 'Roots, Culture, Tradition, History, War, Human Evil'.[59] These apparently asymmetrical acts of appropriation are resisted in *The Kitchen God's Wife* in so far as it promotes an analysis of the referential function of language, of how different entities, signifier/signified and sign/referent are linked together rhetorically and, as such, are liable to a deconstructive questioning. Winnie's story represents this vulnerabilty when her suffering does not signify suffering, at least to Wen Fu and patriarchal China. By the same token, however, Wen Fu's revisionist history is also vulnerable. This vulnerability, moreover, makes available a properly historical model of history. Granted, this model cannot represent history finally, but this is precisely what ensures a future for history and, for that matter, *The Kitchen God's Wife*.

Futurity is emphasized at the end of the text. Pearl is 'caught in endless circles of lies. Or perhaps they are not lies' (409), 'even' after Winnie has told her story, which includes Pearl's 'herstory'. 'I had just been told that Wen Fu might well be the other half of my genetic makeup. ... And then I told her about my illness' (400–1) to a barrage of theories, not cures, from Winnie. One such theory involves Pearl speaking to 'a goddess that nobody knows': 'She is ready to listen. She understands English. You should tell her everything. ... She will wash away everything sad with her tears. She will use her stick to chase everything bad' (413–15). The 'native' has not so much returned here as moved on since the English-speaking Chinese goddess with dyed hair is Winnie's construction. What is more, 'no one would call her Mrs Kitchen God. Why would she want to be called that, now that she and her husband are divorced?' (414). By replacing the Kitchen God, an unfaithful husband who became a fearsome god under dubious circumstances, not with Mrs Kitchen God, but with Lady Sorrowfree, Winnie redresses the gender asymmetry within Chinese mythology apart from an 'upside-down' sexism compatible with patriarchal ideology. The final paragraph of *The Kitchen God's Wife* sees mother and daughter lighting incense to Lady Sorrowfree: 'Of course, it's only superstition, just for fun. But see how the smoke rises – oh, even faster when we laugh, lifting our hopes higher and higher' (415).

The ending of *The Kitchen God's Wife* is 'happy', if only because Winnie and Pearl are seen laughing as the smoke rises and, analogically, their hopes lift. This image of movement contrasts with earlier images of confinement, of caged birds especially, all of them suggesting, through repetition if nothing else, that Tan's narrators are violently determined by a combination of dominant ideologies in China, Japan and America. In Winnie's case especially, these ideologies urge that sexual violence be confined to the female mind/body as if it were a(n incurable medical) condition (of war) about which nothing can be or, indeed, should be done. Granted, nothing can be done about the first rape in the sense that Winnie and by extension the 20,000–80,000 Chinese women in Nanking cannot be un-raped. Not even 'the real good water' of a Chinese magic spring can 'cure' rape, multiple sclerosis and, more generally, the multiple neuroses prevalent in postmodern America.

Ultimately, then, *The Kitchen God's Wife* denies Winnie and Pearl the happy Hollywood ending advocated by Helen, albeit in terms of a pretence, although it does nevertheless suggest, by virtue of the its existence if nothing else, that something can be done about the second rape. In view of the powerful claim made by Wen Fu and Japan that their sex/war crimes did not happen, a claim based in part on the impossibility of 'perfect equivalen[ce]'[60] between and within eyewitness accounts, and moreover, between signifier/signified and sign/referent, *The Kitchen God's Wife* has no alternative but to focus on the 'text/tissue/weave' of history, of why/how it is that the Chinese, in particular Chinese women can be raped twice, both sexually and textually.

Far from rendering this history of ethnic/gender oppression 'a sham' (34), as some critics of postmodernism proclaim, this focus makes possible a radical critique of dominant ideologies: the revisionist fictionalization of the fact of rape and the multi-culturalist factualization of a fiction about rape, two apparently asymmetrical ideologies that ultimately seek to maintain ethnic/gender hierarchies and structures. In other words, *The Kitchen God's Wife* suggests that both ideologies perpetrate the second rape, albeit in different ways, the revisionists, represented in the text by Wen Fu, as well as by Helen (or, so it seems), 'raping' Winnie by denying historical fact, and the multi-culturalists, represented in the text by Helen (or, so it seems), 'raping' Winnie's narrative and, with it, *The Kitchen God's Wife* by denying literary fiction. Most obviously, the intergenerational and intragenerational 'dialogues' in the text provide opportunity of negotiating between revisionism and multiculturalism, effectively 'sabotaging' them by highlighting the linguistic and ideological bases of rape in and by history. Whether sexual or textual, literal or figural, rape functions oppressively in both instances. The acknowledgement of this fact enables Tan to tell the world a 'true story' in this 'realist' text and, for that matter, in her next magic realist text, which also negotiates the literal/figural binary opposition, about the subalternization of Chinese women – Guo, Winnie, Daisy and the 20,000–80,000 women in Nanking – in 'The Kitchen God', *The Kitchen God's Wife* and Chinese history.

The Hundred Secret Senses

AGAIN concerned with the politics of representation, although, in contrast to *The Kitchen God's Wife*, this politics appears not quite so urgent, *The Hundred Secret Senses* (1995) addresses through the intergenerational/intercultural 'dialogue' between two half-sisters, the Chinese-born Kwan Li and the American-born Olivia Yee, theoretico-political questions about the production of truth. Amy Tan introduces this theme in her acknowledgements when she thanks family, friends and colleagues for 'the ... ways in which they contributed to the truth of this fiction'.[1] Given that *The Joy Luck Club* and *The Kitchen God's Wife* offer semi-biographical representations of historical experiences specific to the twentieth century, most obviously the Sino–Japanese War (1937–45) and the Cultural Revolution (1949), Tan's thanks seem to prepare the way for a similar text. But 'the truth in this fiction' is deceptive since *The Hundred Secret Senses* spurns 'the real' via Kwan's stories about ghosts, reincarnation and the supernatural 'World of Yin' (3), unless, of course, the 'moment of truth' in this fiction is that 'reality ... is already in and of itself magical or fantastic' and 'realism is already necessarily a "magic realism"'.[2]

In the tradition of 'American magic realism', a genre that 'has been gaining popularity as a means of literary expression for the majority of ethnic [minority] literatures in the US since the late 1960s',[3] *The Hundred Secret Senses* implies that modern American reality is already in and of itself magical or fantastic. The 'mist[iness]' Olivia attributes to the World of Yin (3), as well as to China (185), an attribute that consigns these two realities to 'the static, ritual-permeated, mythical Time of a China past, where individuals' lives are ... shaped by tradition',[4] also marks modern America: 'When I first arrived in the United States', Kwan reminds her sister, 'you told me rabbits laid eggs once a year and dead people came out of caves to look for them.' According to Kwan, 'Americans do the same thing' (218) in that they also follow 'mystifying' rituals and traditions. *The Hundred Secret Senses* thus redeploys exotic stereotypes, particularly those related to religious and culinary practices, so that the American characters become exotic objects for the Chinese characters. In so doing, it challenges essentialist notions of ethnicity, a challenge reinforced by the main characters' 'multiple personalities' (141). For example: Olivia is Olivia Yee-Laguni-Bishop-Li and, before her twentieth-century persona, Miss Banner (288); and, Kwan is (in) Lili('s body), as well as once being a mid-nineteenth-century Chinese orphan named after 'the famous ghost maiden Nunumu' (27).

More than reversing (and displacing) a range of 'binary states – traditional versus modern, superstitious versus secular, elemental versus materialistic',[5] *The Hundred Secret Senses* raises questions about the production of truth. 'Whatever [Kwan] says, she believes is true' (288), whereas the cynical and 'overly analytical' (18) Olivia suffers a crisis of belief in response to various upsetting experiences, including her father's death, her sister's immigration and, later, institutionalization, and her husband's so-called infidelity: 'Who and what am I supposed to believe?' (222), not an easy question to answer given that Kwan 'pushed her Chinese secrets into [Olivia's] brain and changed how [she] thought about the world' (11). This change is the focus of Olivia's narrative so that by the end of *The Hundred Secret Senses* she knows who/what (she wants) to believe: 'And I listen, no longer afraid of Kwan's secrets. She's offered me her hand. I'm taking it freely. Together we're flying to the World of Yin' (292).

Arguably, however, who/what Olivia believes turns out to be less crucial to *The Hundred Secret Senses* than *how* her belief in the 'supernatural' is produced or constructed by the 'super-natural' effects of ideology and language. These effects deter-mine how a story and a storyteller are read; and, it is the politics of reading that preoccupies *The Hundred Secret Senses* and this chapter. Through the character of Kwan, whose immigrant life spans a period in American history – the 1960s to the 1990s – that saw identity politics complicated by a politics of difference, as well as the growing popularity of 'American magic realism', Tan analogically re-presents a history of the neocolonial relationship between the dominant western(ized) group and other(ed) Americans. Often, this relationship is marked by 'benevolence' that can be traced back to the mid-nineteenth-century Christian missionary project. Kwan's reincarnation links these two histories, as do the descriptions of Tan's other characters, most obviously the 'philanthropic' Louise Kenfield and the 'breast-beating'[6] Olivia. A further link between colonial past and neocolonial present is suggested by Kwan's institu-tionalization at the (in)appropriately named Mary's Help where she undergoes electro-shock treatment. 'Things being what they were back in the early 1960s, the doctors diagnosed Kwan's Chinese ghosts as a serious mental disorder' (14), although, some twenty years later, her stories about ghosts, reincarnation and the World of Yin have made her a local celebrity, parti-cularly in San Francisco's Castro district.

All in all, then, Kwan's relationships seem to depend on the way her 'yin' stories are treated or read. So much more than a character/narrator, 'she' raises questions about the politics of reading, specifically about *how* western(ized) readers respond to that which is radically different or 'supernatural'. Given Kwan's tendency for 'free speech, free association, free car-wash with fill'er-up' (18), it should come as no surprise that the term 'super-natural' (as well as 'yin' and 'ghost') generates different interpre-tative possibilities. Most obviously, 'supernatural' refers to magical events: 'ghosts … leave the mists just to visit [Kwan's] kitchen on Balboa Street in San Francisco' (3); and, 'the *lili-lili* girl' ghost (44) and a noisy 'American ghost' (109) visit Olivia's Californian homes. In its hyphenated form, 'super-natural' refers to anything that supersedes the dominant group's representation of natural reality, a representation that although assumed realistic *has to* be 'super-natural' in the sense that it is different from natural reality. This difference is insurmountable: no representation, whether in the tradition of 'hard realism' (236) or magic realism can overcome it apart from an ideological illusion.

In this respect, then, 'magic' is not specific to other(ed) groups and their literatures. Granted, the supernatural is often represented in these literatures, but the assumption that it functions literally, not figuratively, so that a magic realist text such as *The Hundred Secret Senses* '*express*[es]' and '*reflects* in its language of narration *real* conditions of speech and cognition within the *actual* social relations of a post-colonial culture' risks what is most radical in magic realism.[7] Here, the post-colonial critic Stephen Slemon effectively limits this radicalism by reading magic realism in terms compatible with dominant aesthetic and political categories. Despite these limits, magic realism, which, after all, is an oxymoronic form and, as such, generates different interpretative possibilities, some literal, others figural, none of them settling into a hierarchy or, in Olivia's words, amounting to 'the whole truth' (223), remains remarkably resistant to dominant categories and the binary logic underpinning them. And, it is precisely this resistance that makes possible a post-colonial critique of colonial/neocolonial hierarchies and structures in Tan's magic realist text.

Olivia's opening comments about her 'genetic record' suggest that her world is hierarchical and structured. 'Kwan and I', she assuredly remarks, 'share a father, only that. She was born in China. My brothers, Kevin and Tommy, and I were born in San Francisco after my father, Jack Yee, immigrated here and married our mother, Louise Kenfield' (3). All she says of her sister is that she was born in China. No detailed genealogy is offered, and there is no mention of the village in China where Kwan was born. Contrasting her specific origin, which reliably details genealogical and geographical matters, with Kwan's non-specific origin gives Olivia a secure sense of her American identity in line with binary logic: China/America, abstract/ particular and '"low[/high]-resolution" picture[s]'.[8] Like the American-born daughters in *The Joy Luck Club* and *The Kitchen God's Wife*, Olivia is able 'to *name* things in [her] world to a high degree of topical and local precision',[9] whereas China, 'even' on the China trip featured in the lengthy third part of *The Hundred Secret Senses* is described as 'a fabled misty land' (185).

Olivia's secure sense of 'Americanness' is not disturbed by multicultural America, an adjective that applies to the dominant group, as much as to ethnic minority groups. For example, Louise describes herself as 'American mixed grill, a bit of everything white, fatty and fried' (3), the culinary figure so common in a western exoticist discourses prone to 'foodways stereotyping'[10] being redeployed here in a counter-Orientalist gesture to describe 'Americanness'. For her stereotypical representation of Louise – 'American mixed grill', 'a champion baton twirler', 'a Kelly girl' (3) – and her 'other less-than-appealing Caucasian characters', Tan is charged with reverse racism. To the interview question, 'Is there a problem between you and white characters?', Tan responds with a laugh, also insisting: 'some of these characters have to be foils. I needed a mother who was kind of undependable, so that Kwan could become that fount of love that Olivia is looking for. There was no intention – unless there is something in trying to depict a Caucasian mother as not so great.' And, besides, 'some of [her] best friends are Caucasian',[11] another racist cliché that Tan playfully redeploys.

Like the other mothers in Tan's texts, Louise, once 'wrest[ed] … from the anthropomorphic or humanistic realism in which [she is] bound to be lodged in most interpretations',[12] functions as a figure for a political identity with its historical roots in the mid-nineteenth century: the telescopic philanthropist, who, like Mrs Jellyby in Charles Dickens' *Bleak House* (1853),[13] is 'totally obsessed with helping strangers and ignoring the homefront' (60). Louise's relationships with 'strangers' closer to home are similarly politicized, nowhere more so than in her 'out-relationships'. According to Olivia, the romantic liberalism of the mid-nineteenth-century missionary project persists with Louise: 'Mom thinks that her marrying out of the Anglo race makes her a liberal. "When Jack and I met," she still tells people, "there were laws against mixed marriages. We broke the law for love." She neglects to mention that those laws didn't apply in California' (3). Louise's romantic liberalism also applies to her step-daughter and her boyfriends: 'I suspect she thought of Kwan as a foreign exchange student she would host for a year, a Chinese Cinderella, who would become self-sufficient and go on to have a wonderful American life' (6); and, 'My mother has another new boyfriend, Jamie Jofré. I don't have to meet him to know he'll have charm, dark hair, and a green card' (48).

Not surprisingly, Louise's 'foreign imports' constitute a monolithic group; all are valued for their apparent capacity for 'true love' and 'eternal fidelity' (48) derived from their oppressed ethnicity, even the Italian American Bob Laguni, 'the fluke in [her] history of dating foreign imports – and that's only because she thought Laguni was Mexican instead of Italian' (8). Although not from an 'emerging nation – she would never say "the third world." A colony under foreign dictatorship is excellent', Bob can nevertheless trace his origins or, more properly, his orphan origins back to a country beginning with 'I': 'When emerging nation isn't available, she'll settle for Ireland, India, Iran' and, presumably, Italy (48). The alliteration and the metonymy, not to mention the economic figures – 'imports', 'exchange' and so on – function here to bolster Olivia's satirical description of Louise as an American missionary in her romanticized 'out-relationships' with men promising high returns, specifically with respect to '*amor*' (48) and 'Culture' – the Indian artist Bharat Singh (98) and the Iranian dancer/lover Sharam Shirazi (121).

Olivia's secure sense of 'Americanness' is further reinforced by everyday practices.

> We were a modern American family. We spoke English. Sure, we ate Chinese food, but take-out, like everyone else. And we lived in a ranch-style house in Daly City. My father worked for the Government Accounting Office. My

mother went to PTA meetings. She had never heard my
father talk of Chinese superstition before; they attended
church and bought life insurance instead. (6)

Speaking one language, the standard language, assimilates Olivia
into America, and indulging in everyday practices reinforces the
US as 'a solid community' even though she 'will never meet, or
even know the names of more than a handful of ... fellow-
Americans. ... But [s]he has complete confidence in their steady,
anonymous, simultaneous activity.'[14] Olivia assumes that she is
like everyone else, safe in the conviction that millions of Americans eat Chinese take-away food and so on. While Americans
are 'equal-opportunity eaters'[15] in their consumption of take-
away food from other cultures, they seem less inclined to be
equal-opportunity believers, particularly when it comes to
Chinese superstition. Already 'superstition' implies a hierarchy
that privileges American beliefs over Chinese beliefs, whereby
the former are invariably regarded as 'modern' by Olivia and,
presumably, by everyone else.

However, Olivia's sense of stability is short-lived. Her
father's death from renal failure and her sister's arrival from
China problematize her 'straight record' of things, 'its patterns
of cause and effect, of social relationships and moral values, ...
the patterns of the world [she] seems to know'.[16] In short,
Olivia's 'modern American' and apparently realistic perspective
is rendered vulnerable. For example, the pattern of cause and
effect she utilizes in order to know the world is particularly
'jumble[d]' (4). Indeed, Olivia believes that her bad behaviour
earlier in the day – the accidental decapitation of two pet turtles
– is 'vaguely connected' to Jack's death and Kwan's arrival. The
second effect seems most to concern Olivia: 'the other little girl
... was coming soon to take [her] place' (4). If her bad behaviour
brings about substitution, then perhaps her good behaviour,
praying for Kwan's (non-)arrival, will disrupt the substitutive
process. Olivia is persuaded by this logic: 'I convinced myself I
had become so good that soon Mom would realize that we didn't
need another sister' (8). Red tape and Bob also conspire against
Kwan, the latter for fear of 'any trouble she might cause as a

Communist' (141): 'Mom told me how Bob pressured her, just before they were married, to cancel the paperwork for Kwan. ... "I watched you pray. You looked so sweet and sad, asking God, 'Please send me my big sister from China.'" [Olivia] was nearly six by the time Kwan came to this country' (8). Whether Olivia says what she means or what she does not mean in accordance with causal and 'inverse' (7) logic respectively, both alternatives fail to bring about the anticipated effect.

It is not only Olivia's patterns of cause and effect that are rendered vulnerable by Jack's death and Kwan's arrival; indeed, her social relationships undergo a similar crisis. For instance, Louise reassuringly informs Olivia that she is 'Just like Jack' (4), but this genetic link is tenuous. Neither a skinny body nor an overly analytical mind reliably ties her to her father. Olivia asks: 'what else has been passed along to me through my father's genes. Did I inherit from him my dark moods, my fondness for putting salt on my fruit, my phobia about germs?' (18). It is of no small consequence that her questions go unanswered, particularly in light of the fact that Tan's more critical commentators proclaim that her texts unproblematically endorse ethnic essences via genetically-based plots.[17]

Also failing to provide Olivia (Yee-Laguni-Bishop-Li) with an 'identity that suit[s] her' (141) is another official discourse: the law, notably marriage (and divorce). After seventeen years of marriage to Simon Bishop, Olivia comments: 'We weren't *special*, not like people who truly belonged to each other. We were partners, not soul mates, two separate people who happened to be sharing a menu and a life' (112). Although Olivia criticizes her husband and their marriage, Simon is 'a more sympathetic – and somewhat more fully developed – character than most of the male characters in Tan's other novels. ... [He] is neither monster nor detached observer; he is, instead, a vulnerable man who seems puzzled and even hurt by Olivia's request for a divorce.'[18] Perhaps in response to the charge of 'male bashing', Simon is sympathetically described, albeit by making him Olivia's 'male doppelgänger'. 'Like me', she observes, 'he had a name that didn't fit with his Asian features. ... Both of us had lost a parent before the age of five, he a mother, I a father. We both owned pet turtles; his died after he accidentally dropped them into a chlorinated swimming pool. We both had been loners as kids, abandoned to caretakers – he to two unmarried sisters of his mother's, I to Kwan' (58, 60). Despite these similarities and the correspondences forged via official discourses, specifically scientific and legalistic discourses, Olivia is struck by the arbitrary nature of social relationships. For her, then, blood and marriage are no more a sign of a *'special'* relationship than a shared menu, closet, toothpaste, cereal and so on (19).

The problems Olivia experiences with respect to cause and effect and to paternal-marital relationships are arguably related to language. For example, Olivia's comments regarding Kwan's arrival seem to matter little because meaning is determined apart from her. It seems, then, that Olivia is unable to rely on language to specify a particular meaning/referent. This point is reinforced through mother–daughter conversations. 'Promises to take me to the movies or the public pool were easily erased with excuses or forgetfulness, or worse, sneaky variations of what was said and what was meant: "I hate it when you pout, Olivia," she [Louise] once told me. "I didn't guarantee I'd *go* to the swim club with you. I only said I would *like to*." How could I argue my need against her intention?' (7). Unable to secure a reliable relationship between cause/effect, father/daughter, husband/wife, and intention/meaning, it is no small wonder Olivia acknowledges that arbitrariness is a condition.

More than personal, this condition affects dominant American discourses too. Aunt Betty's 'theory' regarding the circumstances of Jack's death (and Kwan's birth) is a case in point. Olivia knows her father's kidneys killed him: 'Mom said he was born with four instead of the usual two, and all of them were defective.' Aunt Betty theorizes the reason for his excessive number of kidneys. Relying on *Weekly World News* and *Life* magazine for information, Aunt Betty 'said he was supposed to be a Siamese twin. But in the womb, my father, the stronger twin, gobbled up the weaker one and grafted on the two extra kidneys. "Maybe he also had two hearts, two stomachs, who knows"' (5). This theory is of interest for two reasons. First, it is contingent: 'Aunt Betty came up with this scenario around the time that *Life* magazine ran a pictorial about Siamese twins from Russia.' Second, Aunt Betty's theory and by implication *Weekly World News* and *Life* are compromised by a supernatural dimension: 'the stronger twin gobbled up the weaker one' (5). Olivia is forced to concede that Aunt Betty's capacity to explain the circumstances of Jack's death is doubly called into question.

Also called into question is the ideology of the American Dream. Olivia discusses this ideology in relation to the Chinese taxi driver, Rocky: '[His] idea … is to become a famous movie actor, specializing in martial arts.' 'Even if [he] do[esn't] become a movie star in five years, [he] can still come back to China and live like a rich man.' Not perturbed by the prospect of low wages, high expenses, high taxes and high crime, conditions 'unbearable to Americans' but 'ordinary' to Chinese, Rocky preserves his dream of America (178–9). The fact that political rhetoric is so little disturbed by political reality raises a question about the function of the American Dream. Rather than 'feed[ing] fantasies of material possession (though it does this too, of course)' among 'hardworking … [and] simple' (178) Chinese, political rhetoric operates here to 'satisf[y] semiological fantasies about the adequation of sign to meaning seductive enough to tolerate extreme forms of economic oppression'.[19] In other words, the American Dream functions to reconcile political rhetoric and political reality in order to promote the ideological notion among the Chinese that subsistence living generates thousands of American dollars. Perhaps the reality of the American Dream is an easy target, particularly as its tenuous link with political reality is explicitly stated. Moreover, it is hardly surprising that the dream of 'Sisters [and Brothers] … Doing It for Themselves' (178) in America is literally the case for Rocky considering he is from a 'backward' (236) culture.

Yet, *The Hundred Secret Senses* also draws attention to the way in which 'modern' Americans assume the adequation of sign to meaning/referent, particularly in relation to photographic representation. References to photographs are found throughout

Tan's fiction, often at so-called epiphanic moments when American-born narrators in particular are about to discover 'Chineseness' that is apparently reflected in their photographs. However, this reflection is a semiological fantasy. Indeed, 'Chineseness' is not reflected in but *effected* by photographs. This effect is highlighted in *The Joy Luck Club* and *The Hundred Secret Senses* via narrators who are revealed to be equally susceptible to dreams and fantasies as the so-called 'backward' Chinese.

What links these two texts is their representation of the American tourist in China, the 'spiritual tourist' and the 'anti-tourist tourist' respectively.[20] Neither Jing-mei 'June' Woo nor Olivia is in a position to discover 'Chineseness' apart from 'the exoticist/tourist gaze',[21] as it is effected by sights and experiences designated 'camera-worthy' by western guidebooks that cater specially for their complex needs. It thus proves difficult to take anything that either narrator says about 'the real China' literally, particularly not Olivia, whose job as a photographer for the travel magazine that has hired her to collect culinary images of local Chinese cuisine blatantly positions her within several exoticizing discourses. As an 'anti-tourist tourist', Olivia is aware of these discourses, although her awareness does not prevent her from participating in the semiological fantasies she criticizes in others, not only the Chinese taxi driver and his American Dream but also American tourists and their Orientalist dreams.

More serious in her quest for 'Chineseness' than the mass tourists in Guilin, who are described as 'bloated Westerners in jogging suits' frenziedly buying 'touristic kitsch'[22] – 'Mao buttons, the Eighteen Lohan carved on a walnut, plastic Buddhas in both the Tibetan-thin and roly-poly models' – Olivia rejects this 'marred' version of China (171–2). Two blocks on from this depressingly familiar spectacle of mass tourism and westernization is the bird market, again, a familiar spectacle, if this time to the anti-tourist tourist in search of the exotic. 'Scream[ing] with … photo opportunities', the bird market, with its 'ordinary fowl, chickens and ducks, destined for the stew pot', when 'set against a background of beautiful and better-fated birds, might make a nice visual for the magazine article' (172). At this point, Olivia is still in the domain of the familiar, her camera reinforcing the difference between foreign/local, even as it seems to allow her access to the local. But after listening to a local trader's sales pitch, she, now in an apparently unfamiliar domain, exclaims: '"Omigod!" I turn to Simon. "He's selling this owl as food! ... I don't believe this. ... I'm going to be sick"' (173). Sickened by the economic realities of 'real China', its mass production/consumption of plastic Buddhas and rare birds alike, Olivia continues her quest for a China apparently 'unmarred' by 'the detritus of [western] modernization' (184) – tourism and capitalism.

The movement of the narrative from city to country, from Guilin to Changmian, seems to provide such a China. From that all-important distance, Olivia sees Kwan's village 'nestled' among hills (and mountains) that are not green but 'velvety moss-green', 'deep ... emerald' and 'dark jade' (184), her 'exoticist/tourist gaze' becoming even more pronounced when she looks through the viewfinder of her camera: 'I feel as though we've stumbled on a fabled misty land, half memory, half illusion. Are we in Chinese Nirvana? Changmian ... conveys all the sentimental quaintness that tourists crave but never actually see.' But she does (seem to) see it, albeit through the images featured in travel brochures, car commercials and documentaries. Changmian is also familiar to Olivia in that 'it's the setting for Kwan's ['yin'] stories, the ones that filtered into [her] dreams' (185).

Sceptical Olivia is, however, no 'spiritual tourist'; she is in China to do a job, and thus rejects this 'fabled misty land' for its apparent opposite: 'hard realism' (236). But not even this form can escape the semiological fantasies Olivia this time accords to 'well-heeled readers flipping through a chic travel magazine that specializes in ... images of third world countries'. As she explains, 'hard realism would give people the wrong impression, the *all* of China is this way, backward, unsanitary, miserably poor' (236). Whether the images are 'hard' or 'soft', realistic or magical, American readers invariably assume the adequacy of sign to referent made possible by a combination of realistic literary devices, specifically mimesis and synecdoche. Damned if she does and damned if she doesn't, it is no small wonder that Olivia decides to 'Screw the magazine. To hell with the right and wrong impressions. ... I'll just do my best to capture a moment' (237).

Olivia's 'moment' features Du Lili preparing to cook a chicken. 'I circle her, focus, and begin to shoot. But upon seeing my camera, she jumps up to pose. ... So much for spontaneity.' After taking a few posed shots, Olivia persuades Du Lili that she is not really taking pictures. Du Lili is so rapt in finding the best chicken that she seems not to notice Olivia 'skulk[ing] around the courtyard like a thief, trying to look unobtrusive, while ... search[ing] for the best combination of subject, light, background, and framing' (237). Far from 'coincid[ing] with what's given' (236), the photographs resemble a scene from '*Macbeth*' (240). More shocking to Olivia perhaps than the chicken's death is Du Lili's remark: 'I usually cut off the head right away. But this time I let the chicken dance a bit. ... For your photos!' (239), not, as Olivia assumes, for health reasons. Her representation of 'real China' is thus compromised by the Shakespearian 'death-dance' between Du Lili and the chicken, as well as by the formality of the photographs.

Olivia's attempt to capture 'Chineseness' via photography, along with Aunt Betty's theory and Rocky's dream, all of them effected by so-called realistic discourses associated with the American media, specifically magazines, newspapers, films and music, depends on a semiological fantasy that assumes the adequation of sign to referent. In this way, then, *The Hundred Secret Senses* highlights the 'super-natural' dimension of American culture, reinforcing Kwan's remark that 'Americans do the same thing' (218). Rather than pursuing the radicalism of this remark, Olivia, at this point in the text, takes what is arguably the easy option when she merely replaces western truth with eastern truth, logical explanations with magical explanations: 'Maybe there's truth in the lie' (262).

On hearing the magical story of Kwan's childhood, for

example, Olivia acknowledges that it does seem to explain 'the disparity between the photo of the skinny baby our father showed us and the chubby girl we met at the airport. It would also explain why Kwan doesn't resemble my father or my brothers and me in any way' (233). As Kwan tells it, two childhood friends – 'Pancake Kwan' and 'Buncake Lili' – are drowned in a flash flood. Their bodies are recovered and placed in coffins ready for burial. Both girls enter the World of Yin. Lili chooses to stay in this immortal realm with her dead parents, as does Kwan, who expects to be reunited with her dead mother. However, Kwan has to return to the mortal world. 'I tried to return to my body', she explains, 'I pushed and shoved. But it was broken, my poor thin corpse. ... Du Yun and Big Ma were opening the coffin lids. Hurry, hurry, what should I do?' (232). What she does is become Kwan-Lili, a fact confirmed by a ghost-talker: 'The girl who lived in this body doesn't want to come back. And the girl who lives in it now can't leave' (230). Fortunately for Kwan, ghosts and other superstitions are proclaimed reactionary by the new Communist government. Consequently, Big Ma and Du Yun 'pretended [Pancake] had always been this plump girl. Buncake the skinny one' (231).

No less magical than the story of Kwan-Lili's childhood is her explanation of why she had to return to the mortal world: 'I had no choice', she tells her sister. 'How else could I keep my promise to you?' (232), albeit a promise made in 1864, at the end of the Taiping Rebellion in China when Kwan was Nunumu and Olivia was Miss Banner. In keeping with magic realism, particularly its tendency to 'naturalize' the supernatural so that 'the reader does not react to the supernatural in the text as if it were antinomious with respect to our conventional view of reality',[23] Kwan-Nunumu's story compares favourably with the limited historical accounts of the Taiping period. Accounts are limited because even though 'the Taipings were ... the biggest and best-known rebel movement of their day',[24] recruiting, at the height of the Rebellion, over a million 'peasants and landowners, peddlers and teachers, bandits and beggars, and not just Hakkas, but Yaos and Miaos, Zuang tribes, and even the

Puntis who were poor' (31), all of them united against Manchu imperialism and ruling-class Confucianism[25] under the leadership of Hung Hsiu-ch'uan or the Heavenly King, 'a holy man who had been born a Hakka, then chosen by God to be his treasured younger son, little brother to Jesus' (29), no Taiping writings survive. Destroyed by the victorious Manchus, with help from Anglo-French forces, the history of the Taipings is represented in foreign memoirs and documents.[26] Not surprisingly, then, 'the standard [secondary] texts tend toward factual, Westernized accounts of military battles, descriptions of territory gained or lost, and tallies of victories and defeats'.[27]

What Tan does in *The Hundred Secret Senses*, as she did in *The Kitchen God's Wife*, albeit about a different historical period, is represent the 1850–60s from the perspective of a narrator whose ethnic/gender identity, along with her disability, traditionally marginalizes her from history. Anticipating the neoconservative charge levelled at Tan, often by masculinist critics, E. D. Huntley insists that the Hakka perspective of the one-eyed bandit girl, Nunumu, who is orphaned during the Taiping Rebellion, later becoming a servant to a group of western missionaries at the Ghost Merchant's House in Changmian, 'factor[s] the personal element into a historical equation, revealing the frequently overlooked truth that military and political battles are always won or lost at the expense of thousands [and, in this case, millions][28] of individuals whose lives are forever disrupted by the ambitions of a powerful minority and their followers'.[29]

At once personal/political, historical/literary, real/magic, Nunumu's story describes the complex political relations within China, its tribal and class divisions, and between China and the west via an array of characters, all of them differently connected to the trade in opium, weapons and Christianity: Miss Banner, an American, and the daughter of an opium dealer; General Cape, another American, and a mercenary; Yiban Johnson, 'a half-and-half man' (25), 'driven by his devotion to Miss Banner; nervous Miss Mouse; fervent Pastor Amen; opium-eating Dr. Too Late';[30] outspoken Lao Lu; Zeng, a one-eared peddler; and, finally, Nunumu, a 'Hakka, Guest People – hnh! – meaning, guests not invited to stay in any good place too long' (26). Restricted to poor mountainous places that necessitated the women, their feet unbound, also worked the land, the Hakkas became something of a proto-feminist and proto-communist tribe. They were understandably attracted to the Christianized Taiping movement.[31]

In addition to comparing favourably with Chinese history, Nunumu's story is empirically verifiable. The recovery of a journal and a book from the late 1850s, along with Olivia's discovery of some duck eggs buried in the garden of the Ghost Merchant's House, apparently indicates that there is 'some basis for her [sister's] delusions' (284). Journal, book and eggs: Olivia 'ha[s] things … that belong to a woman from a childhood dream' (286). Dream also becomes reality when Simon disappears:

> Whatever she says, she believes is true. Like what she said about Simon, that she hadn't seen him as a ghost, which means he's alive. I believe her. I have to. Then again, if I believe what she says, does that mean I now believe she has yin eyes? … That Miss Banner, General Cape, and One-half Johnson were real people? That she was Nunumu? (288)

Given the historical and empirical verifiability of Kwan's magical stories, when coupled with the unreliability of so-called realistic discourses, Olivia's '[m]aybe there's truth in the lie' (262) is not only unsurprising but also easy. All she has to do is reverse the patterns of the world she seems to know. Such a reversal is, however, tied up with 'the neocolonial production of knowledge';[32] and, it is this production that *The Hundred Secret Senses* resists by offering a reading of magic realism that preserves its radicalism against the views of some post-colonial critics who arguably render the form compatible with dominant aesthetic/political categories.

The fact that Tan's two narrators inhabit discursive realities that are traditionally regarded as oppositional, one American, the other Chinese, one real, the other, magical, an opposition dramatically reinforced in the final part of the text when Olivia reveals that Kwan is (officially) dead, suggests that the relationship between them is more than personal. As with so many of the personal relationships within Tan's texts, the Olivia-Kwan relationship also provides opportunity to analyze colonial/ neocolonial hierarchies and structures, specifically in the context of the theoretico-political debate currently circulating about magic realism. What dominates this debate is the view that '[t]he concept of magic realism is a troubled one for literary theory'.[33] Literary and cultural theorists in Post-colonial Studies in particular acknowledge the 'trouble' it causes to western generic,[34] temporal, spatial,[35] ontological, and epistemological categories. Not surprisingly, then, magic realism is regarded by some post-colonial critics as 'paradigmatic of a space which is trying to cope with the problem of narrativizing decolonization',[36] making it, in Homi Bhabha's view, 'the literary language of the emergent post-colonial world',[37] a view more or less endorsed by Slemon in 'Magic Realism as Post-Colonial Discourse'.

For Slemon, the magic realist text is a 'speaking mirror'. It 'reflects in the language of narration the real conditions of speech and cognition within the actual social relations of a post-colonial culture'. While acknowledging that these relations are 'continuous', the 'two opposing discursive systems ... forestall[ing] the possibility of interpretive closure', he nevertheless closes or limits the post-colonial critique available to magic realism by insisting that this form 'recapitulates a dialectical struggle within a culture's language, a dialectic between "codes of recognition" inherent within the inherited language and those imagined codes ... that characterize a culture's "original relations" within the world'.[38] Slemon may seem to problematize his terms through the use of quotation marks, but, on closer inspection, they merely function to draw attention to the fact that he is quoting from other sources.[39] To link recognized or realistic codes with the dominant group and imagined or magical codes with other(ed) groups, and to organize these codes/groups into a dialectical and ultimately hierarchical structure is to overlook the way in which magic realism promotes radical insights about 'supernaturalism' – in its un/hyphenated form simultaneously.

With respect to Tan's magic realist text, Kwan highlights the supernatural/super-natural relations the dominant group also has with natural reality when she discusses western rituals surrounding Easter and Christmas. To Olivia she says: 'you told me rabbits laid eggs once a year and dead people came out of caves to look for them. ... Yes, and you also said if I did not listen to you, Santa Claus would come down the chimney and put me in a bag, then take me to a very cold place, colder than a freezer.' If, as Kwan observes, 'Americans do the same thing' (218), then binary oppositions like those used by Slemon prove not only inadequate but also ethnocentric, suggesting, as Gayatri Chakravorty Spivak puts it in her critique of magic realism as post-colonial discourse, a 'hidden ethical, political agenda behind claiming that [this] style ... is paradigmatic of a space which is trying to cope with the problem of narrativizing decolonization'.[40] It is in its negotiation of this agenda, or one like it, that magic realism promotes a post-colonial critique of colonial/neocolonial hierarchies and structures.

The debate among (these) post-colonial critics basically depends on *how* a magic realist text is read. The 'how' of reading or the politics of reading also determines the relationship between the modern American Olivia and the superstitious Chinese Kwan. When Olivia reverses the magic/realism hierarchy and concedes that '[m]aybe there's truth in the lie' (262), it is worth considering who in particular benefits from this production or construction of truth. Reversal admittedly benefits Kwan, albeit in a limited way: 'Chineseness' once made it impossible for her to speak; now it is 'the precise reason that makes it only too possible for [her] to speak'.[41] If Kwan represents 'a locus of truth'[42] for her sister (and others), Olivia's bad treatment of her in the past, specifically the 'Chink' jokes, the cheap presents and, above all, Kwan's institutionalization, seemingly negated by the privilege guiltily awarded to her now, then the relationship between the two sisters would do little to upset neocolonial hierarchies and structures. Indeed, it would be an instance of Olivia letting Kwan speak in a 'Chinese' way that is ultimately compatible with the neocolonial production of knowledge.

Crucially, however, *The Hundred Secret Senses* resists this neocolonial set-up, most obviously when one of its most recent forms is satirized: 'New Age profiteering'. According to Olivia, 'you don't have to pay [Kwan] a hundred fifty an hour just to hear her reveal what's wrong with your past life. She'll tell you for free, even if you don't ask' (17). Olivia also stops 'breast-beating' when she acknowledges that it 'wasn't [her] fault that Kwan went to the mental hospital' (13). Both examples suggest that Olivia is beginning to reflect *on* her and by extension the American theoretico-political investment in Kwan's stories about ghosts, reincarnation and the World of Yin. The emphasis given to 'on' – a reflection on rather than a reflection of – invites a reading of magic realism that radicalizes not only its relationship to other realisms, specifically 'hard realism' (236), but also its relationship to 'the real conditions'[43] in and around a colonized/decolonizing space.

More precisely, magic realism 'reflects' in several directions at once, towards the colonized/decolonizing space *and* towards the (neo)colonizing space *and* towards the 'super-natural' ideological and linguistic effects that underpin any realism. These effects put into question an uncritically mimetic conception of literature, not just 'multicultural' literature. Even as they generate the realist illusion of transparency that dominates so many readings of 'multicultural' literature, the latter traditionally being discussed in terms of a 'speaking mirror' or a 'window on the world', these effects also problematize this illusion as it applies to those in the colonized/decolonizing space *and* in the (neo)colonizing space. Critical readings of 'multicultural' literature typically focus on its capacity to *de*mystify the hierarchical relationship between (neo)colonizer and (de)colonized as it is determined by each group's proximity to 'Truth', even in the most 'mistyfying' of literary texts. By pushing the boundaries of 'hard realism' (236) via references to the supernatural/supernatural, the magic realist text demystifies the (neocolonial) notion that it transparently reflects 'Truth', along with demystifying the notion that the (neo)colonizer inhabits a space with 'no geo-political determinations' and so is 'transparent' vis-à-vis the (de)colonized.[44] Arguably, then, the 'moment of truth'[45] in the magic realist text is that 'truth' is produced or constructed by de/mystifying ideological and linguistic effects. What counts as truth thus depends on *how* these productions/ constructions are read.

In Tan's magic realist text, however, reading is a problem, if not the problem for Olivia: 'Who and what am I supposed to believe?' (222) arguably emerges from her inability to distinguish between the literal and the figural. The binary opposition that enables her to designate realistic discourses literal and magical discourses figural is most obviously disrupted by a sister who has 'no boundaries' (20). 'Chopped-off hands flying out of a roofless house, my father floating on the China Sea, the little baby sucking on his mother's heart': 'I'm sure', insists Oliva, 'Kwan meant some of this figuratively. But as a child, I saw everything Kwan talked about as literal truth. ... I didn't have strong enough boundaries between imagination and reality' (12, 45). Geo-political factors also influence Olivia's reading of Kwan's 'yin' stories: 'Maybe in another country Kwan would be considered ordinary. Maybe in some parts of China, Hong Kong, or Taiwan she'd be revered' (17), assuming that the people in these countries believe in ghosts and other super-stitions after being 'redeemed' and/or 'reformed' by Christianity and Communism respectively (224).

Thus far, one sister's immaturity and the other sister's ethnicity seem to explain (a belief in) magic. However, this explanation is interrogated by Olivia when Kwan is institu-tionalized at Mary's Help. 'Things being what they were back in the early 1960s, the doctors diagnosed Kwan's Chinese ghosts as a serious mental disorder' (14). In Tan's texts, 'the American doctor', including Rose Hsu Jordan's 'psyche-atricks' (188) in *The Joy Luck Club* and Pearl Louie Brandt's pathologist-husband in *The Kitchen God's Wife*, is typically represented in terms compatible with 'the Western man of reason and science'.[46] Apparently impartial to 'childish' or 'backward' beliefs in the supernatural, 'he' diagnoses them as a sign of madness. Crucially, however, this diagnosis is based on a contradiction that puts into question the proclaimed objectivity of scientific discourses vis-à-vis 'the Chinese(-speaking) woman'.

The Hundred Secret Senses highlights this contradiction when Kwan's stories about ghosts, reincarnation and the World of Yin are 'read' literally by the doctors at Mary's Help, even though they proclaim such literalism with regard to the supernatural mad. Moreover, such a literal approach to Kwan's 'yin' stories seems mad in that it bypasses their 'super-naturalism' or, more precisely, their literariness. It is quite possible that Kwan is given electro-shock treatment for her (mis)use of the literary dimension of language. Given that she 'believes in free speech, free association, free car-wash with fill'er up' (18), it is hardly surprising that her references to the supernatural, specifically to 'yin' or 'shadow[y]' and 'invisible'[47] phenomena are not consistent. Along with seeing ghosts or 'yin people' (13), a literary,[48] not an anthropological, expression, Kwan describes the doctors as 'American ghosts'. She elaborates: 'I don't see them, don't hear them, don't speak to them' (14). The doctors may as well be invisible to her, as she is to them.

This condition of invisibility, which, in Kwan's case, seems to signify catatonia, as opposed to 'Chinese silent treatment' (14) or, for that matter, the 'unnatural disaster' that marks the experiences of other(ed) groups in America, is frequently represented in 'multicultural' American literature. As Mitsuye Yamada observes in her 1981 essay, 'Invisibility is an Unnatural Disaster: Reflections of an Asian American Woman': 'Like the hero in Ralph Ellison's novel *Invisible Man* [(1947)], I had become invisible to white Americans, and it clung to me like a bad habit.'[49] Another novel, Maxine Hong Kingston's *The Woman Warrior: Memoirs of a Girlhood among Ghosts* (1976), a novel not only crucial to Tan's literary development but also to the development of an Asian American literary canon, opens up 'ghosts' to various meanings, some of which are supernatural, although others are clearly not: 'A Sitting Ghost', 'White Ghosts' and 'Negro students (Black Ghosts)', as well as the US as a 'ghost country' where 'the first generations have had to figure out how the invisible world the emigrants built around [their] childhoods fits into solid America'.[50]

Following *The Woman Warrior*, 'ghosts' function ambivalently in *The Hundred Secret Senses*. They exceed the binary oppositions between literal/figural, real/magic and American/China that are so fundamental to 'the Western white phallocentric system' of which Kwan's American doctors are a part.[51] Theirs is a system that diagnoses 'the Chinese(-speaking) woman' mad regardless of whether she speaks or not. Moreover, 'free speech [and] free association' (18) or 'free' signifiers without *one* meaning/referent (in the natural world) constitute a threat to this system: hence Kwan's electro-shock treatment. Although Olivia criticizes the 'scientific' rationale of the doctors at Mary's Help, she, like them, is threatened by her sister's 'free' signifiers. Rather than responding with physical violence, she attempts to reside in the aporia generated by the insight that 'reality ... is already in and of itself magical or fantastic'[52] as the discourses that constitute 'the real' depend on 'super-natural' effects for their naturalization and literalization. Given that the 'who/what' of belief is effected by ideology and language, as opposed to nature, Olivia's relativism is hardly surprising: 'All the possibilities whirl through [her] brain, and [she] feel[s she is] in one of those dreams where the threads of logic between sentences keep disintergrating. ... All these things are true and false, yin and yang' (222). Ultimately, however, this 'dreamy' or aporetic condition proves unsustainable for various reasons, some self-interested – *her* sister cannot be mad – others political and theoretical.

Aside from the fact that Olivia's critique of Kwan's treatment at Mary's Help depends for its effectiveness on deciding between possibilities, in this case, right and wrong, she *has to* decide who/what to believe because it is simply not feasible to believe all possibilities, particularly when they cancel each other out. Rather than seeing the latter in negative or destructive terms, whereby the 'super-natural' underpinnings of magic/realism make 'Truth' impossible, is it not possible to see the ideological and linguistic analysis of 'truth' more positively, especially as merely reversing the true/false binary opposition with respect to magic/realism does little to problematize (neo)colonial hierarchies and structures? Does a radical critique of these violent hierarchies and structures not begin to emerge when the 'how' or production and construction of 'truth' is analyzed? Inviting a positive response to both questions, Tan's magic realist text, if not magic realism generally, promotes not the destruction but the deconstruction of 'truth'.

Olivia's narrative moves in this deconstructive direction when she begins a linguistic analysis of 'yin' stories. A (mis)use of language, specifically mistranslation and the misapplication of grammatical rules, does in part account for the naturalization and literalization of the supernatural. For example, Miss Banner's 'magical' story of her brothers' deaths depends on her poor Chinese. After a few more Chinese lessons from Kwan-Nunumu, Miss Banner tells this story again: 'her little brothers did not chase a chicken into a hole, they died of chicken pox and were buried in the backyard' (41). Similarly, Simon refers to a late girlfriend in the present tense, giving the impression to his 'betrayed' wife that Elza Marie Vandervort is 'in the present time' (62). A similar tactic is employed throughout *The Hundred Secret Senses* with respect to Kwan, who, at the time of Olivia's narration, is (officially) dead despite telling her 'yin' stories in the first person. Language, then, as opposed to nature, effects the supernatural, although, as Olivia later observes, not in a reliable way since signifiers are 'free' in the sense that they are resistant to *one* meaning/referent.

This resistance 'even' extends to numbers – perhaps the most reliable system of signs. For instance, '*Yi-ba-liu-si*' or '1864' produces two contradictory meanings: 'Lose hope, slide into death' and 'Take hope, the dead remain' (26). Contradiction also marks other numbers related to age in particular. It turns out that Du Lili is both older and younger than Kwan, a contradiction Olivia assumes she can easily resolve by questioning these two women about their ages. It is the logical thing to do, but, then again, such a question reinforces the fact that she 'can no longer trust [her] perceptions, [her] judgements' (264). What is more, how can Olivia possibly ask these women if they are telling the truth about their ages, lest she be thought ridiculous? As Olivia remarks, albeit in a different context: 'how can I ask? "Hey, tell me, is my sister really my sister? Is she a ghost or just insane?"' (234). Similarly, how can she ask Du Lili if she is seventy-eight or fifty, 'ancient' or 'young as a spring chicken' (235)? This time, however, neither grammar nor logic helps Olivia to determine whether this idiom is true with respect to Du Lili's age. Moreover, this analogical link between a woman and a chicken brings all manner of meanings into play, meanings that compromise Olivia's ability to 'know for sure' (235).

More specifically, the literal reading of the idiom assumes that Du Lili is a chicken. This is clearly absurd, as the conversation between Olivia and Simon makes plain. '"Maybe Du Lili used an expression like – well, as 'young as a spring chicken.' His voice has the assured one of masculine reason. "Maybe you took her literally to mean she thought she was a chicken." "She didn't say she was a chicken." My temples are pounding' (235). Having dismissed the notion that Du Lili is literally a chicken, Olivia reads the idiom figuratively, no easy task given that there are at least three interpretative possibilities. First, it could mean that Du Lili feels youthful in spite of her years. Second, it could convey the sense that she is neither old nor young. Third, it could imply that Du Lili 'ain't no spring chicken' (241). Olivia assumes that by discounting the literal reading she limits the interpretative possibilities. However, her figural reading of the spring chicken idiom produces more as opposed to less possibilities, none of which bring Olivia any closer to knowing Du Lili's age since they contradict each other. And, besides, even if she did 'know for sure', '[w]hat difference would it make?' (235). Does it make a difference whether Du Lili is old or young? Does it make a difference whether magical representation is meant figuratively or literally? If magic makes senses to Du Lili, 'why question the world in which [she] live[s]?' (222). As Olivia remarks, '[a]ll these things are true and false, yin and yang. What does it matter?' (222). Far from resolving things, 'what does it matter?' intensifies Olivia's crisis because it moves at once towards literal and figural possibilities. She asks, '[w]ho can tell me the truth?' (233), but '[w]hat does it matter?' suggests that the truth she first asked for no longer matters. In this way, then, she asks and does not ask for a concept of difference with respect to truth and falsehood.[53]

All in all, then, Olivia's linguistic analyses of Kwan's and others' 'yin' stories highlights the impossibility of reliably deciding between the figural and the literal, which is not surprising given that she is dealing with an oxymoronic form that resists *one* meaning/referent. But Olivia *has to* decide who/ what to believe, and, as occurs in so many of Tan's texts, she seems to have a 'big spiritual epiphany' while in China about 'what's important in ... life - laughter, unanticipated joy, Simon ... even Simon. And, yes, love, forgiveness, a healing inner peace ... [no] big rifts or major regrets' (263–4). Like Tan's other texts, *The Hundred Secret Senses* represents China as an epiphanic site for its American-born character consistent with Orientalist ideology. At the same time, however, it radically problematizes this representation. For example, *The Joy Luck Club* problematizes Jing-mei 'June' Woo's 'bloody' epiphany through recourse to cultural, not natural forms, specifically a myth, a shampoo and a Polaroid photograph, whereas *The Hundred Secret Senses* is more blatant in this regard: 'Fuck this shit' (263). Indeed, Olivia's 'big spiritual epiphany' is, as she says, 'a joke on me. And I can't even laugh about. How stupid I feel. I can no longer trust my perceptions, my judgments' (264).

Arguably, Olivia's 'big spiritual epiphany' is also a 'joke' in 'the Chinese American tradition of *jaw jieh* (catching pigs), "a time-honored practice of bullshitting white people into buying up ... junk"'[54] or, in this case, buying into 'Chinese superstition' by reading it as an expression or a reflection of 'Truth' and other similarly capitalized concepts unavailable in postmodern America. Admittedly, 'Chineseness' is sometimes 'the literal truth' for Tan's American-born narrators. For example, Olivia, by the end of her narrative, does ascribe a literal meaning to 'yin' stories, concluding that 'truth lies not in logic' (319), along with advocating a belief in 'ghosts' (320). At the same time, however, *The Hundred Secret Senses* makes it difficult to take her belief literally, although she seems to (want to), not only because her reliability as a narrator is repeatedly questioned, most obviously by her 'exoticist/tourist gaze',[55] but also because the 'moment of truth' in this magic realist text is that 'reality … is already in and of itself magical or fantastic' and 'realism is already necessarily a "magic realism"'.[56] *The Hundred Secret Senses* suggests that this 'moment of truth' is also a 'super-natural' production or construction, and, for this reason, affirms the oxymoron so fundamental to magic realism. Like any figure, the oxymoron brings together *different* phenomena, in this case, the real and the magical, the literal and the figural, not, as Olivia puts it, to form 'the whole truth' (223) in a dialectical and ultimately hierarchical structure that risks what is most radical in magic realism – namely, its representation of *how* the 'who/what' of belief is dependent on ideological and linguistic effects that deconstruct dominant aesthetic and political categories.

The 'how' of Olivia's belief in Kwan's 'yin' stories thus resists the magic/realism binary opposition underpinning it. In a complex and oxymoronic negotiation of 'truth', she privileges magic because it is real or, more properly, 'follow[s] most of the [magic] conventions of realism'. Linda Kenyon continues: 'you have to believe the narrator',[57] which Olivia does because 'it isn't in her [sister's] nature to lie' (288). And, besides, magic is real(istic), even verging on the 'boring as hell' (129), especially when 'yin people' drop by to offer culinary advice: 'They say, "Ah! This sea bass, too firm, not flaky, maybe cook one minute too much. And these pickel-turnips, not crunchy enough, should make sound like walk in the snow, crunch-crunch, then you know ready to eat"' (128). 'No longer believ[ing her] sister is crazy' (17), along with advocating a belief in 'ghosts', Olivia decides that 'believing in ghosts – that's believing that love never dies. If people we love die, then they are lost only to our ordinary senses. If we remember, we can find them anytime with our hundred secret senses' (320–1).

With this 'sweet' statement *The Hundred Secret Senses* (almost) ends, although it is worth bearing in mind that 'ghosts' are reconfigured. This reconfiguration is important because it articulates the text's complex negotiation of possibilities that are 'secret' and 'ordinary', all of them resisting closure in a final chapter entitled, appropriately enough, 'Endless Songs' that sees Olivia, now named Olivia Li – 'Why not? What's a family name if not a claim to being connected in the future to someone from the past?' – affirming the limitlessness and endlessness of love. The latter is further supported by the fact that Olivia and Simon do not divorce. They are 'still working things out ... practicing [at] being a family' with their fourteen-month-old baby girl, Samantha Li, who Olivia 'want[s] to believe [is] a gift from Kwan' despite the doctor insisting that 'Simon ... had in fact not been sterile. ... Well, what do you know? The earlier tests were wrong. The lab must have made a mistake' (320).

'Endless Songs' reinforces the preoccupation in *The Hundred Secret Senses* with that which resists closure: hence its representation of characters with split and multiple identities in an oxymoronic form marked by difference or 'free speech, free association, free car wash with fill'er up' (18). How Olivia responds to this difference, as embodied, most obviously, in the figure of her dead *or* disappeared *or* 'yin' sister, Kwan, arguably functions as a meta-commentary on the politics of reading. *The Hundred Secret Senses* represents various models of reading 'the other', all of them claiming to be 'benevolent'. From philanthropists and psychiatrists to (some) post-colonial critics: these 'readers' uncritically treat difference in reductive terms. Some readers value difference for its exoticism, a value accorded, as in Louise's case, for what it can do for her, whereas other readers seek to institutionalize the exotically different in accordance with dominant aesthetic and political categories underpinned by binary logic. But binary oppositions between literal/figural, real/magic, America/China and so on, although inescapable, are brought to crisis vis-à-vis Tan's 'yin' story/ teller, as her narrator is forced to acknowledge: Kwan, Olivia observes, 'points to birds flying overhead. If only she said they were elephants. Then, at least, her madness would be consistent' (233). Inconsistency marks Tan's representation of Kwan, an oxymoronic character who believes in superstition for real *and* for tradition (218). All these (and other) possibilities need to be affirmed, if not by Kwan's 'readers', then by Tan's readers, so as to bring about a post-colonial critique of (neo)colonial hierarchies and structures.

In Tan's magic realist text, this critique begins to emerge when the 'who/what' of belief is represented as a production and construction in keeping with deconstruction. Kwan's comments serve to highlight the supernatural underpinnings of discourses her sister designated real(istic). Most obviously, Olivia's binary opposition between 'modern' America and 'misty' China is not only reversed but also displaced. *The Hundred Secret Senses* thus draws attention to the way in which this binary opposition (and others) relates to natural reality only by virtue of 'supernatural' ideological and linguistic effects. This attention to the 'how' of belief, including 'big … epiphanies' (264), ensures that no *one* belief, whether it emerges from science or religion, reason or superstition, 'hard realism' (236) or magic realism and so on, is final with respect to natural reality. None of these discourses constitute 'the literal truth' (12) or, for that matter, 'the whole truth' (223), as they cancel each other out. The impossibility of finality with regard to 'truth' does not mean that believing is over; after all, Olivia does, by the end of *The Hundred Secret Senses*, (want to) believe in 'ghosts'. What it does mean is that 'truth' is a production or construction, and, as such, relies on 'super-natural' effects, including the oxymoron, to bring *different* entities together. The difference fundamental to the oxymoron and by extension to magic realism ensures that the bringing together of linguistic and natural reality so as to produce 'truth' is and, indeed, *has to* be provisional. It is this provisionality that is represented by (those with) *The Hundred Secret Senses*; and, finally, it is the 'secret sense' of the provisionality of produced 'truth', a production also addressed in *The Bonesetter's Daughter*, that empowers a post-colonial critique of colonial/neocolonial relations in the tradition of 'American magic realism'.

The Bonesetter's Daughter

BEFORE the beginning of *The Bonesetter's Daughter* (2001) proper, Amy Tan, in her acknowledgements and epigraph, returns to the matrilineal narrative that she never quite abandoned even in her novel about two half-sisters.[1] Between *The Hundred Secret Senses* and *The Bonesetter's Daughter*, a gap of six years, Daisy Tan sadly died, reason enough for her daughter to re-examine matrilineality in what is regarded as her 'most autobiographical novel to date'.[2] As well as losing her mother, Tan also lost a reader and a 'writer',[3] losses that actually preceded Daisy's death by four years because of Alzheimer's. Commenting on loss or, more precisely, the process of loss, as it informs *The Bonesetter's Daughter*, Tan says: 'I wanted to write about the loss of memory, and the memories you keep in the midst of losing somebody; what you try to keep but end up forgetting, and what you try to discover about the loss.' But she found herself spinning out the novel for years beyond the deadline. 'It almost felt as though, as long as I kept writing the book, [Daisy] would stay alive.'[4]

Although her mother did die in 1999, Tan acknowledges 'two ghostwriters [who] came to [her] assistance during the last draft' of *The Bonesetter's Daughter*. She elaborates: 'The heart of this story belongs to my grandmother, its voice to my mother', both of whom are the focus of Tan's epigraph. 'On the last day that my mother spent on this earth, I learned her real name, as well as that of my grandmother. This book is dedicated to them. Li Bingzi and Gu Jingmei.'[5] This dedication seems to confirm a point made in the text by LuLing Liu Young, whose autobiography comprises a large part of *The Bonesetter's Daughter*. In one of her chapters, LuLing asserts that '[a] mother is always the beginning. She is how things begin' (228). Not only does the text begin with the mother, both in its conception[6] and on its first page proper; it also fails to end quite when it should because of Tan's need to keep her mother alive through writing. Daisy thus affects the beginning and the ending of her daughter's fourth novel, albeit an end without finality in the form of 'ghost writing'.

'Words flow' (308) not only between Tan and her dead ancestresses but also between the various characters in *The Bonesetter's Daughter*. The three main characters, starting with the oldest first, Precious Auntie, her daughter, LuLing, and her granddaughter, Ruth Young are connected through their bones. As stated in the 'Epilogue', 'Ruth ... thinks about her mother as a little girl, about her grandmother as a young woman. These are the women who shaped her life, who are in her bones' (308). In addition to this material connection is a 'spiritual' connection, which, as it turns out, materializes itself through the 'Precious Auntie ghost' (69). According to LuLing, this ghost caused the deaths and near death of her husbands and daughter respectively. Less violently, but no less dramatically, divination via Ruth's 'sand-writing' (67) provides further evidence of the Precious Auntie ghost. She seems to speak through and, at the end of the text, to her granddaughter, no small feat for a dead woman: '"Think about your intentions," Bao Bomu says. "What is in your heart, what you want to put in others." And side by side, Ruth and her grandmother begin. Words flow' (308).

What is interesting about Tan's depiction of 'spirituality' is its materiality, particularly in writing – 'sand-writing' and 'ghost writing'. As with *The Hundred Secret Senses*, the spiritual again depends on 'super-natural' effects of language and ideology. This dependency suggests that neither ghosts nor bones are represented as 'im-mediate',[7] instead functioning like texts or books: 'ghost *writing*' and *divining* bone. As regards the bone/book relationship, for example, it is variously asserted in the text, most obviously via genealogy and repetition/parallelism. More specifically, a bone doctor's daughter, Precious Auntie, is grandmother to Ruth, a 'book doctor' (27), with the similarity between these health-related jobs, as well as the formal similarity between 'bone' and 'book' bolstering this relationship. It is worth pointing out, moreover, that bone/book is unreliable with regard to meaning: 'Who knows' whether the answers gleaned from divination were right, especially as 'the more successful diviners were skilled at saying what the emperors wanted to hear' (301–2). Another way to contact a dead ancestor is through 'sand-writing', although it proves no more reliable that bone divining: 'At times [Ruth] made up the answers to suit herself. But on other occasions, she really had tried to write what her mother needed to hear' (302).

In *The Bonesetter's Daughter*, divination is represented as 'a great linguistic puzzle' (302) that generates both supernatural and 'super-natural' interpretative possibilities. After the publication of *The Hundred Secret Senses*, a text explicitly about the supernatural, Tan revealed that '[she] was pushed to write … by certain spirits – the yin people'.[8] With the publication of *The Bonesetter's Daughter*, she '"c[a]me out" about her beliefs in "yin people" (ghosts) as a source of her fiction'.

> 'I was always ambivalent,' says Tan. 'I was raised with a sense that I could communicate with ghosts, and it did seem to come from something other than myself. I can still find rational ways to explain these things. … But I've gotten so much help in my writing that it's hard to pass these off – it's like being ungrateful; denying the existence of a force greater than oneself. You could say it's ghosts or the supernatural, but those terms are tainted as flaky notions. To me, it's not about physical bodies before or after death; it's a continuous consciousness and a form of love.'[9]

In another interview, Tan describes 'a very strong experience … that happened exactly 24 hours after [her] mother's death': 'I opened my eyes and saw my mother. She was smiling and I could see her head – larger than life – moving towards me like a hologram.'[10] Perhaps such statements are to be expected given all the deaths in her life, of family and friends. Perhaps they give her comfort.[11] Or, then again, perhaps Tan's religious upbringing – her father's Holy Ghost and her mother's Chinese ghosts – also explains her references to the supernatural, particularly 'ghost writing'.

Picking up on Tan's point about her ambivalence, an ambivalence that is articulated in her magic realist text about 'believing in ghosts – that's believing that love never dies', and the debate therein about the literal/figural status of the 'World of Yin' (*HSS*, 3, 320), this chapter pursues, not a supernatural, but a 'super-natural' explanation of ghost writing. After all, Tan explores this latter possibility when she discusses a force greater than herself. Granted, 'force' may be a supernatural phenomenon, but it can just as easily refer to 'super-natural' phenomena, to the influence of cultural forces on identity, as well as to the Chinese tradition of 'talk-story', a communal form of writing in which stories 'flow' between generations. With respect to her mother's Chinese beliefs about 'magical thinking, old societal pressures, the flow of ch'i' (43), Tan highlights their 'influence [on] the development of [her] imagination'.[12] In her words: 'I remember what my mother instilled in me: a belief not so much in ghosts but in the limitlessness of love. And then I know how love releases hope, how hope transforms the unknowable, the intangible into something you can grasp and hold close to your heart.'[13]

The emphasis here on transformation, even the translation of the intangible into the graspable, further opens up 'ghost writing' to supernatural and 'super-natural' interpretative possibilities. Ghosts or 'yin people' may constitute 'the real' for Tan, but how do they function in her texts? Before responding to this question, it is worth remembering that 'yin people' is 'not a Chinese expression at all. ... [Tan] just made it up. "Yin" means invisible or shadow.'[14] Is this literary invention meant either literally or figuratively? What does it mean to accord a literal status to the 'World of Yin', as featured in both *The Hundred Secret Senses* (3) and *The Bonesetter's Daughter* (6)?

What are the aesthetic and the political implications of 'tak[ing] her literary metaphors as Chinese facts' in accordance with the 'information retrieval approach' to 'multicultural' literature?[15]

Arguably, Tan's 'ghosts', like those in other twentieth-century 'multicultural' texts, most obviously, Maxine Hong Kingston's *The Woman Warrior*,[16] 'are signifiers with diverse meanings'.[17] In *The Hundred Secret Senses*, for instance, Kwan Li, the Chinese-born sister who 'believes she has yin eyes[,] ... sees those who have died and now dwell in the World of Yin, ghosts who leave the mists just to visit her kitchen on Balboa Street in San Francisco' (3). Much like *The Woman Warrior*, '[g]hosts exist in old China as they do in ... California'.[18] Given that Kwan also 'believes in free speech, free association, free car-wash with fill'er up' (18), it is hardly surprising that her references to the supernatural are not consistent. Along with seeing ghosts, Kwan refers to the psychiatric staff at Mary's Help as 'American ghosts'. She elaborates: 'I don't see them, don't hear them, don't speak to them' (14). Treated like this, the staff may as well be invisible (yin) to Kwan, as she is to them. Similarly, in *The Bonesetter's Daughter*, 'ghost writing' has both an 'ordinary' and a 'secret' meaning. It is at once a profession, Ruth's profession, and something more intangible, even supernatural.

Giving up the ghost for a moment, this chapter focuses on Ruth's profession and language-related matters generally. Such a focus reiterates the emphasis accorded throughout this study to representation as a main theme in all of Tan's texts, and so it is fitting that this final chapter analyzes her final novel (to date) alongside matters related to the 'text/tissue/weave'[19] of writing. Also briefly returning to her other main thematic preoccupations, to identity and matrilineality as discussed in relation to *The Joy Luck Club*, this chapter reinforces the case made for reading Tan's texts as *literary* texts, as opposed to treating them as reliable or 'im-mediate'[20] statements about 'things Chinese', particularly in view of the fact that the insights – admittedly, the essentialist insights – articulated by Tan's characters are mediated, often with reference to popular representations. Granted, these characters do not always acknowledge the irony of using a photograph, for example, to effect their epiphanies regarding 'Chineseness', but the fact that photographs and other cultural forms are used at all would seem to complicate the debate about essentialism in Tan's texts. To reiterate an argument made throughout this study: essences *have to* be formulated in relation to identity, history and reality, but the fact that they have to be *formulated* at all, and the texts do highlight the ideological and linguistic processes involved in this formulation, ensures that these essences function ambivalently, to say the least.

The question here, then, is whether *The Bonesetter's Daughter* also approaches the issue of essentialism in this ambivalent way. How does it formulate the relationship between identity, matrilineality and language? As a semi-autobiographical novel, written in part to keep Daisy alive, *The Bonesetter's Daughter* does suggest a close relationship between identity and language. This closeness is reinforced in so far as the text represents a Chinese mother with Alzheimer's and an American-born daughter struggling with the difficulties her mother's disease generates, particularly with respect to its impact on identity and matrilineal/familial relationships. Rather than utilizing 'older notions of autobiography as a genre constrained by truth and history, one that is a process of simple transcription, the faithful replication of a "self" presumed to exist prior to writing',[21] Tan negotiates this genre in accordance with more recent insights about the remembered, even dis(re)membered 'self' as produced or de/constructed in writing. In 'Thinly Disguised Memoir', from *The Opposite of Fate*, Tan discusses (her) memory, of how it is 'the kind of memory that is simultaneously the most unreliable *and* the most authentic element a writer can infuse into her work'.[22]

This 'kind of memory' is also at work in *The Bonesetter's Daughter* when, in response to a question about whether Ruth and LuLing are autobiographical, Tan replies: 'No, they're not based on anyone outside of myself and my mother but they are also not based that closely to me and [my] circumstance[s].' She continues:

For example, Ruth is a ghost writer, and although I did
write for business, what she does is write self help books
which I've never really done. She also lives with a man,
they're not married and their relationship is a little iffy
because they haven't really talked about what that commitment means since they're not married – what love means
in their case. He has 2 daughters who Ruth feels are
growing distant from her. I don't have that in my life. And
the story that LuLing tells is nothing like my mother's
life. My mother never came from a place like Immortal
Heart.[23]

Other semi-autobiographical elements include molestation and
muteness, both of which happen to Ruth. A neighbour molests
Ruth, although Tan was molested by 'a respected member of the
community', whose reappearance at a book signing, years later,
left her momentarily mute: '"I was a deer caught in headlights,"
she says. "I could not speak." That muteness ... returned later
after a college roommate was murdered. ... "It happened on my
birthday, and every year for about 10 years on my birthday, I
lost my voice."'[24]

Voices are also lost in *The Bonesetter's Daughter*, annually
in Ruth's case, although Precious Auntie loses hers permanently
after deliberately swallowing a ladleful of boiling ink. Precious
Auntie's name is also lost and, later, 'found', again paralleling
Tan's experience, almost. 'The novel was reshaped when Tan
learned her mother's true maiden name – Li Bingzi – on the day
her mother died. "I was stunned; I'd spent all these years writing
about her life, but I didn't know what name she was born
with."'[25] Although Tan does not discuss this reshaping in detail,
it does seem plausible to argue that the text's preoccupation with
forgetting/remembering the name of Precious Auntie, who is
LuLing's mother, not just her nursemaid, is connected to Daisy's
deathbed revelation.

Aside from the semi-autobiographical elements, *The Bonesetter's Daughter* negotiates a relationship between language
and identity in that many of its characters are in one way or
another connected to writing: from main characters like Ruth

and LuLing, who are both writers and, for that matter, translators, to minor characters like Art and Mr Tang, the respective 'partners' of these women. More specifically, Ruth is a ghost writer or a 'book doctor', 'helping people transfer what's in their brain onto the blank page'. She 'tend[s] to think of [her]self as … a translator' (27), something she should be good at given that 'Ruth had always been forced to serve as LuLing's mouthpiece. By the time she was ten, Ruth was the English-speaking "Mrs LuLing Young" on the telephone, the one who made appointments for the doctor, who wrote letters to the bank' (41–2). LuLing too was her mother's mouthpiece after Precious Auntie was rendered permanently mute after burning her face and mouth. Unable to talk, Precious Auntie relied on 'hand-talk, face-talk, and chalk-talk' instead. 'No one else understood [this] … kind of talk, so [LuLing] had to say aloud what she meant' (4). Along with being a translator, LuLing is a writer. She is trained in the mechanics of Chinese calligraphy to 'an artist's level, first-rate classical' (47), also using this form to write her autobiography that is, in part, *The Bonesetter's Daughter*.

With respect to the minor characters, Art, like Ruth, is also a doctor with a PhD in linguistics, specifically American Sign Language. He 'work[s] at the Center on Deafness at UCSF' and, as Ruth jokingly puts it, is 'an expert on silence'. Like LuLing, then, he too responds to 'facial expressions, hand gestures, body posture and its rhythms' (25). LuLing's companion, Mr Tang, is hired by Ruth to translate her mother's life story. He was also 'a famous writer in China but … his work remained untranslated and unknown' (261) in the United States. Other minor characters connected with writing on LuLing's 'side' include her adoptive family, the Lius, all of them being involved in the business of inkstick production. It is their ink that Precious Auntie consumes after a spurned suitor, the brutish Mr Chang, kills her father and her lover, Baby Uncle, the poetry-writing relative of the inkstick makers. Minor characters on Ruth's 'side' include her authors, Ted and Agapi, and, interpreting 'writing' rather loosely, her best friend, Wendy, who is described as 'a divining rod for strange disturbances in the earth's atmosphere. She was witness to bizarre sights: three homeless albinos living in Golden Gate Park ... a loose buffalo strolling down Taraval Street' (18).

LuLing's narrative also refers to divining, albeit in the different context of the ancient Chinese tradition of divining bones. '*Until recently*', Precious Auntie tells her daughter,

> *these kinds of bones weren't so valuable, because of the scratches. Bone diggers used to smooth them with a file before selling them to medicine shops. Now the scholars call these oracle bones, and they sell for twice as much. And the words on here? They're questions to the gods. ... The diviner put a hot nail to the bone, and it cracked. ... Then he interpreted what the cracks meant.* (142)

In addition to divining, bones were also used for curing. Precious Auntie's father, a famous bonesetter or bone doctor, 'used bones to heal bones' like his ancestors before him, right back to the time of the Sung Dynasty, nine hundred years before. Bonesetting is a 'family heirloom', as is 'the exact location [of the bones], passed from generation to generation, father to son, and in Precious Auntie's time, father to daughter' (143). In addition to this disruption of Chinese patriarchal tradition,[26] the bonesetter '*let* [Precious Auntie] *do whatever a son might do*' (145), including reading, writing, questioning, playing riddles, walking alone, choosing a spouse and having premarital sex out of keeping with the 'Three Obediences and Four Virtues'.[27]

Their traditional worth aside, bones also prove historically and economically valuable. More specifically, the discovery of oracle bones 'offer[s] evidence of unmistakable early religiosity, including ancestral cult, divination, sacrifice, priesthood and shamanism'.[28] This late nineteenth-century discovery 'dissolved' the already 'loose ... Biblical framework' that dominated Europe at this time. With 'the expansion of the Orient further east geographically and further back temporally ... [r]eference points were no longer Christianity and Judaism, with their fairly modest calendars and maps, but India, China, Japan, and Sumer, Buddhism, Sanskrit, Zoroastrianism, and Manu. ... [H]istory itself was conceived of more radically than before'.[29]

The discovery of Peking Man also proved 'important ... to science, history, and all of China' (161). Arguably, Peking Man's bones, which were found, lost and never re-found, hardly surprising given that China was dealing with 'the widespread remnants of warlordism and factionalism, to say nothing of the Japanese invasion' around the time of his excavation,[30] 'loosened' and 'dissolved' the scientific framework. As Harry L. Shapiro observes in *Peking Man*, '[w]hen his existence was first announced in 1926, the news came as a bombshell to the scientific world'.[31] Why a bombshell? Was it because 'no relics of primitive man this far back had ever been found in China, or indeed anywhere else on the mainland of Asia'?[32] Or was it because *Pithecanthropus* or Peking Man, like *Australopithecus africanus*, discovered a year before in South Africa, further undermined the (Eurocentric) assumption that 'Culture' originated somewhere in Europe, an assumption most aptly demonstrated by the phoney *Eoanthropus dawsoni* or Piltdown Man?

Shapiro's *Peking Man* does not exactly constitute 'reflexive'[33] anthropology in that it pays little attention to the ideological/political underpinnings of the race for 'the origin of the species', only momentarily considering 'nationalism and ... chauvinism'[34] as a problem for certain anthropologists. About Piltdown Man, for example, Shapiro is 'puzzle[d]' as to why 'such distinguished and knowledgeable experts ... men of undisputed authority ... could have been taken in by what now appears to have been an obvious fraud. ... But [this is] not [an] easy question ... to answer.'[35] He is similarly puzzled by the invading Japanese army's interest in Peking Man, again explaining it in personal, not political, terms, as 'either the expression of a special drive by Japanese anthropologists eager to have such an extraordinary collection for their own research purposes, or a kind of collector's passion so widespread among the Japanese'.[36] There is no mention in Shapiro's text of the imperialist appropriation of a culture through cultural artefacts, whether for 'booty' or, worse, cultural genocide.

The impact of Peking Man on western historical/scientific frameworks certainly makes him an interesting point of focus.

The question, however, is whether he functions as a bombshell in *The Bonesetter's Daughter*. Far from 'dissolving' Eurocentrism and Orientalism, Peking Man may actually 're-valorize' these essentialist ideologies, especially in view of the fact that Tan elsewhere stands accused of an uncritical 'Valorization of Origin'. According to Sau-ling Cynthia Wong, *The Joy Luck Club* and *The Kitchen God's Wife* 'suggest there is indeed a locus of truth, and that locus is origin. … Origin stays put, long-suffering but autotelic, awaiting re-discovery and homage. … [T]here is a privileging of origin – which … means privileging China and the Chinese'.[37] A text all about ancestral bones, whether they belong to Peking Man or to Precious Auntie, would seem to confirm Wong's point that Tan accords the Chinese body an epiphanic potential, were it not for the fact that both sets of bones are lost, possibly forever.

While Precious Auntie's bones are unlikely to be re-discovered after a landslide destroyed the section of the gorge into which her body was thrown (218), those of Peking Man may possibly re-surface. And, if they do, what form will they take? Will they be 'oxtails[?] Or the … casts of the original' (302), as happened in 1951 when rumours circulated among 'some Chinese palaeontologists that … Peking Man [was] in the United States, at the American Museum of Natural History'? What the museum actually had on display were 'merely the *casts* of Peking Man, not the original fossils.'[38] The fact that there are no original bones, 'merely' casts of fossils or copies of copies in keeping with Jean Baudrillard's notion of simulacrum, and the fact that Peking Man comprises 'at least forty individuals – men, women and children',[39] would seem to make 'him' an odd point of focus for a text that valorizes the origin. But, then again, perhaps Peking Man does not constitute 'a locus of truth', functioning instead as a figure for the hyperreal, the multiple and the fragmentary. Likening the mysterious Peking Man to 'how we learn about our own parents, our ancestors and origins', Tan remarks: 'We discover pieces and then lose them, and so much remains a mystery.'[40] In the text, Mr Tang views Peking Man in a similar way when he asserts that '[s]o much of history is mystery. We don't know what is lost forever, what will surface again. All objects exist in a moment of time. And that fragment of time is preserved or lost or found in mysterious ways' (302).

In *The Bonesetter's Daughter*, bones are not stable points of reference, if they are referents at all, being lost both in the case of Peking Man and Precious Auntie. The instability of bones is further suggested by the different uses and values accorded to them, most obviously by the bonesetters and the 'bonesellers' (the Chang father and son) respectively. A hierarchy between bonesetting and boneselling is discernible in LuLing's narrative: honest trade versus dishonest trade or, more precisely, dishonest trading, and, related to this, the proper versus the improper treatment of ancestors and ancestral bones. Following LuLing's narrative, ancestral bones, including those of Peking Man, should not be used for either bonesetting or boneselling because both would involve separating the bones from the rest of the body. To do either is to risk a curse. In Precious Auntie's words of warning to LuLing: '*A ghost will then come and take us and our miserable bones with it. ... I tell you, the ghosts won't rest until our family is dead. The entire family gone*' (157).

Not afraid of this ancestral curse, LuLing, whose marriage to the Chang son seems certain, offers to disclose the secret location of the ancestral bones to the murderous Chang father. Precious Auntie responds by committing suicide, an act designed to protect her daughter from the Chang family and by implication the family curse. While her suicide does 'work' in these respects, the fact that she killed herself denies her a proper burial. She is dumped in a gorge, and her daughter, unable to recover the bones, suffers the consequences: LuLing believes that she is haunted by 'the Precious Auntie ghost' (69) not only in China but also in the US, a belief apparently confirmed by her husbands' deaths and the playground accident that nearly killed her daughter. As Ruth interprets it, 'the lady with the bloody hair was trying to kill her! So it was true, that day at the playground, she almost died' (70). This interpretation is exaggerated; it is a product of childhood imaginings more than anything else, especially as Ruth only suffers a broken arm and a broken voice.

Apart from this incident, Precious Auntie 'haunts' the characters, if not the text per se, in other ways as well. As regards Ruth's annual muteness, for instance, she blames it on a virus and allergies. Her (adult) 'Days of No Talk' (12) start when she moves in with Art, and are psychosomatic in his opinion. *The Bonesetter's Daughter* also offers a supernatural explanation to do with the Perseids, although Ruth 'did not actually believe that her laryngitis was star-crossed, or that the meteor shower had anything to do with her inability to speak'. Yet, for LuLing, shooting stars or 'melting ghost bodies' are bad luck, a sign that 'a ghost [i]s trying to talk to you' (11), a point paradoxically reinforced by familial muteness. Arguably, Ruth's 'Days of No Talk' relate to Precious Auntie's 'Life of No Talk'.

This relationship is further suggested by the other, non-oral forms of articulation utilized by grandmother and granddaughter. Just as Precious Auntie relied on 'hand-talk, face-talk, and chalk-talk' (4), so too does Ruth rely on 'sand-talk' or, more properly, 'sand-writing' after the playground accident leaves her temporarily mute. '"How does the bean curd dish taste?", LuLing asked one night. And Ruth etched: *Salty*. ... "I thought so too," her mother answered. This was amazing! Soon her mother was asking her opinion on all kinds of matters. ... Ruth had never experienced such power with words.' Along with responding to questions about food, clothes, TV programmes and the stock market, Ruth ventures a question about whether she could have a dog. 'She scratched in the sand: *Doggie*', clearly not anticipating her mother's response: 'She jumped up and her chest heaved. "Precious Auntie," LuLing cried, "you've come back. This is your Doggie [LuLing's childhood nickname]. Do you forgive me?"' (68). Despite her own intentions, it seems that whatever Ruth writes is significant to her family history. And so '*The End*' is translated by LuLing as 'End of the World', the gorge where Precious Auntie's body was dumped, not, as Ruth intended, 'to steer the conversation to a close'. Similarly, 'O-Z' or *The Wizard of Oz*, the film that Ruth wants to see at a neighbour's house, when followed by '*good* ... G-O-O' is translated as 'Goo! *Goo* means "bone" in Chinese. What about bone?

This concern bone-doctor family?' (101). After Ruth is molested by the neighbour, a message is conveyed to LuLing: '*You must move*, Ruth wrote. *Now … [to] Land's End*' in San Francisco (117).

Although *The Bonesetter's Daughter* promotes the idea that sand-writing is 'ghost writing', and so not to be believed, the fact that Ruth's words, in their form and content, do cohere with her family history, would seem to suggest a basis for LuLing's superstitious beliefs. Not only are Ruth's words italicized like Precious Auntie's; they also appear to come from elsewhere: 'Most of the time she thought that sand-writing was just a boring chore, that it was her duty to guess what her mother wanted to hear. … Yet Ruth had also gone through times when she believed that a ghost was guiding her arm, telling her what to say' (100). The end of *The Bonesetter's Daughter* would also seem to reinforce the supernatural interpretation of Ruth's 'ghost writing': '"Think about your intentions," Bao Bomu says. "What is in your heart, what you want to put in others." And side by side, Ruth and her grandmother begin. Words flow. They have become the same person. … They write about what happened, why it happened, how they can make other things happen' (308). Here, Ruth is reconciled with her grandmother and everybody else as well. 'She has a husband who loves her, two girls who adore her, a house she co-owns, dear friends, a life with only the usual worries about leaks and calories' (307). And, in the relationship with her 'difficult, oppressive, and odd' (52) mother, a relationship lacking (physical) affection (43), it seems that for Ruth and LuLing '[i]t was not too late for them to forgive each other and themselves' (308).

Such an ending is familiar to Tan's readers and critics, with many of the latter criticizing 'the family' and the happy Hollywood ending for neoconservatism. Out of all her texts, this criticism, succinctly articulated by Gary Pak as 'your typical Asian American mother/daughter sweet stories, your cross-generational stuff, your intercultural relationship jive',[41] seems most relevant to *The Bonesetter's Daughter*, if only because Tan openly discusses her emotional investment in it. Authorial remarks aside, it is worth noting that the text does continue the 'Tan-ian' tradition of representing familial difficulties, with the mother–daughter relationship standing out in this regard. 'Throughout Ruth's childhood, LuLing's fury escalated until she could barely speak, except to sputter the old threat: "Maybe I die soon!"' (45). This threat is not just a possibility, as it was in Ruth's childhood, but a reality. The fact that 'her mother was dying, first her brain, then her body' (88) would seem to go some way towards problematizing the assumption that *The Bonesetter's Daughter* ends happily, even 'sweetly'. Or, then again, perhaps a mother's degeneration is not such an unhappy event in view of the fact that Alzheimer's allows LuLing 'only [to] recall … being loved very, very much' and to forget 'her woes' (307). Not even death seems to constitute an unhappy event, particularly as the presence of ancestral ghosts is felt.

On one level, supernatural presences or the persistence of an essential identity resistant to change, even a change as radical as death, does make *The Bonesetter's Daughter* a rather 'sweet' story. The ideological and political implications of such a storyline are also worth considering, especially as Tan's texts have been criticized for an uncritical commitment to essentialism. How, then, to respond to the presence of the Precious Auntie ghost? Does she endorse, as Tan's more critical commentators would argue, 'a powerful essentialist proposition': Chinese female identity, whether it is present in family, bones or a ghost, 'triumph[s] over history'?[42] Is *The Bonesetter's Daughter* suggesting that a gendered ethnic essence is resistant to death, never mind culture? To respond positively to these two questions is to accord a literal status to the Precious Auntie ghost, an odd response given that the supernatural is not typically assumed to correspond to reality.

Granted, ghosts may constitute 'the real' for Tan, but how do they function in her text(s)? Indeed, is it possible to interpret the Precious Auntie ghost figuratively? At the risk of stating the obvious, she is, after all, only a character, doubly constructed by language, not only Tan's but also LuLing's. More than this, she is, at least until the 'Epilogue', regarded as a *vengeful* ghost. Her 'presence' thus depends on a performative, in this case, a curse and, more generally, the performativity of language, which, in turn, challenges the assumption of an essential identity that is exterior to language and by implication history and culture. This assumption is challenged further in that 'ghost' gives rise to at least two contradictory interpretative possibilities, appealing to the metaphysics of presence that it simultaneously resists. Indeed, how present can a *ghostly* presence be?

The argument that language effects the Precious Auntie ghost is to some extent problematized by the fact that Precious Auntie, when she was alive, could not speak. Doubly subalternized through muteness and suicide, it seems that here the subaltern woman cannot speak. Like the auntie in Kingston's *The Woman Warrior*, Precious Auntie is a mute(d) 'No Name Woman'.[43] Without a voice and a name, these two 'aunties' are marginalized not only from their families but also from language, history and culture. Paradoxically perhaps, this marginalization is historically achieved, relying on historical representations of femininity that demand 'silence and obedience'[44] from Chinese women. Chinese patriarchal ideology ensures that 'its' women are really already subalternized. Yet, as Gayatri Chakravorty Spivak argues, learning to 'unlearn' or critique dominant ideologies radically problematizes subalternity. More precisely, this critique 'seek[s] to learn to speak to (rather than listen to or speak for) the historically muted subject of the subaltern woman' through a 'systematic unlearning' that 'involves learning to critique [dominant] discourse[s]'.[45]

Arguably, this un-learning occurs in *The Bonesetter's Daughter*. In her (and the text's) opening line, LuLing asserts that '[t]hese are the things I know are true', and she proceeds to name herself and certain members of her family. There is, however, 'one name [she] cannot remember. ... And the name was – ' (3, 6). This unfinished sentence puts into question LuLing's 'Truth' and 'memory for everything' (3), a questioning that is reinforced by Precious Auntie: '*Someday*', she says to her daughter, '*when you know how to remember, I'll give this* [a divining bone] *to you to keep. But for now you'll only forget where you put it'* (142). Significantly, 'someday' does not refer to the time when she wrote her narrative, five or six years before *The Bonesetter's Daughter*. Despite the fact that the second part of LuLing's narrative is preoccupied with remembering – 'these are the things I must not forget' (135), with 'things' referring primarily to her unforgettable 'sad life' (86) – she still does not know how to remember. In short, LuLing simultaneously remembers and forgets. She remembers, even compulsively remembers, with her use of 'must' suggesting an obligation, and her use of repetition (267) strengthening this obligation, although this kind of remembering is LuLing's problem. She has to unlearn this compulsive remembering if she is to learn *how* to remember.

The process of unlearning is in part effected by Alzheimer's. As Ruth's observes, '[d]ementia was like a truth serum' (268). By 'los[ing] her mind, the memory web that held her woes in place', LuLing learns how to remember. 'And though [she] still remembers the past, she has begun to change it. She doesn't recount the sad part. She only recalls being loved very, very much. She remembers that to Bao Bomu she was the reason for life itself' (307). In this 'demented' state, then, LuLing finally recalls Precious Auntie's name on seeing a (the?) divining bone in the San Francisco Asian Art Museum.

Ruth goes through a similar process of unlearning. Like her mother, she has 'memory problems', and compulsively 'count[s] fingers as a memory device' (271, 19). Numbers abound in Ruth's numbered chapters. She enumerates everything, from the ten daily tasks to the top ten songs (40, 122). Not until the end of *The Bonesetter's Daughter* does a chapter on Ruth get a title, albeit a title that relates more to form than to content: 'Epilogue', not 'Truth', 'Heart', 'Change', 'Ghost' and so on, as with LuLing's chapters. This difference between mother and daughter is further reinforced by their different approaches to reality and, indeed, to language. These differences typically form a binary opposition: the superstitious and 'rambling' (14) Chinese mother is opposed to the secular and 'utilitarian' (27) American-born daughter. While LuLing insists that the two of them are 'the same but for opposite reasons', Ruth 'want[s] to be the exact opposite of her mother' (3, 121) for reasons that are at once personal and political. As an American, she has little time for suicide, superstition and other 'Chinese nonsense'. Hence Ruth's 'compulsion with number counting ... was practical, not compulsive; it had to do with remembering things, not warding off some superstitious nonsense' (40).

At odds because of their different attitudes towards reality, mother and daughter are also divided because they speak different Englishes, never mind different languages. LuLing's English is 'poor', much to Ruth's embarrassment. 'Her mother couldn't even say Ruth's name right. It used to mortify Ruth when she shouted for her up and down the block. "Lootie! Lootie!" Why had her mother chosen a name with sounds that she couldn't pronounce?' (41). Ruth's chapters often refer to LuLing's mistakes, her temporal mix ups mainly, as well as those to do with her faculty of selection: 'She would say "ribbon" when she meant "wrapping paper," "envelope" when she meant "stamp"' (42). While Alzheimer's may trigger aphasia, Ruth has no such excuse. When it comes to Chinese, she has a 'resistant brain; lines – dots and dashes, downstrokes and upstrokes, bends and hooks' do not look like 'a beam of light' to her, only 'a sparerib picked clean of meat'. LuLing responds to her daughter's inter-pretation of Chinese calligraphy with 'a snort, the compressed form of her disappointment and disgust' (48–9).

A poor student of Chinese, Ruth's difficulty with the language also comes from the fact that she has been 'living off words for so long that it's hard to think about them beyond what's utilitarian' (27). *The Bonesetter's Daughter* problematizes Ruth's approach to language, even when the words in question seem to lend themselves directly to 'utilitarianism': onomato-poeia, translation and, ultimately, autobiography. What links these three uses of language is their assumed literalism, the apparently straightforward relationship they posit between word/sound, original/translation and story/life. Arguably, Ruth 'unlearns' the unproblematic relationship between word and world so that by the end of the text she is better able to speak to her mother, as well as to her grandmother.

To start with onomatopoeic words like 'crash, boom, bang', simple monosyllabic words that are assumed to have a simple, if not essential relationship with sound: Ruth observes that 'onomatopoeia was a jumble of syllables, not at all like the simple sounds it was supposed to represent' (27). Significantly, Ruth's realization about the difference between 'onomatopoeia' and 'crash' comes after a discussion with Art about his favourite word. '"Vapors,"' he said at last. ... "[T]he sound of the word, how it forms on your lips, teeth, and tongue – vaporzzzzzz – it lilts up, then lingers and fades. It's perfectly matched to its meanings' (26). Here, then, onomatopoeia works and does not work; one minute, words match meanings and, a few minutes later, this match is questioned because of the difference between words, including 'onomatopoeia' and, quite possibly, 'crash', and sounds. Onomatopoeia thus proves unreliable, which is hardly surprising given that (annual and permanent) muteness afflicts the bonesetter's daughter and granddaughter.

Just as onomatopoeia is problematized, so too is translation, specifically Ruth's utilitarian model of translation. Describing her ghost-writing skills to Art, she 'tend[s] to think of [her]self as more of a translator, helping people transfer what's in their brain onto the blank page ... straightforward[ly] recasting ... their words' (27, 37). Her 'transliterate' (261) approach to translation is apparent here despite co-authoring books on 'Self-Help, Wellness, Inspirational, New Age' (36), books that seem at odds with Ruth's strategy of enumeration. Two authors comment on this discrepancy: '"Stop thinking in terms of constraints," [Ted] told her. "If you write this book with me, you have to believe in its principles. Anything is possible, as long as it's good for the world"'; and, '"Darling," Agapi said, "why does it always have to be a list of five and ten? I can't always limit myself to such regular numbers"' (35–6, 38). Mr Tang also criticizes her translation skills, albeit indirectly, when he says: 'I don't like to just transliterate word for word.' Although both translators are also successful writers, she a ghost writer, he 'a famous writer in China' (261), Mr Tang's model of translation is ultimately privileged, not least because he, rather than Ruth, translated

LuLing's life story. He also completed this task in two months, whereas she is seen struggling for an hour to translate one sentence.

Although comforted by rigid systems of classification, quite possibly in response to the crisis generated by a suicidal mother and a ghostly grandmother, Ruth does nevertheless look forward to a future when she could 'finally ... stop counting' (131). Counting is far reaching, negatively affecting her body, which is described as inflexible, almost to the point of rigor mortis (23), as well as her relationships. In her partnership with Art, for example, she is 'offered ... a percentage ownership in the flat. ... She was supposed to decide on the percentage interest she should have, then call the lawyer and set up the paperwork. But how could you express love as a percentage?' (89).

Quantitative cohabitation is as problematic as quantitative (co-)authoring. Near the beginning of *The Bonesetter's Daughter*, Ruth reveals that she 'wanted to write a novel in the style of Jane Austen, a book of manners about the upper class, a book that had nothing to do with her own life' (27). Would her lists of fives and tens really suit such an endeavour? This question does not necessarily assume a romantic model of writing, understood as somehow beyond the constraints of form. After all, Austen's novels are regarded as conservative, even 'decorous', in terms of their form and content. What the question does invite, however, is a consideration of the author as a figure in crisis, in part brought on by 'The Doppler Effect of Communication': 'There is always a distortion between what a speaker says and what a listener wants it to mean' (22). Given that communication is prone to such 'distortion', particularly between mother and daughter, Ruth often articulating her impatience with LuLing's rambling, her 'side routes ... going into excruciating details over the infinite meanings of Chinese words' (14), it seems unlikely that the 'utilitarian' Ruth would render herself vulnerable to 'The Doppler Effect', never mind other linguistic 'distortions'. For this reason, then, it seems highly unlikely that she could progress from book doctor to 'book writer' in the style of Austen.

The Bonesetter's Daughter also offers another reason for

Ruth's utilitarianism: 'Writing what you wished was the most dangerous form of wishful thinking.' More specifically:

> Years before she had dreamed of writing stories as a way to escape. She could revise her life and become someone else. She could be someone else. In her imagination she could change everything, herself, her mother, her past. But the idea of revising her life also frightened her, as if by imagination alone she were condemning what she did not like about herself and others. (27)

Why this attitude to story writing? One possible explanation is that Ruth understands the performative power of words, particularly her mother's words: '"Maybe I die soon!" ... No matter how often she heard them, they never ceased to grab her by the throat' (88). On reading her teenage diary, Ruth insists that, on the one hand, it proves her existence but, on the other hand, it 'nearly killed them both', particularly the hurtful words addressed to her prying mother: 'You talk about killing yourself, so why don't you ever do it? I wish you would. Just do it, do it, do it! Go ahead, kill yourself! Precious Auntie wants you to do it, and so do I' (121, 123–4). LuLing does attempt suicide, and her daughter, reduced to hysteria because 'she had wished for this, caused this to happen' (125) is also rushed into hospital. For Ruth, the relationship between word and world is close, only too close given that writing simultaneously effects life and death. Not surprisingly, then, she imposes constraints and limits on language, even if such an act makes difficult the mother–daughter relationship.

Although they speak different languages, utilize different models of language and operate on different axes of language, LuLing on the metaphoric axis and her daughter, by implication, on the metonymic axis, Ruth does nevertheless want to hear about her mother's life, as she nears death. She now wants to be taken through 'all the detours of the past, ... the multiple meanings of Chinese words, how to translate her heart' (131). The subsequent chapter is entitled, appropriately enough, 'Heart', a title that refers to LuLing's birthplace – Immortal Heart – and, presumably, to her heart. Here, it would appear that Ruth has successfully translated her mother's heart, although, crucially, Mr Tang, *not* Ruth, translates this chapter. His is an 'odd' (261) model of translation, at least to Ruth. For example, he requests a photograph of LuLing so that he can translate her autobiography 'more naturally'. As he puts it, '[s]eeing her would help me say her words in English the way she expressed them in Chinese' (261).

Mr Tang's 'natural' model of translation seems to posit an essential relationship between translation and original and, for that matter, between LuLing's life story and life. Or does it? Would his translation not have progressed more 'naturally' if he had seen her rather than a photograph of her? Photographs function in complex ways in Tan's texts, *effecting*, not reflecting, an essential 'Chineseness'. If 'Chineseness' is so obviously in the Chinese mother(land), as *The Joy Luck Club*'s Jing-mei 'June' Woo[46] and *The Hundred Secret Senses*' Olivia Yee[47] both seem to assume, then why do they rely on photographs at all? What kind of ethnic essence depends on a photograph to literalize or naturalize it? By having Mr Tang's 'natural' model of translation depend on a photograph, thereby suggesting a relationship between languages, as opposed to a relationship between story and life, *The Bonesetter's Daughter* also problematizes essentialist assumptions about language (in its relation to identity).

Despite Ruth's aversion to Mr Tang's 'odd' model of translation, it is significant that she too is seen staring a photograph of LuLing and Precious Auntie before writing a story that comes from the 'heart'. Ruth has finally unlearnt counting and other rigid systems of classification, supplementing it with something altogether more open, if not 'flow[ing]' (308). She is thus in a better position to speak not only to her mother but also to her grandmother, even listening to the voice of this previously mute(d) 'No Name Woman'. In *The Bonesetter's Daughter*, then, the subaltern woman can speak, a point reinforced formally via romanized, not italicized, speech: '"Think about your intentions," Bao Bomu says. "What is in your heart, what you want to put in others." And side by side, Ruth and her grandmother begin.

Words flow' (308). Although Ruth listens to and to some extent speaks for Precious Auntie, the fact that *their* words flow suggests a non-hierarchical relationship between them. 'They write about what happened, why it happened, how they can make other things happen. They write stories of things that should not have been. They write about what could have been, what still might be. They write of a past that can be changed' (308). Moreover, the fact that their 'flowing' words are not included in the 'Epilogue', a chapter title that typically signifies closure and finality, not, as is here, movement and futurity, further reinforces this argument for a non-hierarchical relationship between Ruth and Precious Auntie.

'Words flow' (308) not only applies to Ruth but also to *The Bonesetter's Daughter* as a whole, despite the claims of Tan's more critical commentators that rigidity, more so than fluidity, characterizes her texts. Indeed, these critics insist that her writing adheres to binary logic in terms compatible with essentialist ideologies, most obviously neo-Orientalism and neo-racism. For example, Wong argues that *The Joy Luck Club* ends with 'a powerful essentialist proposition: despite much wavering throughout the crisscrossing narratives, "family" and "blood" eventually triumph over history'.[48] Does *The Bonesetter's Daughter* simply substitute 'bone' for 'blood' to end the curse and, in the process, 'sweetly' reconcile (grand)mother and daughter, as well as text and reader? Wong's argument would also seem relevant here, were it not for the fact that *The Bonesetter's Daughter* is preoccupied with riddles, particularly linguistic riddles, even being named after a woman who 'play[ed] riddles' (145).

Before the 'Epilogue', LuLing and Ruth, with their respective 'partners', visit the Asian Art Museum in San Francisco. One of the exhibits on display is a (the?) divining bone. Reinforcing the argument that LuLing has finally leaned how to remember, she finally recalls Precious Auntie's name: '"Liu Xin[g] … family name Gu." Ruth wanted to shout for joy, but the next instant she realized her mother had said the Chinese word for "bone." Dr Gu, Dr Bone, bone doctor' (301). After some debate over whether 'Gu' refers to the family trade or the family name, the matter is more or less settled, to Ruth's obvious relief. 'Ruth began to cry. Her grandmother had a name. Gu Liu Xin. She had existed. She still existed. Precious Auntie belonged to a family. LuLing belonged to that same family, and Ruth belonged to them both. The family name had been there all along, like a bone stuck in the crevices of a gorge' (305).

'Gu' is not just *like* a bone, however; it is also the Chinese word for 'bone', which goes some way towards explaining why 'Gu' is effective with regard to the ancestral curse. The traditional way to do end a curse would be to '[r]eturn the bones' (156). Significantly, LuLing does not go to China to carry out this duty, perhaps because Tan's other texts, most obviously *The Joy Luck Club*, have been criticized for endorsing 'the return of the native' as a solution to the 'multiple neuroses' that pre-occupy the American-born characters in particular. Here, it is not Precious Auntie's bones that are returned, but her name. The 'return' of the name, then, seems to be sufficient to end the curse, at least to LuLing's (dying) mind. Moreover, the fact that Precious Auntie is supportive of her granddaughter, sitting beside her as she writes, also seems to signal that the curse is at an end.

As it turns out, however, 'Gu' is not just the word for bone, but '"old," "gorge," … also "thigh," "blind," "grain," "merchant," lots of things. And the way "bone" is written can also stand for "character." That's why we use that expression "It's in your bones." It means, "That's your character"' (304). Interestingly, 'character' also means lots of things, referring to identity as it is formulated both 'inside' and 'outside' a narrative, as well as to a sign used in a system of writing. 'Gu' as 'bone' and 'character' proves particularly interesting as far as the debate about Tan's essentialism is concerned. The many meanings of 'Gu' problematize essentialism, the latter relying on the assumption of one meaning. Moreover, the fact that 'Gu' means 'character' suggests that identity, even a 'bony' identity, has its basis in language. An essential 'Chineseness' would thus seem to be complicated by language, an unreliable language at that, opening Tan's text to various interpretative possibilities. In this respect, then, *The Bonesetter's Daughter* is rather like a divining bone, posing questions but not necessarily final answers; it is something of 'a linguistic puzzle' (302), playing with words, not just 'Gu' but also 'ghost writing', as it too means many things, including a job, a form of divining and a figure for Tan's writing.

As her 'most autobiographical novel to date',[49] it should come as no surprise that theories of writing and matters related to language generally preoccupy *The Bonesetter's Daughter*. Here, autobiography, like translation, is understood as a relationship between languages and by extension between texts, which, in turn, opens it up to various and, at times, contradictory interpretative possibilities, some literal, others figural. 'Ghosts' may well constitute 'the real' for Tan, also coming to her assistance during writing, but as she articulates in interviews and, for that matter, in *The Bonesetter's Daughter*, 'ghost' and 'ghost writing' can be variously interpreted. 'Ghost' could be a figure for transgressive women marginalized from their families most obviously, as well as from history and language like Kingston's mute(d) 'No Name Woman'. 'Ghost writing' could refer to Ruth's and, quite possibly, Tan's theory of writing, of how it exists in an intergenerational and intertextual network. Indeed, Ruth describes LuLing's autobiography as a 'quilt' (270), a figure used by women writers especially, often ethnic minority women writers in North America, as well as some post-colonial writers,[50] to emphasize, among other things, the intertextuality of writing. Writing thus understood involves, as Tan phrases it, 'force[s] greater than oneself'.[51]

Whether supernatural or 'super-natural', these forces are represented in *The Bonesetter's Daughter*. '[E]verything, even ink, had a purpose and a meaning' (172), making subjective intention just one of many possible forces motivating writing. For example, Ruth may mean dog when she writes dog, but, crucially, there are no guarantees, especially as dog also means 'doggie' or a nickname. Similarly, Gu means bone, old, gorge, thigh, blind, grain, merchant, character and a surname. Clearly, then, 'words flow' (308), with Ruth learning openness to other meanings, including those of her mother and grandmother. It is with this flexible and reciprocal or communal model of writing that *The Bonesetter's Daughter* ends, inviting the reader also to respond to this flexibility or, at least, to 'unlearn' a 'utilitarian' or literal approach to the text(s). Such a reading responds to the text(s) 'as literature – as a story, language, memory'[52] without giving up the ghosts that haunt Tan's writing, from her dead ancestresses to other Chinese and Chinese American women subalternized and rendered invisible 'yin people' by dominant ideologies that, even at their most 'benevolent', preserve violent ethnic/gender hierarchies and structures. By negotiating the 'text/tissue/weave'[53] of this history of subalternization, *The Bonesetter's Daughter* follows *The Joy Luck Club, The Kitchen God's Wife* and *The Hundred Secrets Senses* in a feminist rewriting of history, effectively transforming a legacy of silence and oppression into 'a legacy of strength'[54] by drawing attention to the de/construction of ethnic/gender stereotypes.

Critical overview and conclusion

THIS study could not conclude without mentioning the film adaptation of *The Joy Luck Club* (1993), co-written and co-produced by Amy Tan, as well as her two children's books, *The Moon Lady* (1992) and *The Chinese Siamese Cat* (1994).[1] This crossing over into the genres of 'chick flick' and 'kid lit' also offers a useful way into an overview of the Tan critical canon because responses to the film in particular reiterate the debates currently circulating about 'the Amy Tan phenomenon'[2] vis-à-vis ethnic/gender stereotyping. Again, *The Joy Luck Club*'s relationship to Orientalism and multiculturalism is targeted for discussion, arguably more so than feminist/womanist issues because the film devotes less attention to the way in which both immigrant and diasporic Chinese American women are *doubly* 'colonized' by their ethnicity and their gender.[3] More of an 'ethnic film' than a 'chick flick', then, this 'emotional sibling'[4] to *The Joy Luck Club* – 'we keep all the characters, all the stories' through the use of 'wraparound' and 'a lot of voice-over'[5] – is nevertheless discussed in gendered terms, its popularity and melodramatic content inviting comparison to the soap opera, a femininized form not famed for its realism and authenticity.

Described as 'fake', 'untruthful',[6] 'shallow',[7] 'phony' and 'unnatural',[8] often, as it happens, by male critics, not necessarily Asian American masculinist/nationalist critics, 'the signifiers of ethnicity, of "Chineseness", including the sceneries, costumes, mannerisms, verbalisms, acts of violence', being only too conspicuous in this regard, *The Joy Luck Club* is once again 'written off as a mythification, a degradation and distortion that has little to do with the "real" China and "real" Chinese people'.[9] Even when the 'real' China is represented, specifically Guilin, a region renown for its natural beauty that is lingeringly represented in the final wartime scene especially, the (test-)audience assume it is 'fake'.[10] This response to the Chinese sceneries is interesting because it problematizes the real/fake binary opposition so often utilized to criticize Tan's texts without sufficient attention to the fact that they necessarily mediate the 'real' China, often in 'mistyfying'[11] terms by narrators/characters (and some readers/viewers) who are not always responsive to the irony of using photographs and other cultural forms to render the Chinese mother(land) 'im-mediate'.[12]

The ironic dimension of Tan's texts, an irony that is, admittedly, less easily achieved in a Disney film, especially as the Studio seldom relinquishes creative control to novelists-turned-screenwriters,[13] complicates the 'mythification' of 'Chineseness'. For this reason, the film is not so easily 'written off', particularly as Tan's texts are *about* this 'mythification' (and the impact it has on personal/political relationships). As Tan observes, somewhat playfully: it is '*as if* this *reel* life were more real than real life. But that's what movies are all about'.[14] Tan's 'reel' China, like the photographed China in her literary texts, arguably reinforces the notion of mediated 'Chineseness'.

Interestingly, the film also features a number of photographs. At the Woos' party, in the opening scene, for instance, Waverly organizes a group photograph of the Joy Luck 'aunties' and their daughters. In this photograph, Jing-mei is seen holding a brief case, whereas the other characters hold on to each other. The asymmetry of the scene suggests her sense of alienation not only from the group but also from her recently deceased mother, Suyuan, along with reinforcing the *asymmetrical* structure of the film's (and the novel's) narrative. This asymmetrical 'family' photograph appears on screen again at the end of the film, after the dockside scene, and, more crucially, after the main cast is listed. Before the credits roll, a second 'family' photograph appears on screen of all *four* Joy Luck mothers and their daughters. Thus placed, *outside* the filmic narrative, these two photographs function ambiguously. On the one hand, Suyuan's presence in the second photograph lends itself to the happy Hollywood ending, so often desired by the characters in Tan's texts and, indeed, her readers/viewers. On the other hand, however, Suyuan's continued absence from the first photograph disrupts such an ending, as does the ambiguity over whether the second photograph is of the characters or the actors. Similar to its literary 'sibling', the film version of *The Joy Luck Club* resists an ending (and reading) it also ratifies via its depiction of a (cinematic/photographic) 'reel' China and by extension a mediated, if not a 'melodramatized'[15] 'Chineseness'.

Unperturbed by this 'melodramatization' of 'Chineseness' achieved cinematically by multiple flashbacks to 'old' China, shot in '"primitive", most earthly colours ... with semi-dark lighting and accompanied by a slow, melodious soundtrack',[16] Tan's diverse audience, from Chinese Americans and 'arthouse buffs' to 'young, blue-collar bucks',[17] seem not to mind the 'Western Oriental dialogue' and other so-called 'grotesquely outlandish'[18] filmic features relating to China's past and present. Many of these features are usefully, if, at times, problematically, discussed in '*Joy Luck*: The Perils of Transcultural "Translation"', by George K. Y. Tseo: Lindo's 'exceptional perception' and her reference to 'near immaculate conception';[19] Ying-ying's 'husband's outward expression of his conduct [that] is totally at odds with Chinese behaviour';[20] An-mei's 'gain[ing] an upper hand over the strong-willed and shamelessly manipulative adults of the clan'; and, moving from 'old' to 'new' China, Jing-mei's behaviour on meeting her sisters at the dockside in Shanghai. 'To top things off', remarks Tseo,

> Jing-mei makes her way through the crowd at the dock and, just when she reaches her sisters, sets her suitcase down on the ground. ... Anybody watching this scene who had lived or simply travelled substantially in China would know that in all probability when, after the hugs, Jing-mei bent down again to pick up her luggage nothing would be there. Had things really happened as depicted in the film

Jing-mei's sisters' first urgent words to her might have been, 'Don't put that suitcase down!'[21]

But is such a 'real happening' the focus of *The Joy Luck Club*, particularly when neither the film nor the novel is about the 'real' China, only, to quote Tseo, 'a mythical conception of a country far away',[22] and, moreover, to quote director Wayne Wang, the 'very strong, universal'[23] representation of the family and the intergenerational/intercultural gap? Tan also discusses the film's wide appeal: 'Certainly, the movie's context is Chinese-American. But the subtext ... involves emotions we all have.'[24] This subtext works to powerful effect, even affecting Tseo: 'Ultimately, *The Joy Luck Club* is about mothers and daughters. ... The truth conveyed by Tan shone through even the movie's thin characterization, which may be why so many young women left the theaters in tears. To them the scenes must have triggered self-recognition.'[25]

Arguably, 'self-recognition' is more common than Tseo realizes, supporting Wang's point about the wide appeal of the film among women, not just young American women but also old Chinese women,[26] as well as 'young, blue-collar bucks', so used to deriding films not featuring Sylvester Stallone. As it happens, *The Joy Luck Club* outgrossed Stallone's *Demolition Man* in a season of 'multi-hanky' films including *Philadelphia*, *Shadowlands* and *Schindler's List*. On an $10.6 million budget from Disney, approximately half of *Schindler's List* and a fifth of *Jurassic Park*, this 'eight-hanky' classic made $32 million at the box office, a rare achievement for an 'ethnic film' with multiple protagonists, none of them big-name stars, multiple voice-overs, multiple flashbacks and subtitles.

'Multiple-hanky' scenes include the film's narrowing, not closing – Suyuan is dead, as she was in the novel – of the intergenerational/intercultural gap. This narrowing is depicted when the two generations, to paraphrase Suyuan, see themselves and each other. This seeing is all that the Chinese mothers hope for their American-born daughters, and it seems to be successful as the latter come to realize their 'worth', as described in the swan-feather story that opens the film (and is repeated by

Jing-mei three times in total), albeit with limited reference to the dominant American ideologies that powerfully determine Chinese American history, 'even' for the middle-class diasporic generation.

This sense of self worth is emphasized in Lena's and Rose's narratives in particular, if only because the film departs from the novel by having the increasingly sophisticated Lena leave money-orientated Harold and start afresh with a family-orientated and presumably 'tender' man, and by having Rose 'refresh' her marriage with unfaithful Ted after she proclaims that her increasingly 'tragic' persona is 'full of shit'. Unlike Lena and Rose, Waverly is no 'doormat'[27] in her relationship with Rich, her 'spotty' husband-to-be, only with her powerful mother. While it is 'so easy' for Waverly to blame Lindo for her loss of self worth, she does ultimately take responsibility for this loss – 'I did it to myself' – and is thus able to form a better relationship with her mother. As Suzanne D. Green observes in relation to their 'mirror scene' at Trevor's hair salon: 'The facial expressions, the quick hug they exchange ... and the laugh they share all serve to show to the audience that these women have bonded as perhaps never before.'[28]

Although poignant, such bonding does not match the emotional intensity of Suyuan's forced abandonment of her Chinese daughters. This experience also provides occasion for the other Chinese mothers to narrate the profound loss they felt after, in Lindo's and An-mei's cases, losing a mother through marriage and suicide respectively, and, in Ying-ying's case, losing a baby through infanticide, not abortion (as in the novel). Ying-ying's drowning of the son she bore to a husband who flaunts his affairs with other women/whores, the two terms being synonymous for him, as they are presumably for An-mei's stepfather, who also (erotically) objectifies his wife with violent consequences, makes 'a harsher statement about the depths of [Ying-ying's] pain'. This said, Green argues that this particular change is unnecessary since abortion is painful enough, leading her to wonder whether the avoidance of such 'a divisive and controversial issue' signals 'the filmmakers' desire to avoid a public outcry by anti-abortion fundamentalists over the inclusion of abortion in a mainstream film'. She continues: 'the film offers a particularly unsettling insight: that some American viewers might find the depiction of abortion more disturbing than an instance of infanticide, a more remote (and arguably culturally ordained) practice'.[29] This shift from the filmmakers to film viewers, both of them negotiating political concerns, albeit in different ways, Tan (and Wang) for fear of promoting Orientalist stereotypes,[30] precisely the stereotypes that the inclusion of the infanticide scene at once ratifies *and* resists, suggests that *The Joy Luck Club* once again performs a difficult balancing act. If allowed to dominate, the emotional draw of the film, like that of the novel,[31] can undermine the critical or 'unsettling' potential of this 'not strictly … feel-good movie'.[32]

Describing a similar balancing act, David Henry Hwang, also a successful crossover writer, principally for his play/film *M. Butterfly*, argues that *The Joy Luck Club* 'confound[s] expectations and confuse[s] conventionality', not least because of its mainstream appeal. 'Because of the economic realities, Hollywood can no longer look at an Asian-American project and say we can't do this piece' and, reversing the perspective, Hwang continues: 'As a community … we cannot sustain a picture of any budget by ourselves; in order for any of these things to be successful, they have to cross over.'[33] Economic realities, then, force Hollywood and the Asian American community to cross over into 'unfamiliar' territory to the mutual benefit of both or, more precisely, to the financial benefit of Hollywood and a debatable number of Asian Americans.

Yes, *The Joy Luck Club* and *M. Butterfly*, along with Ang Lee's *The Wedding Banquet* and Chen Kaige's *Farewell My Concubine*, have brought their writers various degrees of fame and fortune. And, yes, this people-based 'new Chinoiserie',[34] so popular in America and to a lesser extent 'elsewhere in the world [where] the ghost stories, the action films, and the kung fu films seem to be more popular',[35] has widened the repertoire for Asian American actors who had heretofore been more or less ignored by Hollywood. But, is this interest in 'Chineseness' just a fad from a minority, a 'model minority', who, as long as they 'kissass', to borrow Frank Chin's terminology, are permitted access to white middle-class opportunities, especially compared to 'badass' African Americans?[36] If Tan and her 'Americanized' or, more accurately, 'Hollywoodized' peers do affirm 'white racist'[37] discourses, most obviously Orientalism and multiculturalism, as Chin and other Asian American critics maintain, then, rather than marking a significant shift in the ideological/ political assumptions of Hollywood and by extension mainstream American culture, the 'new Chinoiserie' and, moreover, responses to it demand critical attention.

From the perspective of the marketplace, the six-figure dollar advances and sales, as well as the various nominations – the National Book Award for Fiction, the National Book Critics Circle Award and the *Los Angeles Times* Book Prize – and awards, including the Bay Area Book Reviewers Award and the Commonwealth Club Gold Award for *The Joy Luck Club*, Tan's best-selling texts have contributed to the popularizing of Asian American literature both inside and outside the academy. Appearing on university syllabi in America, Europe,[38] Hong Kong and elsewhere, usually on courses in 'multicultural' and/ or women's writing, 'the Amy Tan phenomenon' is increasingly scrutinized by scholars in essays, dissertations, journal articles and books. In 1995 and 1996 respectively, two American journals, *Paintbrush* from Truman State University and *Hitting Critical Mass* from the University of California, devoted editions exclusively to Tan, and, in 1998, Greenwood Press published E. D. Huntley's *Amy Tan: A Critical Companion*, the only other monograph available at present. Published three years before *The Bonesetter's Daughter*, Huntley's *Amy Tan* covers three novels arguably in a way more suited to the interests of highschool students and first-year undergraduates.[39] This said, its introductory chapters would appeal to a wider range of students not familiar with 'The Life of Amy Tan' and 'Amy Tan and Asian American Literature', and two (out of three) relatively short sections on 'Alternate Reading', specifically on 'Cultural Criticism' and 'Feminism', when considered alongside Huntley's critique of 'ethnic labelling',[40] would provide a good basis for a more complex reading of Tan's texts.

If practised uncritically, ethnic labelling privileges ethnicity, understood as Chinese and, sometimes, Chinese American, but not American, over cultural issues to do with the literary de/construction of identity, history and reality, a privileging that also overlooks the fact that '[b]eing Chinese American means living with duality and division, with contrast and opposition'.[41] Perhaps in response to this practice, some critics depart from the norm by reading Tan's texts *not* alongside others that are similarly labelled, including, first and foremost, Maxine Hong Kingston's *The Woman Warrior* and those by Julia Alvares, Christine Bell, Sandra Cisneros, Louise Erdrich, Cristina Garcia, Toni Morrison, Bharati Mukherjee and Gloria Naylor. For example, Stephen Souris and Walter Shear briefly analyze *The Joy Luck Club* apart from the 'ethnic canon' on the basis that it harps back to modernist experiments with the 'decentred multiple monologue' as practised by Sherwood Anderson, William Faulkner, Ernest Hemingway and Virginia Woolf.[42] Harping back even further, one critic suggests that Ying-ying St. Clair's 'The Moon Lady' is 'Wordsworthian' in its exploration of human origins.[43] Also analyzing *The Joy Luck Club* apart from 'the prevalent categorical difference of the "ethnic other"', Rey Chow situates the film 'within our postmodern explorations of human origins *in general*' by juxtaposing it with *Jurassic Park*.[44]

Whether studied independently of or jointly with other 'multicultural' (and) American texts, Tan's fiction is prized and generally praised. Her 'visions' are often described in terms of food, precious stones and other equally exotic, 'magic[al] and 'myster[ious]'[45] figures: 'Pure enchantment' (*JLC*, back cover) writes the *Mail on Sunday* of Tan's first novel, which perhaps explains why the *New York Times'* Orville Schell is so enchanted that he confuses characters, families and Joy Luck Clubs, also explaining away his confusion by insisting that it reflects the confusion of immigration/diaspora. For Schell, 'the *recherches* to old China are so beautifully written that one should just allow oneself to be borne along as if in a dream. ... She has written a jewel of a book'.[46] Philip Howard from *The Times* observes that *The Kitchen God's Wife* 'portrays Chinese society, both now and throughout this century, as a web of superstitions, secrets and hierarchies'.[47] Natasha Walter and Michèle Roberts in the *Guardian* and the *Independent* respectively argue that *The Hundred Secret Senses* is 'sugary'[48] and 'works like a dream'.[49] Also reviewing for the *Guardian*, Joan Smith says of *The Bonesetter's Daughter*: 'I don't think Tan intends to suggest that contemporary America is shallow and insipid, compared to the savagely vivid world of her recent ancestors, but that is certainly the effect.'[50]

Despite the difference between text and writer, a difference emphasized in theories about 'the death of the author', a concept explored somewhat anecdotally by Tan in *The Opposite of Fate*,[51] a number of her critics focus on the issue of intentionality, the main reason for this being an ideological/political agenda apparently compatible with neoconservative, neo-Orientalist and neo-racist discourses: '*The Joy Luck Club* and Amy Tan's Quest for Stardom in the Market of Neo-Racism'. Surprisingly perhaps, this is not a masculinist/nationalist proclamation, but (part of) the title of an essay by a female Asian American critic familiar with postmodern debates about ethnicity and gender. According to Sinkwan Cheng, text/writer are interchangeable, nowhere more so than when Jing-mei 'June' Woo has her 'bloody' epiphany towards the end of *The Joy Luck Club*. '[S]tanding in for the author', this character 'ties together a political quest with a familial quest'. Cheng continues: 'It is interesting ... to note that Tan's textual quest for reunion with her "Sinocentric" mother and with her ethnic roots coincide with the author's social and economic quest for fame and wealth in the market of postmodern capitalism.'[52] Admittedly, Jing-mei quests for ethnic/gender essences in the Chinese mother(land), but can the same be said of the text(s) and, indeed, of Tan?

Throughout this study the focus has been on *how* ethnic/gender essences are de/constructed ideologically and linguistically and, on this basis, Cheng's argument about Tan's text(s) '*reimporting biological determinism to naturalize cultural discriminations'*[53] is rendered vulnerable. Rather than using the texts as a basis for discussing Tan's intention or, as another critic phrases it, 'design' and 'consciousness',[54] the emphasis here is on why authorial intention should be an issue at all. Is it because Tan is a celebrity, clearly alive despite 'AmyTanmustdie' and other death threats, and, for now, participating in 'the entertainment model – the interviews in magazines, radio, TV'?[55] Does 'the birth of the celebrity' signal, not the death, but the return of the author, the 'multicultural' author in particular as her semi-autobiographical literature makes possible a return to the 'origin', if not the 'Origin' and other similarly capitalized concepts such as 'Roots, Culture, Tradition, History, War, Human Evil'[56] and, ultimately, 'Truth' not available to those outside the glamorous world of 'Amy Tan, Inc.'?[57]

The assumption that Tan's texts return the author and, in the process, recover the author's ideological/political intentions and other 'Truths' is not only resisted by the texts themselves, *if* they are 'treated as literature – as a story, language, memory',[58] and by the narrators/characters therein, all of whom 'question what they should believe',[59] but also by the 'author' herself or, more properly, the 'author persona'. In an interview, Tan discusses the necessity of having a persona, an author persona, which, like her musician persona in the 'The Rock Bottom Remainders', a charity band of best-selling writers, including Stephen King, involves self-performance, although not always as a 'rock chick': 'It's like becoming actively schizophrenic', Tan remarks. 'The part of you that is important for writing you sort of put away – "Take a nap now. Mama's gonna go out and do her thing!"'[60] Between public and private personas, between fact and fiction, between writer and text: this schizophrenia simile problematizes the assumption that Tan's ideological/political intentions are recoverable from the texts in a reliable way.

Granted, uncovering intentions, particularly suspect intentions, is a matter of great urgency, nowhere more so perhaps than when 'a new and more insidious form of censorship ... [creeps] into the fold [of American literature], winning followers by wearing the cloak of good intentions and ethnic correctness'.[61]

This censorship regarding the content, form and function of literature, not just 'multicultural' (and) American literature, disturbs and terrifies Tan enough for her address the question of intentionality, most (in)directly in *The Opposite of Fate*: 'I believe', says Tan before she shifts into the third person, that 'writers today must talk about their intentions, if for nothing else, to serve as an antidote to what others define as what their intentions should be.'[62] Only too alert to the fact that intentions, even good intentions are vulnerable to (mis)appropriation, and so 'don't always go the way we intend',[63] Tan understands this vulnerability in a way that is as contradictory as (her) literary writing. In her words: 'writing provides the sort of freedom and danger, satisfaction and discomfort, truth and contradiction that I can't find anywhere else in life'.[64] Preserving these contradictions is the responsibility of writers *and* readers vis-à-vis ageism, classism, homophobia, racism, sexism and so on. For Tan, then, the question of intentionality, whether intentions are 'good', 'bad' or 'in-between', although partly a private/personal responsibility, is more effectively addressed at the structural/institutional level.

Although an interesting contribution to the Tan critical canon, mainly because it offers a different perspective on the 'sweet' or idealized/romanticized analyses of matrilineality and intergenerational/intercultural reconciliation, Cheng's 'Fantasizing the *Jouissance* of the Chinese Mother: *The Joy Luck Club* and Amy Tan's Quest for Stardom in the Market of Neo-Racism' is nevertheless uncritically embroiled in the very same 'intentionalist' fantasy it seeks to criticize. Just as Jing-mei quests for a 'truth' in the Chinese mother(land), so too does Cheng quest for the truth in the text in keeping with biographical criticism and, ultimately, the real/fake debate. Her movement from Jing-mei to Tan, from inside to outside, is achieved with such apparent ease because Cheng stops her reading of *The Joy Luck Club* just before the end, specifically at Jing-mei's 'bloody' epiphany, a common practice among Tan's critics, whether they view the texts positively or negatively. For example, Sau-ling Cynthia Wong, in '"Sugar Sisterhood": Situating the Amy Tan

Phenomenon', also argues that 'the ending of the novel itself offers a powerful essentialist proposition: despite much wavering throughout the crisscrossing narratives, "family" and "blood" eventually triumph over history'.[65] A plot based on blood or, as David Leiwei Li notes in 'Genes, Generations, and Geospiritual (Be)longings', 'a plot based on genes is a plot of irreversible lineage, the native-born Asian-American women cannot but inherit the inclinations of their immigrant progenitors. ... [A] plot based on genes is also about ancestral origin, it demands a geocultural allegiance unaffected by personal experience, political history, or place of residence.'[66]

Their differences notwithstanding, these three critics (and others)[67] represent a way of reading that is apparently different from the other, more dominant reading of Tan's text(s). While Cheng, Wong and Li resist idealizing/romanticizing the texts and the intergenerational/intercultural relationships therein by highlighting the neo-racist/Orientalist/conservative implications of Tan's happy Hollywood endings, and while they highlight the postmodern or 'poststructural and multicultural celebrations of diasporic subjectivity',[68] along with discussing 'micronarratives'[69] and 'equivocation',[70] these three critics nevertheless offer a way of reading that endorses closure and the related concepts of reconciliation, wholeness and oneness. Arguably, it does not really matter which of these two readings is privileged, the political or the personal, the 'dark' or the 'sweet', because both ultimately view Tan's texts as modernist.

A modernist reading is only possible if these texts are ended prematurely at the epiphanies involving 'blood' (*JLC*, 288; *KGW*, 397), 'bones' (*BSD*, 301) and the Chinese mother(land) (*HSS*, 263). By ending at the epiphanies and by marginalizing that which is 'post' – namely, the last two paragraphs in *The Joy Luck Club* about the Polaroid photograph of Jing-mei and her sisters, and, more generally, the references to the construction of ethnic/gender essences in culture, not nature, albeit via de/naturalizing tropes and figures – the modernist reading fails to take into account the possibility that Tan's texts resist the answers the narrators provide about questions relating to an embodied 'Chineseness'. Whether through violence, disease (*KGW*) or reincarnation (*HSS*), the 'body' invariably functions unreliably, a point further endorsed by the fact that 'bone' or '*Gu* ... can mean many things: "old," "gorge," "bone," also "thigh," "blind," "grain," "merchant" ... "character"' (*BSD*, 304).

A third way of reading that is responsive to the postmodern dimension of Tan's texts, to their status as 'story, language, memory', as opposed to 'truth', if not 'Truth', is offered by a number of critics, including Judith Caesar in 'Patriarchy, Imperialism, and Knowledge in *The Kitchen God's Wife*', Wendy Ho in 'Swan-Feather Mothers and Coca-Cola Daughters: Teaching Amy Tan's *The Joy Luck Club*', Lisa Lowe in 'Heterogeneity, Hybridity, Multiplicity: Marking Asian American Differences', Melanie McAlister in '(Mis)Reading *The Joy Luck Club*', Malini Johar Schueller in 'Theorizing Ethnicity and Subjectivity: Maxine Hong Kingston's *Tripmaster Monkey* and Amy Tan's *The Joy Luck Club*' and Rey Chow in 'Women in the Holocene: Ethnicity, Fantasy, and the Film *The Joy Luck Club*'.

While all of these critics problematize reductive, if not premature, readings of the texts, offering instead analyses that rigorously remain in the 'text/tissue/weave'[71] of Tan's writing, Chow's essay on the film is worth mentioning in a more detail, especially as many of the other essays have been referenced already. Once again, the body, specifically An-mei Hsu's scarred body, is the object of discussion. Along with providing 'a narrative hinge', explains Chow, '[t]he scar signifies not so much the continuity of ethnic "origin" as its seriality – rather than being a definite beginning, the origin "exists" only insofar as it is in a series, a relation, a mark-made-on-the-other.'[72] Rather than ending her analysis of *The Joy Luck Club* prematurely, at the point where Jing-mei returns to the Chinese mother(land), Chow moves from the modern to the postmodern, from the reliable body to the scarred/defective body, from autonomy to relationality. For her, the scarred body is neither self-sufficient nor immediate with regard to meaning/reference. It is a metaphor, bringing different entities together, including different generations, different cultures, different filmic canons and, ultimately, 'us and them'. As scarification involves violence, it resists the romantic reconciliation of 'us and them', also compelling 'us' to analyze the fantasy whereby 'they', as figures of 'Truth' and other capitalized concepts, 'must be understood not as a separatist subculture but rather as our contemporary culture, with its continual, even if very old, attempts to (re)imagine, (re)make, and (re)invent itself'.[73] As a figure for matrilineality, *The Joy Luck Club* and the 'ethnic film' vis-à-vis dominant views of 'ethnicity' as originary, An-mei's scar implies that the 'origin' is really already scarred, making it impossible to recover in any reliable and final way.

From this overview of the Tan critical canon, very roughly divided into three approaches – 'sweet', 'dark', deconstructive – it should be clear that much depends on how *The Joy Luck Club*(s), *The Kitchen God's Wife*, *The Hundred Secret Senses* and *The Bonesetter's Daughter* are read. This 'how' is principally affected by where the readings end: at the stereotypes and the ethnic/gender essences, a 'happy' place if only to the extent that it stabilizes the texts in accordance with dominant aesthetic and political categories, or, at the 'text/tissue/weave' of these stereotypes and essences. The fact that so many of Tan's narrators desire the former ending, a world where the Kweilin fairy story really did 'end ... on a happy note' (*JLC*, 25), and the family romance really did end 'happily ever after, just like in those stories' (*KGW*, 85), perhaps explains why some critics also privilege the happy Hollywood ending. But does this ending not marginalize the texts' ideological/political commitment to representing those aspects of Chinese and Chinese American history, specifically an immigrant/diasporic femininity 'scarred' by rape (*KGW*), electro-shock therapy (*HSS*) and other forms of violence that persist 'even' in an American 'happily ever after'? Commenting on this persistence in a way that it is arguably relevant to all of Tan's narrators, Jing-mei says of the Kweilin fairy story: 'Over the years, she told me the same story, except for the ending, which grew darker and darker, casting long shadows into her life, eventually into mine'; and, later, 'The endings always changed. ... The story always grew and grew' (*JLC*, 21, 25).

The fact that endings change and grow, and that they do so darkly, puts into question the happy Hollywood ending and, moreover, the presumed happiness of the happy ending when it reinforces stereotypes and essences in and around Tan's texts. For these reasons, then, is it not better to end at the 'end', at the place where the texts draw attention to the issue of representation? At times, Tan's narrators acknowledge this issue, although it is often left to the reader to respond to the irony involved in using a variety of cultural forms, including films, myths, photographs, romantic stories and, in one instance, a shampoo, to de/construct stereotypes and essences. This emphasis on form thus invites a reading of a mediated 'Chineseness' that exceeds the real/fake debate and, with it, the inside/outside model of ideology critique.

A more crucial debate is generated by Tan's texts, one that does not explain away stereotypes and essences therein, but rather accounts for their persistence and their de/construction. Essences cannot help but persist, as Tan's narrators clearly demonstrate through suspect remarks about themselves and others. No 'real' or 'authentic' position is available to them for at least two related reasons, one ideological/political, the other, formal. Granted, they desire authenticity, which they typically associate with a remembered and/or narrated China, 'even' in the two texts that 'return the native'. On their China trips, *The Joy Luck Club*'s Lindo Jong and Jing-mei (266, 272), as well as *The Hundred Secret Senses*' Olivia Yee and Kwan Li (236, 184), concede that they are too American(ized) to be 'one hundred percent' or 'true Chinese', despite abandoning the signifiers for 'Americanness', including 'fancy jewellery', 'loud colors', 'makeup' and a judgemental attitude. Crucially, these signifiers for 'Americanness', specifically the fancy accessories and clothes worn by the Chinese mothers, signify a working-class 'Chineseness' to the American-born daughters. Given that ethnic signifiers are relative and liable to misreading, as when Jing-mei mistakes a Dutch or a Swedish man for an American (273), it is hardly surprising that ethnic essences prove irrecoverable.

Their irrecoverability is further reinforced because of

hybridity, noted by a good number of Tan's commentators in terms of 'the Chinese American experience', as marked by 'schizophrenia',[74] 'double consciousness',[75] 'betweeness',[76] 'biculturalism' and a 'series of dualities – two identities, two voices, two cultures, and even two names – that represent an uneasy stance somewhere between the traditional Chinese culture ... and the contemporary American culture'.[77] Huntley's *Amy Tan* usefully draws attention to the heterogeneity of both cultures in terms of settings, the temporal, geographical and imagined territories, 'from post-feudal China to war-time China, to the America of the 1950s, to modern China under communist domination', to 'Chinatown and mainstream California', specifically in and around San Francisco.[78] Despite the inescapable draw that Chinese nationalism, American assimilationism and other essentialist discourses exert on those in Tan's texts, the various reassurances these discourses offer through closure and the related concepts of reconciliation, wholeness and oneness, the texts draw back from essentialism through their representation of various hybridized experiences, including 'the Chinese American experience' and, more generally, 'the post-colonial experience' and, more generally still, 'the postmodern condition.'

Tan's texts are hybrid constructions and, as such, operate between these two 'posts', neither assuming priority because this would effectively marginalize their complex and strategic negotiation of essentialism. Too much emphasis on the ethnic(/gender) issues would marginalize the formal issues and vice versa, giving rise to readings that degenerate into 'real versus fake' and, ultimately, 'us versus them'. A reading that preserves hybridity by responding to the 'text/tissue/weave' of Tan's writing, that is, to the figure of the torn quilt with which this study began, acknowledges 'China' as 'a story, language, memory'. It is constructed, continually constructed, and, for this reason, cannot finally resolve the narrators' various struggles in all four literary texts with identity, history and reality, although, admittedly, the belief that 'Chineseness' is in their blood, bones and body functions to reassure, albeit provisionally since it depends on de/naturalizing tropes and figures.

Finally, then, how these de/naturalizing tropes and figures are read proves crucial to studying all of Tan's texts. Authorial comments about the difference between symbols and images, a difference Tan associates with a 'Nabokovian' approach to literature, may at the very least encourage an 'Hmm'[79] about symbolism and the ideological assumption underpinning it that literature reliably means/references, and 'multicultural' literature even more so since its place in the western literary canon and, for that matter, at the American airport news-stand, seems often to depend on its affirmation of dominant aesthetic categories, including mimesis, catharsis, didacticism and so on. Thus understood, literature, any literature, is reduced to 'a very limited rhetoric', becoming 'sort of the cart and horse to take people into the right directions, a model America'.[80] Undoubtedly, literature moves people emotionally, *The Joy Luck Club*s being exemplary in this regard in that they appeal to the desire for 'happily ever after' or, less 'sweetly', for solutions to personal/political problems, particularly to the disenfranchizement brought about by ethnic/gender oppression and the postmodern condition. Literature also moves people critically in that it promotes questions about writing and reading, specifically about how literary language holds few guarantees with regard to meaning and reference apart from ideology. Thus understood, literature directs people back to itself and, crucially, to their relationship with it.

By representing this text/reader relationship, sometimes directly, at other times, indirectly via references to a whole range of relationships between generations, cultures, languages, histories, realities and so on, often relationships that are violently determined by dominant narratives, institutions and systems of representation, Tan's fiction moves in at least two contradictory directions, not towards right and wrong, but rather in a 'post' direction that arguably makes possible a progression from formal issues to ideological/political issues. As this study has argued, particularly in the chapter on *The Bonesetter's Daughter*, Tan's writing is about writing and reading, about *how* meaning/reference happens, and, moreover, *has to* happen, although not merely as a violent act of appropriation. By focusing on 'how', specifically on its ideological and linguistic underpinnings, 'what' is rendered provisional and open to change, which, in turn, makes possible reciprocal relationships in and around the texts. And, perhaps reciprocity is all that the 'swan-feather' mother and Tan's (m)other figures hope for through the synecdochical gift of a feather from a creature representing change. Less a symbol, more an 'image' in so far as the feather does not mean this or refer to that, but operates instead at the level of 'textuality and seriality, and ... a kind of continual storytelling'[81] that ensures a future for debate and dialogue both 'inside' and 'outside' *The Joy Luck Club*(s), *The Kitchen God's Wife*, *The Hundred Secret Senses* and *The Bonesetter's Daughter*.

Notes

Chapter 1

1 Amy Tan, *The Bonesetter's Daughter* (London, Flamingo, 2001), 270. Hereafter page numbers and abbreviations for Tan's novels (*JLC*, *KGW*, *HSS* and *BSD*) appear in parentheses in the text. Interestingly, Tan also uses the figure of a quilt to describe the process of her own writing: 'It is a crazy quilt … pieced together, torn apart, repaired again and again, and strong enough to protect us all.' Amy Tan, 'The Ghosts of My Imagination', in *The Opposite of Fate* (London, Flamingo, 2003), 266. Hereafter essays from *Opposite* will appear in the notes.

2 See John Thieme, 'Patchwork, Patchwork Quilting', in *Post-Colonial Studies: The Essential Glossary* (London and New York, Arnold, 2003), 207–8.

3 Gayatri Chakravorty Spivak, 'The Post-modern Condition', in Sarah Harasym (ed.), *The Post-colonial Critic: Interviews, Strategies, Dialogues* (New York, Routledge, 1990), 25.

4 Amy Tan quoted in Curt Schleier, 'The Joy Luck Lady', www.detnews.com (3 November 1995) [Accessed June 1997].

5 Tan, 'The CliffsNotes Version of My Life' and 'Persona Errata', in *Opposite*, 7, 120.

6 Susan Kepner, 'The Amazing Adventures of Amy Tan', *San Francisco Focus* 36.5 (May 1989), 58.

7 See 'My Love Affair with Vladimir Nabokov', in *Opposite*, 225, when Tan describes a scene on a *funiculaire*, and then says: 'I made it up.'

8 Amy Tan quoted in David Stanton, 'Breakfast with Amy Tan', *Paintbrush: A Journal of Multicultural Literature* 12 (Autumn 1995), 9.

9 'The "model minority" stereotype of Asian Americans is a two-edged sword, breeding not only incomplete and inaccurate images of Asian American success but resentment and hostility on the part of other racial groups.' Angelo N. Ancheta, *Race, Rights, and the Asian American Experience* (New Brunswick, New Jersey, Rutgers University Press, 1998), 12. This incompleteness and inaccuracy not only applies to different Asian American groups but also to different members of the same group. For instance, 'Asian American success' is more readily available to those with diasporic as opposed to immigrant identities. This difference is represented in Tan's texts when middle-class American-born daughters criticize what they perceive to be their mothers' working-class (and) Chinese behaviour.

10 Mitsuye Yamada, 'Invisibility is an Unnatural Disaster: Reflections of an Asian American Woman', in Cherríe Moraga and Gloria Anzaldúa (eds.), *This Bridge Called my Back: Writings by Radical Women of Color* (New York, Kitchen Table: Women of Color Press, 1981), 37.

11 Yamada, 'Invisibility', 35.

12 Victor Bascara quoted in King-kok Cheung (ed.), *An Interethnic Companion to Asian American Literature* (Cambridge, Cambridge University Press, 1997), 2, 4.

13 Tan, 'The Language of Discretion', in *Opposite*, 287.

14 Jinqi Ling, *Narrating Nationalisms: Ideology and Form in Asian American Literature* (Oxford, Oxford University Press, 1998), 4–5.

15 Amy Tan quoted in Maya Jaggi, 'Ghosts at my Shoulder', *Guardian Weekend* (3 March 2001), 31.

16 King-kok Cheung, 'The Woman Warrior versus The Chinaman Pacific: Must a Chinese American Critic Choose between Feminism and Heroism?', in Marianne Hirsch and Evelyn Fox Keller (eds.), *Conflicts in Feminism* (New York, Routledge, 1990), 246.

17 Nineteenth-century Chinese working-class men were rendered 'virtual slaves' in the gold mines and on the railroads. Sucheng Chan, 'Asian Americans: Resisting Oppression, 1860s–1920s', in Sucheng Chan, Douglas Henry Daniels, Mario T. García and Terry P. Wilson (eds.), *Peoples of Color in the American West* (Lexington, Massachusetts & Toronto, D. C. Heath Company, 1994), 367. Nineteenth-century Chinese working-class women were often 'the victims of an organized trade in which they were kidnapped, lured or purchased by Chinese "slave" traders'. After arriving in the United States, they 'were taken to the barracoon to be turned

over to their owners or stripped for inspection and sold to the highest bidders'. Mary E. Young, *Mules and Dragons: Popular Culture Images in the Selected Writings of African-American and Chinese-American Women Writers* (Westport, Connecticut, Greenwood Press, 1993), 85. 'The institution of bride-price in China, rather than dowry, with which the English and Euro-Americans were far more familiar in their own society, also led to the widespread discussion [in nineteenth-century America] of all Chinese marriage as a form of slavery. ... All women, whether prostitutes or wives were "purchased"' and all men, as "coolies", were also enslaved.' Sucheta Mazumdar, 'Through Western Eyes: Discovering Chinese Women in America', in Clyde A. Milner II (ed.), *A New Significance: Re-envisioning the History of the American West* (Oxford, Oxford University Press, 1996), 164.

18 'Confucius (551–479 BC) wrote very little about women, but his classification of women with slaves and small human beings ("hsiao ren") so clearly revealed his attitude.' Amy Ling, *Between Worlds: Women Writers of Chinese Ancestry* (New York, Pergamon Press, 1990), 3.

19 Lord Macartney quoted in Stuart Creighton Miller, *The Unwelcome Immigrant: The American Image of the Chinese, 1785–1882* (Berkeley, California University Press, 1969), 43.

20 Gary Hoppenstand, 'Yellow Devil Doctors and Opium Dens: The Yellow Peril Stereotype in Mass Media Entertainment', in Jack Nachbar and Kevin Lause (eds.), *Popular Culture: An Introductory Text* (Bowling Green, Ohio, Popular, 1992), 281–2.

21 Young, *Mules*, viii.

22 Amy Tan quoted in Gretchen Giles, 'Ghost Writer', www.metroactive.com [Accessed June 1997].

23 Jaggi, 'Ghosts', 33, 31: 'When Tan was 16, "my mother was so frustrated – and I really did do things that would have driven any parent crazy – she snapped and held a cleaver to my throat. I was so numb and angry, for 20 minutes I acted as though I didn't care if she sliced my throat."' About this time, Tan was molested by the man appointed to counsel her through her father's illness and death. '"I broke down sobbing. I was hysterical with grief." Then the man changed tack: "He started to tickle me, threw me on to the bed and moved to other parts of my body. It felt so wrong, but I thought, how can it be? This man is a respected member of the community."'

24 Tod Jones, 'Ghost Writer: Amy Tan Explores Themes of Love, Loyalty and the Hereafter', www.pricecostco.com [Accessed June 1997].

25   Ling, *Between Worlds*, 15.

26   Tan, 'Required Reading and Other Dangerous Subjects', in *Opposite*, 316, 310–11, 308, 306. Tan admits that such an attitude is context dependent on page 317 of this essay: 'If not for a few circumstances that led me to where I am now, would I have become one of those activists for ethnically correct literature? If I hadn't found my voice in a published book, would I too have shouted … that there is strength in marginalism? If I had written book after book … and none of them had been published or reviewed, would I also have been tempted to feel there was a conspiracy in the publishing industry? Would I have believed that those Asian-Americans who did get published and reviewed had sold their souls and were serving up a literary version of chop suey for American palates?'

27   Shirley Geok-lin Lim, 'Semiotics, Experience, and the Material Self: An Inquiry into the Subject of the Contemporary Asian Woman Writer', in Sidonie Smith and Julia Watson (eds.), *Women, Autobiography, Theory: A Reader* (Madison, Wisconsin, Wisconsin University Press, 1998), 444.

28   Mitsuye Yamada, 'Asian Pacific American Women and Feminism', in Cherríe Moraga and Gloria Anzaldúa (eds.), *This Bridge Called my Back: Writings by Radical Women of Color* (New York, Kitchen Table: Women of Color Press, 1981), 71.

29   Lim, 'Semiotics', 444.

30   Amy Tan quoted in Annie Taylor, 'The Difference a Day Made', *Guardian* (8 February 1996), 15.

31   Tan, 'Mother Tongue', in *Opposite*, 278–9.

32   Elaine H. Kim, *Asian American Writers: An Introduction to the Writings and their Social Contexts* (Philadelphia, Texas University Press, 1982), 174.

33   Tan, 'Mother', 276.

34   Amy Tan quoted in Dorothy Wang, 'The Joy Luck Club', *Newsweek* (17 April 1989), 69.

35   Tan quoted in Jones, 'Ghost Writer'.

36   Tan, 'CliffsNotes', 18. *Opposite* also includes a short piece entitled 'Confessions' (212–14), where Tan discusses her mother's violent behaviour.

37   David Streitfield, 'The "Luck" of Amy Tan', *Washington Post* (8 October 1989), F8.

38   Tan quoted in Jaggi, 'Ghosts', 31.

39   Tan, 'Mother', 274.

40   Slavoj Žižek, 'Multiculturalism, Or, the Cultural Logic of Multinational Capitalism', *New Left Review* 225 (1997), 44.

41   Žižek, 'Multiculturalism', 44.

42   Melanie McAlister, '(Mis)Reading *The Joy Luck Club*', *Asian America: Journal of Culture and the Arts* 1 (1992), 104.

43   See Ancheta, *Race*, 7–12.

44   Jaggi, 'Ghosts', 29.

45   See Tan, 'Persona Errata', in *Opposite*, 113–20, for a list of eleven 'errata' circulating about her on the Web.

46   Tan, 'Required Reading', 305.

47   Tan, 'Mother', 271.

48   Tan quoted in Kepner, 'Amazing Adventures', 58.

49   Tan quoted in Stanton, 'Breakfast', 6.

50   Amy Tan quoted in 'The Salon Interview: The Spirit Within', www.salon1999.com [Accessed June 1997].

51   McAlister, '(Mis)Reading', 106. For a discussion of information retrieval as colonialist theory, also see Spivak, 'Criticism, Feminism, and The Institution', *Post-colonial Critic*, 9.

52   Tan quoted in Stanton, 'Breakfast', 7–8.

53   McAlister, '(Mis)Reading', 106.

54   Roman Jakobson quoted in Boris Eichenbaum, 'Introduction to the Formal Method', trans. I. R. Titunk, in Michael Rivkin and Julie Ryan (eds.), *Literary Theory: An Anthology* (Oxford, Blackwell, 1998), 8.

55   Tan quoted in Stanton, 'Breakfast', 7.

56   McAlister, '(Mis)Reading', 106.

57   Sau-ling Cynthia Wong, '"Sugar Sisterhood": The Amy Tan Phenomenon', in David Palumbo-Liu (ed.), *The Ethnic Canon: Histories, Institutions, and Interventions* (Minneapolis, Minnesota University Press, 1995), 191.

58   Patricia Marby Harrison, 'Genocide or Redemption? Asian American Autobiography and the Portrayal of Christianity in Amy Tan's *The Joy Luck Club* and Joy Kogawa's *Obasan*', *Christianity and Literature* 46.2 (Winter 1997), 157. Emphasis added.

59   Tan quoted in Giles, 'Ghost Writer': 'I think I got the storytelling primarily from my father, as much as from my mother. ... He was

a Baptist minister and his idea of quality time with his children ...
was to read his sermons aloud to me and see what I thought and if
there were any words I didn't understand. His sermons were like
stories, they were very personable.'

60   Tan, 'A Note', in *Opposite*, 3.

61   Sinkwan Cheng, 'Fantasizing the *Jouissance* of the Chinese
      Mother: *The Joy Luck Club* and Amy Tan's Quest for Stardom in
      the Market of Neo-Racism', *Savoir: Psychanalyse Et Analyse
      Culturelle* 3.1–2 (February 1997), 104.

62   Patricia L. Hamilton, '*Feng Shui*, Astrology and the Five Elements:
      Traditional Chinese Belief in Amy Tan's *The Joy Luck Club*',
      MELUS 24.2 (Summer 1999), 128, 127.

63   Derek Walters quoted in Hamilton, '*Feng Shui*', 137.

64   Hamilton, '*Feng Shui*', 137.

65   Hamilton, '*Feng Shui*', 127.

66   Wong, '"Sugar"', 197.

67   Wong, '"Sugar"', 182.

68   Wong, '"Sugar"', 182.

69   A late T'ang poet, 'The Lady in the Moon', in Cyril Birch and Donald
      Keene (eds.), *Anthology of Chinese Literature* (London, Penguin,
      1965), 337; E. T. C. Werner, *Myths and Legends of China*
      (London, Sinclair Browne Ltd., 1922), 185; and, Tao Tao Liu,
      'Chinese Myths and Legends', in Carolyne Larrington (ed.), *The
      Feminist Companion to Mythology* (London, Pandora, 1992), 234.

70   Roland Barthes, 'Myth Today', *Mythologies*, trans. Annette
      Lavers (London, Vintage, 2000), 123.

71   Tan admits to 'sloppy copy editing' specifically in relation to the
      number four in *The Joy Luck Club*. In an interview, she notes the
      tendency of some readers to accord her metaphors/images with a
      symbolic interpretation, here, a Buddhist interpretation of the
      number four. Her response to this mythologizing of *The Joy Luck
      Club* is also relevant to the more general debate about misrepre-
      senting Chinese myths: 'I don't intentionally plant symbols. I
      have metaphors; I love metaphors, images. But the images are very
      evocative; it's more sensuality and not a symbol to *stand in* for
      something. Vladimir Nabokov had a real hatred of symbolism, and
      I don't go that far, but I sort of identify with it; this is paraphrasing
      him wildly, of course, but he said something like, "Green is not a
      symbol for growth and regeneration. Green is the color of leaves. I
      said the trees were green because they're green!" (laughs).

Sometimes that's what I want to say.' Tan quoted in Stanton, 'Breakfast', 11–12. Also see Patricia Holt, 'Between the Lines: Students Read a Lot into Amy Tan', *San Francisco Chronicle* (18 August 1996), 2: 'The truth is', remarks Tan, 'I do indeed include images in my work, but I don't think of them as symbols, not in the Jungian sense.'

72   Wong, '"Sugar"', 182.

73   Liu, 'Myths', 246.

74   Liu, 'Myths', 239.

75   Wong, '"Sugar"', 187.

76   Wong, '"Sugar"', 195. According to Wong, it is (only) *The Woman Warrior* that 'ceaselessly deconstructs its own narrative authority'.

77   Barthes, 'Myth', 120.

78   Barthes, 'Myth', 119.

79   Wong, '"Sugar"', 180.

80   Wong, '"Sugar"', 187–8.

81   Wong, '"Sugar"', 192.

82   Wong, '"Sugar"', 195.

83   Wong, '"Sugar"', 196.

84   David Leiwei Li, 'Genes, Generation, and Geospiritual (Be)long-ings', *Imagining the Nation: Asian American Literature and Cultural Consent* (Stanford, Stanford University Press, 1998), 111.

85   Li, 'Genes', 116.

86   Wong, '"Sugar"', 182. Also see 204n: 'the inland location of the episode and the lack of corroboration in ethnographic literature (e.g., Shizhen Wang) make the kind of veil lifting … described by Tan an extremely unlikely occurrence.'

87   Rey Chow, 'Violence in the Other Country: China as Crisis, Spectacle, and Woman', in Chandra Talpade Mohanty, Ann Russo and Lourdes Torres (eds.), *Third World Women and the Politics of Feminism* (Bloomington, Indiana University Press, 1991), 91.

88   Wong, '"Sugar"', 202.

89   Edward W. Said, *Orientalism: Western Conceptions of the Orient* (London, Penguin, 1995), 20–1.

90   Chow, 'Violence', 91.

91   Said, *Orientalism*, 3.

92 Said, *Orientalism*, 21.

93 For a fuller discussion of the 'double session of representation' see Spivak, 'Practical Politics of the Open End', in *Post-colonial Critic*, 108–9.

94 Donna Landry and Gerald MacLean, 'Introduction: Reading Spivak', in Donna Landry and Gerald MacLean (eds.), *The Spivak Reader* (New York, Routledge, 1996), 6.

95 Lisa Lowe, 'Heterogeneity, Hybridity, Multiplicity: Marking Asian American Differences', *Diaspora* 1.1 (Spring 1991), 39.

96 Rey Chow, *Writing Diaspora: Tactics of Intervention in Contemporary Cultural Studies* (Bloomington, Indiana University Press, 1993), 52.

97 Said, *Orientalism*, 21.

98 Tan quoted in Schleier, 'The Joy Luck Lady'.

99 Tan quoted in Stanton, 'Breakfast', 10.

100 Wong, '"Sugar"', 179.

101 See *Opposite*, 339, 317–19, for further details about Tan's literary influences/experiences: the fairy stories and the biblical stories she read in the 1950s and 60s; the literary texts – Hemingway, Faulkner, Fitzgerald, Dreiser, Sinclair Lewis, Virginia Woolf, Evelyn Waugh and, at summer school, Richard Wright, James Baldwin and Ralph Ellison – she studied at university in the 1970s; and, from 1985 onwards, Flannery O'Connor, Isabel Allende, Louise Erdrich, Eudora Welty, Laurie Colwin, Alice Adams, Amy Hempel, Alice Walker, Lorrie Moore, Anne Tyler, Alice Munro, Harriet Doerr, and Molly Giles. At this time Tan also read Gabriel García Márquez, Raymond Carver, David Leavitt, Richard Ford and Tobias Wolff. Other literary preferences include *Jane Eyre* for its 'gothic atmosphere' and *Lolita* 'for [its] language' (221, 353).

102 Tan quoted in Stanton, 'Breakfast', 8.

103 Tan quoted in E. D. Huntley, *Amy Tan: A Critical Companion* (Westport, Connecticut, Greenwood Press, 1998), 8.

104 'Neocolonial' is used here as a shorthand term to highlight the problem of internal colonization in North America as represented by Louise Erdrich, Alice Walker, Toni Morrison, Jamaica Kincaid and Isabel Allende. The differences between these writers notwithstanding, all four represent traumatic histories. In Erdrich's *Tracks* (1988), for instance, reference is made to 'the pressures of land loss, confinement on reservations, spread of epidemic diseases, forced assimilation efforts and intra-tribal conflicts'. From Walker's

The Third Life of Grange Copeland (1970) to *Possessing the Secret Joy* (1992), 'sexism in the black movements of the 1960s, domestic violence and father–daughter rape [along with] female genital mutilation' are addressed. *The Bluest Eye* (1970), Morrison's first novel, addresses 'the question of how self-love is to be achieved for a black girl in a society which hardly values her very existence, let alone her thoughts or her beauty'. Following on from this, she discusses 'the issue of female friendship in *Sula* (1974) [and] black people's relation to the African American past', to 'their folk heritage in *Song of Solomon* (1977), slavery and motherhood in *Beloved* (1987) and black modernity in *Jazz* (1991)'. Helena Grice, Candida Hepworth, Maria Lauret and Martin Padget, *Beginning Ethnic American Literatures* (Manchester, Manchester University Press, 2001), 37–8, 82–3. Representing different relationships to colonial powers, to the UK and the US, Kincaid's *At the Bottom of the River* (1983) through to *The Autobiography of my Mother* (1996) and *My Brother* (1997) focus on difficult family relationships exacerbated by 'a history of slavery and colonialism [that] colors every aspect of life, where relationships are "redolent … in every way of the relationship between captor and captive, master and slave, with its motif of the big and the small, and the powerful and the powerless, the strong and the weak"'. Diane Simmons, 'Jamaica Kincaid', www.galenet.com [Accessed March 2004]. While Allende's earlier writing represents Latin America, specifically dictatorships, violent upheavals, torture, pain and poverty, her later writing, *The Infinite Plan* (1991), for example, focuses on North America. In an interview with Katy Butler from the *Los Angeles Times* (10 October 1999), Allende, now living in California and a friend and neighbour of Tan's, comments on the racist past and present: 'The racism. There is always racism. In that era [the mid to late nineteenth century] there were signs all over saying no dogs or Mexicans or Chinese allowed. Now, it is more hidden. … There is an overt fear of the immigrant.' Like Tan, Allende's texts 'undercut exoticism with irony, romance with anxiety, the supernatural with the sceptical'. Jaggi, 'Ghosts at my Shoulder', 29.

105 See Frank Chin, 'Come All Ye Asian American Writers of the Real and the Fake', in Jeffery Paul Chan, Frank Chin, Lawson Fusao Inada, and Shawn Wong (eds.), *The Big Aiiieeeee! An Anthology of Chinese American and Japanese American Literature* (New York, Meridian, 1991), 8: Discussing Kingston and Tan, Chin argues that they, like 'other Chinese American publishing sensations from the past, from the first book ever published in English, in America, by a Chinese American – *My Life in China and America*, by Yung Wing, 1909 – to Jade Snow Wong's *Fifth*

Chinese Daughter', 1945, 'are Christian [and] the only form of literature written by Chinese Americans that major publishers will publish (other than the cookbook) is autobiography, an exclusively Christian form'.

106   Ling, *Between Worlds*, 130.

107   Huntley, *Amy Tan*, 18–19, 32: 'In an essay about Kingston and the Chinese oral tradition, Linda Ching Sledge provides a useful definition of talk story: "a conservative, communal folk art and for the common people, performed in the various dialects of diverse ethnic enclaves and never intended for the ears of non-Chinese. Because it served to redefine an embattled immigrant culture by providing its members immediate, ceremonial access to ancient lore, talk story retained structures of Chinese oral wisdom (parables, proverbs, formulaic description, heroic biography, casuistical dialogue) long after other old-county traditions had died."' In Kingston's and Tan's texts, talk-story is 'postmodernized' and, moreover, Americanized. Although still communal, popular and empowering, talk-story utilizes, as Tan puts it in 'Mother', 271, 'all the Englishes [she] grew up with'. Furthermore, talk-story lends itself to various political/ideological interpretations, some reactionary, others radical, as well as 'embrac[ing] elements of biography and autobiography, history and mythology ... personal reminiscence and memoir'.

108   Maxine Hong Kingston, *The Woman Warrior: Memoirs of a Girlhood Among Ghosts* (London, Picador, 1976), 164, 184.

109   Tan quoted in Giles, 'Ghost Writer': 'Stories from my mother came more naturally, and I'd listen as she and my aunts sat at a table covered with newspapers, shelling fava beans or chopping vegetables and gossiping about the family'.

110   David Leiwei Li, 'The Naming of a Chinese American "I": Cross-Cultural Sign/ifications in *The Woman Warrior*', *Criticism* 30.4 (Fall 1988), 499.

111   Kingston, *The Woman Warrior*, 9.

112   See Tan, 'Last Week', *Opposite*, 80: 'It wasn't until I was in my thirties that I learned that my mother, at age nine, had seen her own mother kill herself. ... I recently learned that in China today, a third of all deaths among women in rural areas are suicides. Nationwide, more than two million Chinese women each year attempt suicide, and 300,000 succeed. ... More than two million *reported* attempts. How many attempts are not reported?' Also see, 'My Grandmother's Choice', again in *Opposite*, 99–104, where Tan, basing her 'musings' around a 1924 photograph of four

female family members from three generations, describes the 'terrible fate' of these women, as told to her by Daisy.

113 Mazumdar, 'Western Eyes', 164.

114 Daisy Tan quoted by Tan in Hermione Lee, 'Scattered Fragments of a Broken China', *Independent on Sunday* (14 July 1991), 26.

115 Tan, 'Last Week', 70–1.

116 Tan, 'Language', 281.

117 'The first known Chinese woman in the United States was Afong Moy, who was displayed sitting amid Chinese paraphernalia at the American Museum, the Brooklyn Institute, and various other New York locations between 1834 and 1847. In the latter year she shared the star billing with Tom Thumb. When Afong Moy left for Boston, Barnum's Chinese Museum catered to the New Yorker's curiosity by producing Pwan-ye-koo and her maid-servant in 1850. The small bound feet of both women were a prime feature of the advertisements announcing their displays. In both these cases the allure of the women was heightened by the suggestion that they were upper class; the illustrations of the women showing them sitting demurely, their contours obscured by brocades and silk clothing.' Mazumdar, 'Western Eyes', 159.

118 'For as early as 1851, Frank Soule, in his *Annals of San Francisco*, could write that although most of the people in the city were "generally orderly, obedient and useful," the Chinese were an exception. They were "bringing with them a number of their women who were among the filthiest and most abandoned of their sex." At this time there were only seven Chinese women in San Francisco, and at least two of them worked as domestics; there were well over a thousand other prostitutes of various nationalities. But this did not deter a municipal committee from visiting Chinatown in 1854 and declaring that most Chinese women were prostitutes.' Mazumdar, 'Western Eyes', 160. The complimentary figures of the prostitute and the bachelor dominated nineteenth-century American culture.

119 Ancheta, *Race*, 25: 'The Page Law of 1875 was directed at preventing the entry of prostitutes, but immigration officials effectively limited the entry of nearly all Chinese women by classifying them as prostitutes.'

120 Sylvia Yanagisako, 'Transforming Orientalism: Gender, Nationality, and Class in Asian American Studies', in Sylvia Yanagisako and Carol Delaney (eds.), *Naturalizing Power: Essays in Feminist Cultural Analysis* (New York, Routledge, 1995), 290–1.

121 Judy Yung, 'Unbinding the Feet, Unbinding their Lives: Chinese Immigrant Women in San Francisco, 1902–1931', in Shirley Hune, Hyung-chan Kim, Stephen S. Fugita and Amy Ling (eds.), *Asian Americans: Comparative and Global Perspectives* (Pullman, Washington State University Press, 1991), 70, 76, 79, 83. Yung contends that immigrant Chinese women, most of whom were the 'wives of merchants or United States citizens', although 'present[ing] a submissive image in public, ... were known to "wear the pants" at home'. 'Rul[ing] the household and assum[ing] the responsibility of disciplinarian, culture-bearer, and of maintaining the integrity of their families', when coupled with 'a new sense of freedom, accomplishment, and camaraderie' from work, facilitated the advent of the 'new woman' in twentieth-century Chinese America.

122 Cheng, 'Fantasizing', 98.

123 Yung, 'Unbinding', 76.

124 Jaggi, 'Ghosts', 29.

125 Tan quoted in Jaggi, 'Ghosts', 32.

126 Chin, 'Asian American Writers', 26.

127 Frank Chin, 'This is Not an Autobiography', *Genre* 18 (Summer 1985), 111.

128 Maxine Hong Kingston quoted in Phillipa Kafka, *(Un)Doing the Missionary Position: Gender Asymmetry in Contemporary Asian American Women's Writing* (Westport, Connecticut, Greenwood Press, 1997), 13.

129 Chin, 'Asian American Writers', 18.

130 Chin, 'Autobiography', 125, 112.

131 Frank Chin, 'Confessions of the Chinatown Cowboy', *Bulletin of Concerned Asian Scholars* 4.3 (1972), 67.

132 Daniel Y. Kim, 'The Strange Love of Frank Chin', in David L. Eng and Alice Y. Hom (eds.), *Q & A: Queer in Asian America* (Philadelphia, Temple University Press, 1998), 271. Also see Elaine H. Kim, '"Such Opposite Creatures": Men and Women in Asian American Literature', *Michigan Quarterly Review* 29 (1990), 76–8: 'The only good woman in Chin's stories is young, Chinese American, and dead. The old women – the mothers and the aunts – are like mortuary furniture, with their pasteboard faces, rattling jewellery, old makeup falling in chips from their hairlines as they speak.' It is Kim's contention that 'The female body in Chin's work is conquered through a pitiless misogynistic

gaze and through fornication as revenge.'

133 Young, *Mules*, 103. Discussing Frank Chin's *The Chickencoop Chinaman*, Young remarks of his protagonist's name: 'Tam is a sobriquet for Tampax. "I speak the natural born ragmouth speaking a motherless bloody tongue."'

134 Chin, 'Autobiography', 112, 122–3.

135 Ling, *Between Worlds*, 1.

136 Harrison, 'Genocide?', 150.

137 Cheung, 'Woman Warrior', 239.

138 Maxine Hong Kingston, 'Cultural Mis-readings by American Reviewers', in Guy Armirthanayagam (ed.), *Asian and Western Writers in Dialogue* (London, Macmillan, 1982), 56.

139 Kingston, 'Mis-readings', 58, 64.

140 Tan quoted in Stanton, 'Breakfast', 7.

141 Kafka, *(Un)Doing*, 6.

142 Jean-François Lyotard, *The Postmodern Condition: A Report on Knowledge*, trans. Geoff Bennington and Brian Massumi (Manchester, Manchester University Press, 1984), 81–2.

143 Tan, 'Required Reading', 308–9, 316.

144 Tan, 'Required Reading', 308, 315, 322.

145 Tan, 'Mother', 271.

146 Tan, 'Language', 287.

147 Tan, 'Nabokov', 221.

148 Jaggi, 'Ghosts', 29.

149 Tan quoted in 'The Salon Interview'.

Chapter 2

1 Nicci Gerrard and Sean French, 'Sexual Reading', *Observer*, Review (27 September 1998), 2.

2 Gary Pak quoted by Navtej Sarna, 'From the Far Corners', *TLS* (22 March 2002), 22.

3 Gerrard (and French), 'Sexual Reading', 2.

4 Wendy Ho, 'Swan-Feather Mothers and Coca-Cola Daughters: Teaching Amy Tan's *The Joy Luck Club*', in John R. Maitino and

David R. Peck (eds.) *Teaching American Ethnic Literatures: Nineteen Essays* (Albuquerque, New Mexico University Press, 1996), 327.

5   Amy Tan, *The Joy Luck Club* (London, Minerva, 1989), 41. Hereafter page numbers appear in parentheses in the text.

6   Hardy C. Wilcoxon, 'No Types of Ambiguity: Teaching Chinese American Texts in Hong Kong', in Julie Brown (ed.) *Ethnicity and the American Short Story* (New York, Garland Publishing, 1997), 143. Also see Schleier, 'The Joy Luck Lady'. In this interview, Tan says: 'What I believe my books are about is relationships and family. I've had women come up to me and say they've felt the same way about their mothers, and they weren't immigrants.'

7   Tan, 'Nabokov', 221–7.

8   Tan quoted in Stanton, 'Breakfast', 12.

9   Vladimir Nabokov quoted by (Gerrard and) French, 'Sexual Reading', 2.

10 Tan, 'Nabokov', 226.

11 Rocío G. Davis, 'Identity in Community in Ethnic Short Story Cycles: Amy Tan's *The Joy Luck Club*, Louise Erdrich's *Love Medicine*, Gloria Naylor's *The Women of Brewster Place*', in Julie Brown (ed.) *Ethnicity and the American Short Story* (New York, Garland Publishing, 1997), 3, 6.

12 Wong, '"Sugar"', 201. Wong is not alone in according Tan's text(s) a 'darker side'. Other Asian American critics, including Sinkwan Cheng, Frank Chin, and David Leiwei Li, also highlight its commitment to various conservative ideologies. This said, 'dark' is used throughout this chapter (and elsewhere in this study) to describe the difficulties raised by Jing-mei 'June' Woo's narrative in particular: death and, with it, the ideological/political issue of 'subaltern representation' in terms of its benefits and, crucially, its limitations.

13 Gayatri Chakravorty Spivak, 'Can the Subaltern Speak?', in Cary Nelson and Lawrence Grossberg (eds.) *Marxism and the Interpretation of Culture* (London, Macmillan, 1988), 276, 278.

14 Spivak, 'Questions of Multiculturalism', *Post-colonial Critic*, 63.

15 Spivak, 'Can the Subaltern Speak?', 280, 295.

16 For a fuller discussion of 'the double session of representation', see Spivak, 'Practical Politics', 108–9. Also see 'Chapter 1 of this book, 23–4.

17 Tan, 'Thinly Disguised Memoir', *Opposite*, 109.

18   M. M. Bakhtin, 'Discourse in the Novel', *The Dialogic Imagination: Four Essays*, trans. Caryl Emerson and Michael Holquist (Austin, Texas University Press, 1981), 304.

19   Paul de Man, 'Dialogue and Dialogism', *The Resistance to Theory* (Minneapolis, Minnesota University Press, 1986), 107.

20   De Man, 'Dialogue', 109.

21   Ben Xu, 'Memory and the Ethnic Self: Reading Amy Tan's *The Joy Luck Club*', in Amritjit Singh, Joseph T. Skerrett, Jr., Robert E. Hogan (eds.), *Memory, Narrative, and Identity: New Essays in Ethnic American Literatures* (Boston, Northeastern University Press, 1994), 269.

22   Spivak, 'Subaltern Talk: Interview with the Editors', *Spivak Reader*, 292. Emphasis added.

23   Anne E. Brown and Marjanne E. Goozé, 'Introduction', in Anne E. Brown and Marjanne E. Goozé (eds.), *International Women's Writing: New Landscapes of Identity* (Westport, Connecticut, Greenwood Press, 1995), xxiii.

24   Rocío G. Davis, 'Wisdom (Un)heeded: Chinese Mothers and American Daughters in Amy Tan's *The Joy Luck Club*', *Cuadernos de Investigacion Filologica* 19–20 (1993–94), 98.

25   Gloria Shen, 'Born of a Stranger: Mother–daughter Relationships and Storytelling in Amy Tan's *The Joy Luck Club*', in Anne E. Browne and Marjanne E. Goozé (eds.), *International Women's Writing: New Landscapes of Identity* (Westport, Connecticut, Greenwood Press, 1995), 233.

26   Bonnie TuSmith, *All My Relatives: Community in Contemporary Ethnic American Literatures* (Ann Arbor, Michigan University Press, 1993), 68.

27   Li, 'Genes', 111–12.

28   Li, 'Genes', 111.

29   Ho, 'Swan-Feather', 331. These links are not meant to render equivalent the experiences of war, immigration and diaspora, only to contest the notion that American circumstances are unaffected by ethnic/gender oppression.

30   Spivak, 'Post-modern', 25.

31   Spivak, *In Other Worlds: Essays in Cultural Politics* (London, Routledge, 1987), 201.

32   Spivak, 'Can the Subaltern Speak?', 295.

33   Spivak, 'Subaltern Talk', 292.

34   Spivak, 'Subaltern Talk', 288–9. '[H]owever old-fashioned its articulation', specifically with regard to the terms 'identity' and 'consciousness', the Subaltern Studies group do, nevertheless, as Spivak observes in 'Can the Subaltern Speak?', 284–5, 'construct ... a definition of the people ... that can be only an identity-in-differential.' In her 'against-the-grain' reading of the Subaltern Studies group's work, she argues for its 'strategic use of positivist essentialism in a scrupulously political interest'. It 'strategically adher[es] to the essentialist notion of consciousness, that would fall prey to an anti-humanist critique, with an historiographical practice that draws many of its strengths from that very critique. This would allow them', Spivak continues in Other, 205–7, 'to use the critical force of anti-humanism ... even as they share its constitutive paradox: that the essentializing moment, the object of their criticism, is irreducible.'

35   See Spivak, 'Subaltern Talk', 289–93, where she clarifies the difference between talking and speaking: 'in a certain kind of rhetorical anguish ... I said, "the subaltern cannot speak!" This is always read as a rational remark about subalterns as such – Meaghan Morris has made the witty comment that my critics rewrite the sentence as: "the subaltern cannot talk."' Spivak continues: 'Problems arise if you take this "speak" absolutely literally as "talk." ... The actual fact of giving utterance is not what I was concerned about. What I was concerned about was that even when one uttered, one was constructed by a certain kind of psychobiography, so that the utterance itself ... would have to be interpreted in the way in which we historically interpret anything. ... So, "the subaltern cannot speak," means that even when the subaltern makes an effort to the death to speak, she is not able to be heard and speaking and hearing complete the speech act. ... It seems to me that finding the subaltern is not so hard, but actually entering into a responsibility structure with the subaltern, with responses flowing both ways: learning to learn without this quick-fix frenzy of doing good with an implicit assumption of cultural supremacy which is legitimized by unexamined romanticization, that's the hard part.'

36   Spivak, 'Can the Subaltern Speak?', 308, 277.

37   Chin, 'Asian American Writers', 26.

38   M. M. Bakhtin, Rabelais and His World, trans. Hélène Iswolsky (Bloomington, Indiana University Press, 1984), 10.

39   Chris Boldt, 'Why is the Moon Lady in Amy Tan's The Joy Luck Club Revealed to be a Man?', Notes on Contemporary Literature

24:4 (September 1994), 10. Emphasis in original.

40   Wenying Xu, 'A Womanist Production of Truths: The Use of Myths in Amy Tan', *Paintbrush: A Journal of Multicultural Literature* 12 (Autumn 1995), 60–1.

41   Ling, *Between Worlds*, 3: 'The Three Obediences enjoined a woman to obey her father before marriage, her husband after marriage, and her eldest son after her husband's death.' Ling also refers to the 'Four Virtues', which 'decreed that she be chaste; her conversation courteous and not gossipy; her deportment graceful and not extravagant; her leisure spent in perfecting needlework and tapestry for beautifying the home'.

42   Yamada, 'Invisibility', 37.

43   Yamada, 'Invisibility', 37.

44   Tan, 'CliffsNotes', 9–10.

45   Ling, *Between Worlds*, 132.

46   McAlister, '(Mis)Reading', 104.

47   Spivak, 'Multi-culturalism', 59.

48   Patricia Gately, 'Ten Thousand Different Ways: Inventing Mothers, Inventing Hope', *Paintbrush: A Journal of Multicultural Literature* 12 (Autumn 1995), 53.

49   Lowe, 'Heterogeneity', 34.

50   Wong, '"Sugar"', 196.

51   Cheng, 'Fantasizing', 97.

52   Chow, *Writing Diaspora*, 52.

53   Lyotard, *Postmodern Condition*, 74.

54   As regards intergenerational interchangeability, see TuSmith, *All My Relatives*, 67: 'mother and daughter are one and the same'; and, Kim, '"Opposite Creatures"', 82: 'daughters and mothers are each other'. As regards intragenerational interchangeability, see Ling, *Between Worlds*, 138: the older generation of women 'seem interchangeable', not surprising really given that 'the role of mother supersedes all other roles and is performed with the utmost seriousness and determination'; and, Shen, 'Born of a Stranger', 235: the mothers 'have similar personalities – strong, determined, and endowed with mysterious power'.

55   Kim, '"Opposite Creatures"', 82.

56   TuSmith, *All My Relatives*, 68. Also see Ling, *Between Worlds*, 136, as well as Victoria Chen, 'Chinese American Women,

Language and Moving Subjectivity', *Women and Language* 18.1 (1995), 6: 'Seeking the motivation behind a hurtful remark ... leads Tan to an understanding of and sympathy for the mother whose seeming rejection is but a self-defensive mask for her own vulnerability and love'; and, 'in the mother's language, "truth" is characterized by the logic of the opposite; this "indirect" approach works only if one knows how to hear the statement within the context of a certain kind of relationship. Saying the opposite is what the mother felt obligated to perform; in fact, it was the only language that she could use in order to demonstrate her affection and care for her daughter.'

57 Said, *Orientalism*, 190.

58 Tan, 'Language', 281.

59 Ho, 'Swan-Feather', 339.

60 Stephen Souris, '"Only Two Kinds of Daughters": Inter-Monologue Dialogicity in *The Joy Luck Club*', *MELUS* 19.2 (Summer 1994), 113.

61 Steven P. Sondrup, 'Hanyu at the Joy Luck Club', in Mabel Lee and Hua Meng (eds.) *Cultural Dialogue and Misreading* (Sydney, Australia, Wild Peony, 1997), 405.

62 Ho, 'Swan-Feather', 338.

63 Souris, '"Two Kinds"', 107, 105.

64 Orville Schell, 'Your Mother is in Your Bones: *The Joy Luck Club*', *New York Times Book Review* (19 March 1989), 28.

65 Sondrup, 'Hanyu', 403.

66 See Tan, 'Mother', 274, as well Chapter 1 of this book, 8.

67 Wong, '"Sugar"', 188.

68 Marina Heung, 'Daughter-Text/Mother-Text: Matrilineage in Amy Tan's *Joy Luck Club*', *Feminist Studies* 19.3 (1993), 605.

69 Jeffery Paul Chan, Frank Chin, Lawson Fusao Inada, and Shawn Wong, 'Introduction', *The Big Aiiieeeee!*, xi.

70 Heung, 'Daughter-Text', 605.

71 Sondrup, 'Hanyu', 404.

72 Wong, '"Sugar"', 182.

73 Tan, 'Language', 286.

74 Walter Benjamin, 'The Task of the Translator', *Illuminations*, ed. Hannah Arendt and trans. Harry Zohn (London: Fontana Press, 1973), 73, 76.

75   Benjamin, 'Translator', 72, 77.

76   De Man, 'Conclusions: Walter Benjamin's "The Task of the Translator"', *Resistance*, 91. This is de Man's translation, and it contrasts with that of Harry Zohn, which reads: 'fragments are part of a vessel'.

77   Kingston, *Woman Warrior*, 184.

78   See Stanton, 'Breakfast', 12.

79   Tan quoted in 'The Salon Interview'.

80   Malini Johar Schueller, 'Theorizing Ethnicity and Subjectivity: Maxine Hong Kingston's *Tripmaster Monkey* and Amy Tan's *The Joy Luck Club*', *GENDERS* 15 (Winter 1992), 80.

81   Ben Tong quoted in David Leiwei Li, 'Can Maxine Hong Kingston Speak? The Contingency of *The Woman Warrior*', in *Imagining the Nation: Asian American Literature and Cultural Consent* (Stanford, Stanford University Press, 1998), 55.

82   Chow, 'Violence', 92.

83   Li, 'Genes', 116–17.

84   Schueller, 'Theorizing Ethnicity', 75.

85   'Wash and Go' is a British hair-care product that conveniently combines shampoo and conditioner in one.

86   TuSmith, *All My Relatives*, 68.

87   Tan quoted in Stanton, 'Breakfast', 8.

88   Spivak, 'Practical Politics', 109.

Chapter 3

1   Daisy Tan paraphrased by Amy Tan in Maya Jaggi, 'Of Mothers and Daughters', *Guardian* (10 July 1991), 19.

2   Daisy Tan quoted by Amy Tan in Lee, 'Scattered Fragments', 26.

3   Spivak, 'Post-modern', 25.

4   Amy Tan, *The Kitchen God's Wife* (London, Flamingo, 1991), 78, 207–8. Hereafter pages numbers appear in parentheses in the text.

5   Kafka, *(Un)Doing*, 23.

6   Iris Chang, *The Rape of Nanking: The Forgotten Holocaust of World War II* (New York, BasicBooks, 1997), 6.

7   Chang, *Rape*, 199. Also see note 13 below.

8   While Japan's reasons for forgetting its war crimes are perhaps
    obvious, the west's and China's are less so. Cold War alliances
    between the west and Japan, alongside western and Chinese
    collaboration with Japan during the Sino-Japanese War, help
    explain the general amnesia about the Rape of Nanking. Collabor-
    ation is discussed in *The Kitchen God's Wife*, 283, 327, an
    unintentional(?) collaboration by the west, and, through the
    character of Winnie's entrepreneurial father, Jiang Sao-yen, an
    intentional(?) collaboration.

9   Chang, *Rape*, 53. Also see Robert Whymant, 'Japan War Veterans
    Lift Lid on Atrocities', *The Times* (4 August 1997), 15: 'A
    sergeant-major raped and murdered a number of Chinese women.
    Then ... he sliced off pieces from the women's thighs, fried them
    and made a meal for the members of the unit.'

10 See Sulia Chan, 'CAMJ Intended to Set the Historical Record
    Straight', *Chinese American Forum* 3.4 (4 March 1988), 21: 'For
    nearly five decades after 1945, Japan has consistently chosen to
    have a selective memory regarding the War ... omitting Pearl
    Harbor and its war atrocities committed in China and Southeast
    Asia from its school text books, thus shielding its future
    generations from an unpalatable past. In this context ... if you
    don't vigilantly remind the world of humanity's evil aberrations,
    then the perpetrator would inevitably and eventually assume the
    role of the victim by distorting, revising or rewriting history.' Also
    see Chang, *Rape*, 201: 'In 1990 Ishihara Shintaro, a leading
    member of Japan's conservative Liberal Democratic Party and the
    author of best-selling books such as *The Japan That Can Say No*,
    told a *Playboy* interviewer: "People say that the Japanese made a
    holocaust there [in Nanking], but that is not true. It is a story
    made up by the Chinese. It has tarnished the image of Japan, but it
    is a lie."'

11 Ron Aronson in Spivak, 'Post-modern', 24.

12 De Man, 'The Resistance to Theory', *Resistance*, 11.

13 'Textual violence' is used here and throughout this chapter in a
    similar way to Chang's argument about holocaust denial con-
    stituting a 'Second Rape'. For Chang, holocaust deniers' texts
    'rape' for a second time by denying the fact of the first Rape of
    Nanking. As she puts it, on page 14 of *Rape*: 'This book describes
    two related but discrete atrocities. One is the Rape of Nanking
    itself, the story of how the Japanese wiped out hundreds of
    thousands of innocent civilians in its enemy's capital. Another is

the cover-up, the story of how the Japanese, emboldened by the silence of the Chinese and the Americans, tried to erase the entire massacre from public consciousness, thereby depriving its victims of their proper place in history.' Similarly, *The Kitchen God's Wife* represents 'two related but discrete atrocities', albeit with Winnie as the victim of twelve years of sexual violence, which her rapist-husband tries to 'erase' via appeal to stereotypes of Chinese femininity as perpetuated in a range of texts from classical stories to legal documents. It is also possible to understand these 'two structures of violence', one sexual, the other textual, in the context of an unwritten remark that Spivak attributes to Derrida. In 'Strategy, Identity, Writing', *Post-colonial Critic*, 36, Spivak says: 'On the one hand, writing does entail a generalized system of violence. On the other hand, there exist structures of violence in the world which cannot be reduced to just the violence of writing. He [Derrida] said something that stuck in my mind, that there is a constant negotiation between these two structures of violence'. Arguably, Chang's *Rape* negotiates between these two structures of violence, as does (this chapter on) *The Kitchen God's Wife*, the phrases 'Second Rape' and 'textual violence' deliberately and self-consciously blurring the boundaries between two structures of violence in order to highlight the violent impact of (holocaust) denial on Chinese women like Winnie, all the time acknowledging that this blurring is a powerful rhetorical strategy, and, as such, preserves the difference not only between world and text but also between the Rape of Nanking and *The Kitchen God's Wife*.

14   See Chapter 1, 8–10.

15   Tan quoted in 'The Salon Interview'.

16   Ling, *Between Worlds*, 7.

17   The Japanese Ministry of Education quoted in Chang, *Rape*, 207: 'the violation of women is something that has happened on every battlefield in every era of human history. This is not an issue that needs to be taken up with respect to the Japanese army in particular.' The Ministry is also quoted in Richard Lloyd Parry, 'Japan Rejects Professor's Fight for Freedom of Speech', *Independent* (30 August 1997), 10: 'it is common throughout the world for troops to rape women during wartime'.

18   Ling, *Between Worlds*, 3.

19   Chin, 'Confessions', 66.

20   Yamada, 'Asian Pacific', 71.

21   Wong, '"Sugar"', 199. Wong argues that some readers, following

Winnie's lead, 'obscure ... the role of the West in causing' these historical catastrophes. This chapter, however, questions this obfuscation within *The Kitchen God's Wife*.

22   Kafka, *(Un)Doing*, 28.

23   Kafka, *(Un)Doing*, 28.

24   Xu, 'Memory', 263.

25   Chow, 'Violence', 82.

26   Chang, *Rape*, 4–5.

27   Wong, '"Sugar"', 199.

28   Mervyn Rothstein, 'A New Novel by Amy Tan', *New York Times* (13 June 1991), C13. In 'What She Meant', *Opposite*, 207–11, Tan discusses her mother's comment in more detail, also recalling 'her *demand*' that she 'tell [Daisy's] true story'. Emphasis in original.

29   Spivak, 'Strategy, Identity, Writing', 36.

30   Judith Caesar, 'Patriarchy, Imperialism, and Knowledge in *The Kitchen God's Wife*', *North Dakota Quarterly* 62.4 (1994–95), 169–70.

31   Kafka, *(Un)Doing*, 35.

32   Wong, '"Sugar"', 198.

33   Gately, 'Ten Thousand', 53.

34   Wong, '"Sugar"', 200–1.

35   Li, 'Genes', 116–17.

36   Ben Tong quoted in Li, 'Can Maxine Hong Kingston Speak?', 55.

37   Kafka, *(Un)Doing*, 36.

38   Kafka, *(Un)Doing*, 36.

39   Caesar, 'Patriarchy', 169.

40   See Chin, 'Asian American Writers', 26. Chin charges Tan with a reverse sexism, also considered assimilationist, for her demoniza-tion of Chinese men, the Christian terminology deployed to describe the demonic and devilish Wen Fu in particular proving significant. In Chin's words: 'America and Christianity represent freedom from Chinese civilization. In the Christian yin/yang of the dual personality/identity, Chinese evil and perversity is male. And the Americanized honorary white Chinese American is female.'

41   Xu, 'A Womanist Production of Truths', 60.

42   For a fuller discussion of gender asymmetry in *The Kitchen God's Wife* see Kafka, *(Un)Doing*, 17–50.

43 Kafka, *(Un)Doing*, 23.

44 Kafka, *(Un)Doing*, 23.

45 Wong, '"Sugar"', 196.

46 Wong, '"Sugar"', 195.

47 See Gary Chalk, 'The Kitchen God', in *Tales of Ancient China* (London, Frederick Muller, 1984).

48 Caesar, 'Patriarchy', 169.

49 Robb Forman Dew, 'Pangs of an Abandoned Child', *New York Times Book Review* (16 June 1991), 9.

50 Kafka, *(Un)Doing*, 46.

51 Roland Barthes, 'The Reality Effect', in *The Rustle of Language*, trans. Richard Howard (New York, Hill and Wang, 1986), 143, 148.

52 Barthes, 'The Reality Effect', 141.

53 Caesar, 'Patriarchy', 169.

54 Chow, 'Violence', 83.

55 Chow, 'Violence', 84.

56 Huntley, *Amy Tan*, 33, 73.

57 Spivak, 'The Problem of Cultural Self-representation', in *Postcolonial Critic*, 51.

58 Ling, *Between Worlds*, 7.

59 Wong, '"Sugar"', 200.

60 Xu, 'Memory', 263.

Chapter 4

1 Amy Tan, *The Hundred Secret Senses* (London, Flamingo, 1995). Hereafter page numbers appear in parentheses in the text.

2 Frederic Jameson, 'On Magic Realism in Film', *Critical Inquiry* 12.2 (Winter 1986), 311.

3 Magdalena Delicka, 'American Magic Realism: Crossing the Borders in Literatures of the Margins', *Journal of American Studies of Turkey* 6 (1997), 25.

4 Wong, '"Sugar"', 186.

5 Wong, '"Sugar"', 185.

6   Spivak, 'The Intervention Interview', *Post-colonial Critic*, 121.

7   Stephen Slemon, 'Magic Realism as Post-Colonial Discourse', *Canadian Literature* 116 (1988), 12. Emphasis added.

8   Wong, '"Sugar"', 186.

9   Wong, '"Sugar"', 186.

10 See Sau-Ling Cynthia Wong, 'Big Eaters, Treat Lovers', in *Reading Asian American Literature: From Necessity to Extravagance* (Princeton, New Jersey, Princeton University Press, 1993), 65–6: 'It is commonplace in foodway studies that food is an ethnic sign. … "Mainstream Americans frequently use foodways as a factor in the identification of subcultural groups and find in the traditional dishes and ingredients of 'others' who eat differently from themselves a set of convenient ways to categorize ethnic and regional character" (3, Brown and Mussell).' Wong continues: 'One should add, too, that foodways stereotyping occurs both ways: ethnic Americans are just as fond of ridiculing Americans' taste in food, or the lack thereof. This is especially true in the era when consuming highly processed foods is identified by many immigrants with an "American" way of life.'

11 Tan quoted in 'The Salon Interview'.

12 Rey Chow, 'Women in the Holocene: Ethnicity, Fantasy, and the Film *The Joy Luck Club*', in Carmen Luke (ed.), *Feminism and the Pedagogies of Everyday Life* (New York, SUNY Press, 1995), 214. In 'The Salon Interview', Tan criticizes the anthropomorphic assumption in relation to Kwan, Olivia and Simon: 'Kwan comes strictly from my imagination. … I've already had interviews wondering if Olivia's relationship with her husband, Simon, is like my marriage, and I think, "Wait a minute, that's not my husband, that's not my relationship." Certainly all of us have gone through fights with partners in our life, but that's not drawn from my relationship per se. But I know I'm going to be subject to that assumption.'

13 See Charles Dickens, 'Chapter Four: Telescopic Philanthropy', in *Bleak House* (Oxford, Oxford University Press, 1998), 47, 52: 'She [Mrs Jellyby] was a pretty, very diminutive, plump woman, of from forty to fifty, with handsome eyes, though they had a curious habit of seeming to look a long way off. As if … they could see nothing nearer than Africa! … "It *must* be very good of Mrs Jellyby to take such pains about a scheme for the benefits of Natives – and yet – Peepy and the housekeeping!"'

14 Benedict Anderson, *Imagined Communities: Reflections on the Origin and Spread of Nationalism* (London, Verso, 1983), 26.

15   McAlister, '(Mis) Reading', 104.

16   Catherine Belsey, *Critical Practice* (London, Routledge, 1980), 68–9.

17   See Li, 'Genes'.

18   Huntley, *Amy Tan*, 126.

19   Paul de Man, *Allegories of Reading: Figural Language in Rousseau, Nietzsche, Rilke, and Proust* (New Haven, Yale University Press, 1979), 262.

20   For a fuller discussion of these two types of tourist see Graham Huggan, 'Transformations of the Tourist Gaze: Asia in Recent Canadian and Australian Fiction', in *The Post-colonial Exotic: Marketing the Margins* (London, Routledge, 2001). Jing-mei is a 'spiritual tourist' in that her China trip represents the fulfilment of her late mother's 'long-cherished wish' (*JLC*, 288) to reunite her family. The trip thus resembles a kind of pilgrimage, particularly for Jing-mei, who, while there, has a 'bloody epiphany', albeit via a Polaroid photograph. Olivia is an 'anti-tourist tourist' in that her China trip is professional, not personal: 'a travel magazine, *Lands Unknown* … has accepted Simon's and my proposal for a photo essay on village cuisines of China' (*HSS*, 136).

21   Huggan, *Post-colonial Exotic*, 180.

22   L. Turner and J. Ash quoted in Huggan, *Post-colonial Exotic*, 196.

23   Amaryll Chanady quoted in Delicka, 'American Magic', 26.

24   John King Fairbank, *The Great Chinese Revolution 1800–1985* (London, Pan, 1986), 81.

25   Fairbank, *Chinese Revolution*, 73.

26   Fairbank, *Chinese Revolution*, 79.

27   Huntley, *Amy Tan*, 121.

28   Fairbank, *Chinese Revolution*, 81: 'Modern estimates are that China's population had been about 410 million in 1850 and, after the Taiping, Nien, Muslim, and other smaller rebellions, amounted to 350 million in 1873.'

29   Huntley, *Amy Tan*, 121.

30   Huntley, *Amy Tan*, 127.

31   Huntley, *Amy Tan*, 136: '*Taiping tianguo*, or "a Heavenly Kingdom of Great Peace" in which the faithful would labor together for the good of the community. In [t]his kingdom, everyone would have equal access to education, and footbinding and slavery would be outlawed. In addition, undesirable habits such as gambling,

drinking alcohol, and smoking tobacco would be forbidden.'

32   Spivak, 'The New Historicism', in *Post-colonial Critic*, 160.

33   Slemon, 'Magic Realism', 9.

34   Slemon, 'Magic Realism', 9: 'In none of its applications to literature has the concept of magic realism ever successfully differentiated between itself and neighbouring genres such as fabulation, metafiction, the baroque, the uncanny, or the marvellous.' Also see Peter Hinchcliffe and Ed Jewinski (eds.), 'Introduction', in *Magic Realism and Canadian Literature: Essays and Stories* (Waterloo, Waterloo University Press, 1985), 8: magic realism also 'borders not only on dadaism and surrealism, but on the fantastic, the gothic, the grotesque, and – finally – the marvellous'.

35   Slemon, 'Magic Realism', 9: 'Since Franz Roh first coined the term in 1925 in connection with Post-Expressionist art, it has been most closely associated, at least in terms of literary practice, with two major periods in Latin-America and Caribbean culture, the first being that of the 1940's and 1950's; and the second being that of the "boom" period of the Latin-American novel in the late 1950's and the 1960's.' However, these temporal and spatial definitions are problematized by the fact that '"magical realism" … has been used to great effect by some expatriate or diasporic subcontinentals writing in English'. Gayatri Chakravorty Spivak, 'Poststructuralism, Marginality, Postcoloniality and Value', in Padmini Mongia (ed.), *Contemporary Postcolonial Theory: A Reader* (London, Arnold, 1996), 202.

36   Gayatri Chakravorty Spivak, *Outside in the Teaching Machine* (London, Routledge, 1993), 13.

37   Homi K. Bhabha, 'Introduction: Narrating the Nation', in Homi K. Bhabha (ed.) *Nation and Narration*, (London, Routledge, 1990), 7.

38   Slemon, 'Magic Realism', 10, 12.

39   Slemon, 'Magic Realism', 23n: 'codes of recognition' comes from Coral Ann Howell; and, 'original relations' comes from R. E. Watters.

40   Spivak, *Outside*, 13. In addition to Spivak, Aijaz Ahmad has criticized this view, here linked to Slemon, but in Ahmad's *In Theory: Classes, Nations, Literature* (London, Verso, 1992), 69, to Bhabha and some of his 'collaborators': 'It is doubtful, of course, that "magical realism" has become "the literary language of the emergent postcolonial world", any more than the "national allegory" is the unitary generic form for all Third World narrativities, as Jameson would contend. Such pronouncements are now routine features of the metropolitan theory's inflationary

rhetoric.'

41   Spivak, 'Multi-culturalism', 60.

42   Wong, '"Sugar"', 196.

43   Slemon, 'Magic Realism', 12.

44   Spivak, 'Can the Subaltern Speak?', 271, 275.

45   Jameson, 'Magic Realism', 311.

46   Kafka, *(Un)Doing*, 28.

47   Tan quoted in Giles, 'Ghost Writer': 'Yin' means invisible or shadow.'

48   See Giles, 'Ghost Writer': 'The word *ghost* itself is so very tainted with assumptions and negative connotations that you're whacked out if you believe that such things exist," [Tan] says briskly. ... "The best I can do is to call them yin people. That's not a Chinese expression at all," she chuckles. "I just made it up."'

49   Yamada, 'Invisibility', 36–7.

50   Kingston, *Woman Warrior*, 67, 91, 149, 148, 13. Kingston's various, even contradictory, interpretations of 'ghost' do generate problems for some critics, but it is her translation of *'kwei'* or 'gwai' into 'ghost' that has generated the most criticism. As Kim comments in *Asian American Literature*, 310–11n: 'Jeffery Paul Chan has criticized Kingston's use of the word "ghosts," which, he, like many white critics (see Walter Clemons, 'East Meets West', *Newsweek*), says refers to white people. According to Chan, Kingston mistranslates "gwai" as Christian missionaries do, as "devil" or "ghost," when it actually means "asshole," because she is catering to a "white interpretation" of Chinese ('Jeffery Paul Chan, Chairman of S.F. State Asian American Studies, Attacks Review,' San Francisco *Journal*, May 4, 1977).'

51   Kafka, *(Un)Doing*, 28.

52   Jameson, 'Magic Realism', 311.

53   See de Man, *Allegories*, 3–19, for a discussion of grammar and rhetoric.

54   Tong quoted in Li, 'Can Maxine Hong Kingston Speak?', 55.

55   Huggan, *Postcolonial Exotic*, 180.

56   Jameson, 'Magic Realism', 311.

57   Linda Kenyon, 'A Conversation with Robert Kroetsch', *The New Quarterly* 5.1 (1985), 10.

Chapter 5

1 Amy Tan, *The Hundred Secret Senses* (London, Flamingo, 1995), 19: 'In many respects, Kwan's been more of a mother to me than my real one.'

2 Jaggi, 'Ghosts', 29.

3 See Chapter 1, 6–7.

4 Tan quoted in Jaggi, 'Ghosts', 29.

5 Amy Tan, *The Bonesetter's Daughter* (London, Flamingo, 2001). Hereafter page numbers appear in parentheses in the text.

6 Jaggi, 'Ghosts', 29: '*The Bonesetter's Daughter* … was conceived in response to the diagnos[i]s … of her mother Daisy with Alzheimer's'.

7 Wong, '"Sugar"', 195.

8 Tan quoted in 'The Salon Interview.'

9 Tan quoted in Jaggi, 'Ghosts', 32.

10 Amy Tan quoted in Sue Corrigan, 'It's your Funeral', *Mail on Sunday* (20 May 2001), sec. 'Night&Day', 82. Also see, 'A Question of Fate', in *Opposite*, 41–60, where Tan, referring to the murder of a close friend, describes how she heard this dead man's voice in her everyday life, as well as in 'dream-lessons'. *Opposite* also includes 'Room with a View, New Kitchen, and Ghosts' (235–38), another 'musing' about a ghost who haunted her San Francisco home, although, at the end of this piece, she prefers to remain 'silent' about whether she actually believes in ghosts.

11 Tan quoted in Corrigan, 'Funeral', 82. After describing her mother's death, of how she appeared to communicate with deceased relatives and, later, appeared as a hologram, Tan states: 'Even if that is all delusion, it's still a wonderfully comforting thought'.

12 Amy Tan quoted in 'Amy Tan on Writing *The Hundred Secret Senses*', www.putnam.com [Accessed June 1997].

13 Tan quoted in 'Amy Tan on Writing.'

14 Tan quoted in Giles, 'Ghost Writer.' Also see Chapter 4 of this book, 118.

15 Claudia Kovach Smorada, 'Side-Stepping Death: Ethnic Identity, Contradiction, and the Mother(land) in Amy Tan's Novels', *Fu Jen Studies* 24 (1991), 33. See Chapter 1 of this book for a discussion of the multiculturalist factualization of fiction, 10–11. This approach

to 'multicultural' literature is also discussed in Chapter 3, 92 and Chapter 4, 113.

16 See Chapter 4, 118–19.

17 Yuan Yuan, 'The Semiotics of China Narratives in the Contexts of Kingston and Tan', *Critique* 40.3 (Spring 1999), 299.

18 Esther Mikyung Ghymn, *Images of Asian American Women by Asian American Women Writers* (New York, Peter Lang, 1995), 17.

19 Spivak, 'Post-modern', 25.

20 Wong, '"Sugar"', 195.

21 Harrison, 'Genocide?', 150.

22 Tan, 'Memoir', 110.

23 *'The Bonesetter's Daughter* – An Interview with Amy Tan', www.firewandwater.com [Accessed December 2002].

24 Tan quoted in Jaggi, 'Ghosts', 31.

25 Tan quoted in Jaggi, 'Ghosts', 33. Also see Tan, 'Last Week', 69–97, where Tan, attempting to write her mother's obituary, lists Daisy's names: Li Bingzi (maiden name), Du Lian Zen (adopted name), Du Ching (school name and first married name), Daisy Tan, (second married name), Daisy Tan Chan (third married name), and Daisy C. Tan (the name she used after her third marriage was annulled). 'As to her fourth "marriage,"' Tan continues, 'to T. C. Lee, the dapper eighty-five-year-old gentleman whom our family in Beijing feted when he and our mother "honeymooned" in China, well, the truth was, she and T. C. never really married.'

26 Harry L. Shapiro, *Peking Man* (London, George Allen & Unwin Ltd., 1976), 33: 'Lei Hiao (420–477 AD), for example, recommended dragon bones of five colors as best, and those of black color the least desirable. Those collected by women were described as useless.'

27 See Chapter 2, 45 and Chapter 3, 78, for a fuller discussion of the 'Three Obediences and Four Virtues'.

28 Julia Ching, *Chinese Religions* (London, Macmillan, 1993), 15.

29 Said, *Orientalism*, 120.

30 Fairbank, *Chinese Revolution*, 213.

31 Shapiro, *Peking Man*, 11.

32 Shapiro, *Peking Man*, 11.

33 Judith Okely, 'Anthropology and Autobiography: Participatory

Experience and Embodied Knowledge', in Judith Okely and Helen Callaway (eds.), *Anthropology and Autobiography* (London, Routledge, 1992), 2, 11. Okely is keen to dissociate 'reflexive' from 'mere navel gazing', arguing that '[s]elf-adoration is quite different from self-awareness and critical scrutiny of the self'. Noting changes in anthropology in the late twentieth century, specifically the early 1970s, Okely proposes that the field is becoming increasingly critical about 'political concerns of intrusion and partisanship, questions of national, ethnic origins ... and gender'.

34   Shapiro, *Peking Man*, 49.

35   Shapiro, *Peking Man*, 48.

36   Shapiro, *Peking Man*, 15.

37   Wong, '"Sugar"', 196–7.

38   Shapiro, *Peking Man*, 25–6.

39   Shapiro, *Peking Man*, 11.

40   Tan quoted in Jaggi, 'Ghosts', 33.

41   Pak quoted in Sarna, 'Far Corners', 22.

42   Wong, '"Sugar"', 194.

43   Kingston, *Woman Warrior*, 9.

44   Veronica Wang, 'Reality and Fantasy: The Chinese-American Woman's Quest for Identity', *MELUS* 12.3 (1985), 24.

45   Spivak, 'Can the Subaltern Speak?', 295.

46   See Chapter 2, 65–7.

47   See Chapter 4, 108–10.

48   Wong, '"Sugar"', 194.

49   Jaggi, 'Ghosts', 29.

50   See Chapter 1, 1.

51   Tan quoted in Jaggi, 'Ghosts', 32.

52   Tan quoted in 'The Salon Interview'.

53   Spivak, 'Post-modern', 25.

54   Tan quoted in Jaggi, 'Ghosts', 32.

Chapter 6

1   *The Moon Lady* is adapted from Ying-ying St. Clair's first chapter in *The Joy Luck Club*. For a discussion of student responses to this chapter see Carol Booth Olson and Pat Clark, 'Using Amy Tan's "The Moon Lady" to Teach Analytical Writing in the Multi-cultural Classroom', *Paintbrush* 12 (Autumn 1995). For Olson's and Clark's students – 9th graders at an inner-city school in Santa Ana, California – 'lostness', and how it is brought about, both personally and politically, is central to 'The Moon Lady'. A similar theme preoccupies *The Chinese Siamese Cat*, also available at www.tampines.org [Accessed July 2003], a story about how Siamese cats, which are really Chinese cats, got their dark markings by being used as 'writing brushes' by a despotic Magistrate. The story ends happily, but not before it deals with the cats' complicity in their own and the people's oppression, and, related to this, the power of writing and re-writing.

2   Wong, '"Sugar"', 174.

3   See Suzanne D. Green, 'Thematic Deviance or Poetic License? The Filming of *The Joy Luck Club*', in Barbara Tepa Lupack (ed.), *Vision/Re-Vision: Adapting Contemporary American Fiction by Women to Film* (Bowling Green, Ohio, Bowling Green State University Popular Press, 1996), 222–3: 'The film version of *The Joy Luck Club* does not illustrate the double jeopardy that the women experience, the dual marginalization of being both female and ethnically different than the majority of their American society. ... In her novel, Tan spends a great deal of time dealing subtextually with the problem of femininity that is subject to the expectations of men, in part because of gender and in part because of ethnicity.'

4   Amy Tan quoted in Jaggi, 'Ghosts', 32: The film is 'an emotional sibling to the book; it was never intended to be a twin, a filmic clone'.

5   Ron Bass quoted in Amy Tan, 'Joy Luck and Hollywood', in *Opposite*, 181–2: 'We use a wraparound that allows us to tell the stories through an ensemble, no single lead.'

6   Adam Mars-Jones, 'Scenes from the Grief Brief', *Independent* (11 March 1994), 25.

7   Geoff Brown, 'Welcome to the Great Wail of China', *The Times* (10 March 1994), 35.

8   George K. Y. Tseo, '*Joy Luck*: The Perils of Transcultural "Translation"', *Film Quarterly* 24.4 (1996), 339.

9   Chow, 'Women', 212.

10 Tan, 'Hollywood', 200–1: 'one of the most curious comments I heard during a test-audience focus-group session involved the scenes shot in China. To me, these scenes are stunning – so stunning they strain credulity. A woman in the focus group said, "All the scenes were gorgeous – until we got to China. You should get rid of those matte paintings. You can tell they're fake." I turned to Wayne [Wang] and poked him. "See? We didn't have to suffer in China. We could have used better matte paintings."'

11 See Chapter 2, 66–7 and Chapter 4, 109 for a discussion of Tan's 'mistyfication' of China.

12 Wong, '"Sugar"', 195.

13 See Tan, 'Hollywood', 183: Jeffrey Katzenberg of Disney and its Hollywood Pictures 'gave us what we wanted – creative control – and he expressed enormous respect for Wayne [Wang] as a film-maker. We would be able to make our movie like an independent production, and we'd be supported by Hollywood Pictures'.

14 Tan, 'Hollywood', 201. Emphasis added.

15 Chow, 'Women', 214.

16 Eleanor Ty, 'Exoticism Repositioned: Old and New World Pleasures in Wang's The Joy Luck Club and Lee's Eat Drink Man Woman', in Larry E. Smith and John Rieder (eds.), Changing Representations of Minorities East and West (Hawaii, Hawaii University Press, 1996), 63, 66. Primitive, orange and dark China, as Ty notes, contrasts with modern, blue and light America. This lighting scheme is most obviously utilized in the contrast between the candlelit scenes in 'old' China and the bright, even clinical lighting in the scene at the hair salon. It is worth noting that this opposition is to some extent undone by the subdued lighting in the party scenes at the Woos' Californian house.

17 Sheila Johnston, 'The Tears of Living Dangerously', Independent (11 March 1994), 25.

18 Tseo, 'Joy Luck', 340, 341.

19 Tseo, 'Joy Luck', 340. It is worth pointing out that the 'exceptionality' of Lindo's perception regarding the distance between herself and her mother brought about by the marriage contract is lessened by an explanation similar to that of the novel: 'Because I was promised to the Huangs' son for marriage, my own family began treating me as if I belonged to somebody else. My mother would say to me when the rice bowl went up to my face too many times, "Look how much Huang Taitai's daughter can eat."

My mother did not treat me this way because she didn't love me. She would say this biting back her tongue, so she wouldn't wish for something that was no longer hers' (*JLC*, 51). Moreover, the reference to the servant girl's 'near immaculate conception' is, again following the novel, explained by the conversation Lindo oversees/overhears between the expectant parents.

20   Whether this outward expression is *totally* at odds with Chinese behaviour is questioned by the behaviour of Daisy Tan's first husband, who, as Tan observes, in, for example, 'Pretty Beyond Belief', in *Opposite*, 216, 'openly brought his girlfriends home to humiliate her'.

21   Tseo, 'Joy Luck', 340–2.

22   Tseo, 'Joy Luck', 343.

23   John C. Tibbetts, 'A Delicate Balance: An Interview with Wayne Wang about *The Joy Luck Club*', *Film Quarterly* 2.1 (1994), 4.

24   Tan, 'Hollywood', 190.

25   Tseo, 'Joy Luck', 343.

26   Wang quoted in Tibbetts, 'Delicate', 5: 'One of the saddest scenes … was June's reunion in China with her two older sisters. When we were filming the scene, what was amazing was that during the rehearsal the whole row of extras could hear the dialogue. They were completely in tears. An older woman came up to me later and told me she had to leave her baby during the war and never found it again. She really broke down. There's a lot there that the Chinese can identify with.'

27   Green, 'Deviance', 224.

28   Green, 'Deviance', 216–17.

29   Green, 'Deviance', 214.

30   See Tan, 'Hollywood', 189–92 on '*The Asian Question*'.

31   See Chapter 2, 35–6.

32   Green, 'Deviance', 224.

33   David Henry Hwang quoted in Matt Wolf, 'America makes Pacific Overtures', *The Times* (4 November 1993), 37.

34   Rob Gifford, 'Light on a Bamboo Screen', *Independent* (25 March 1994), 19.

35   Wang quoted in Tibbetts, 'Delicate', 3, 6.

36   Chin, 'Confessions', 60.

37   Chin, 'Confessions', 60.

38   See Rocío Davis, 'An Introduction to Asian American Literature in Europe', *Hitting Critical Mass: A Journal of Asian American Cultural Criticism* 4.1 (Fall 1996).

39   Huntley, *Amy Tan*. Huntley's three novel chapters offer a fairly traditional literary analysis of 'Plot Development', 'Narrative Strategies', 'Narrative Point of View', 'Character Development', 'Setting', 'Literary Devices' and 'Major themes and Issues'.

40   Huntley, *Amy Tan*, 39.

41   Huntley, *Amy Tan*, 39, 75–6.

42   Souris, '"Two Kinds"', and Walter Shear, 'Generational Difference and the Diaspora in *The Joy Luck Club*', *Critique: Studies in Contemporary Fiction* 34.3 (Spring 1993).

43   See John C. Hawley, 'Assimilation and Resistance in Female Fiction of Immigration: Bharati Mukherjee, Amy Tan, and Christine Bell', in Leslie Bary *et al.* (eds.), *Rediscovering America 1492–1992: National, Cultural and Disciplinary Boundaries Re-examined* (Baton Rouge, Louisiana, Louisiana State University Press, 1992).

44   Chow, 'Women', 214–15.

45   Yem Sui Fong, 'Review of *The Joy Luck Club*', *Frontiers* 11.2–3 (1990), 123.

46   Schell, 'Your Mother', 28.

47   Philip Howard et al., 'Review of *The Kitchen God's Wife*', *The Times* (6 June 1992), 41.

48   Natasha Walter, 'Teacher of the Heart', *Guardian* (9 February 1996), 14.

49   Michèle Roberts, 'Sister Act: American Dreams and a Chinese Fairy Godmother', *Independent* (10 February 1996), 10.

50   Joan Smith, 'China Girls', *Guardian* (10 February 2001), 44.

51   See Tan, 'CliffsNotes', 7: 'I remember being asked by a young woman what I did for a living. "I'm an author," I said with proud new authority." "A contemporary author?" she wanted to know. And being newly published at the time, I had to think for a moment before I realized that if I were not contemporary I would be the alternative, which is, of course, dead. Since then I have preferred to call myself a writer. A writer writes – she writes in the present progressive tense. Whereas an author, unless she is clearly said to be "contemporary," is in the past tense. ... To me, the word *author* is chilling as rigor mortis, and I shudder when I hear

myself introduced as such when I lecture at universities. This is probably due to the fact that when I was an English major at a university all the authors I read were, sad to say, not contemporary.'

52   Cheng, 'Fantasizing', 96.

53   Cheng, 'Fantasizing', 119. Emphasis in original.

54   Wong, '"Sugar"', 185, 187, 191.

55   Tan quoted in Stanton, 'Breakfast', 10.

56   Wong, '"Sugar"', 200.

57   See Huggan, 'Margaret Atwood, Inc., or, Some Thoughts on Literary Celebrity', in *Post-colonial Exotic*, 209–27. At the beginning of this chapter, Huggan discusses 'a rather different form of the exotic – celebrity glamour. But celebrity glamour, as I shall argue, shares several features with other, better known variants of exoticist discourse, among them the creation of a commodified mystique that veils the material conditions that produce it'.

58   Tan quoted in 'The Salon Interview'.

59   Tan, 'A Note', 2.

60   Tan quoted in Stanton, 'Breakfast', 11.

61   Tan, 'Required Reading', 309.

62   Tan, 'Required Reading', 321.

63   Tan, 'To Complain is American', in *Opposite*, 365.

64   Tan, 'Required Reading', 322.

65   Wong, '"Sugar"', 194.

66   Li, 'Genes', 116.

67   Wong, '"Sugar"', 202: 'Asian American critics are busily engaged in defining a canon dissociated as much as possible from Orientalist concerns, through teaching, practical criticism, and other professional activities if not conscious, explicit theorizing. Although there is obviously no end point in the canon-formation process, there are already signs that the "Asian American" canon, the one arising from contestations within the community, differs considerably from the one shaped by the publishing industry and the critical establishment.' The latter canon, and Tan's un/witting participation in it, is presumably for Wong not disassociated from Orientalist concerns.

68   Li, 'Genes', 117.

69   Cheng, 'Fantasizing', 120–1n.

70   Wong, '"Sugar"', 203.

71   Spivak, 'Post-modern', 25.

72   Chow, 'Women', 205, 213.

73   Chow, 'Women', 218. Hence she reads *The Joy Luck Club* alongside *Jurassic Park*.

74   See Sheng-mei Ma, 'Immigrant Schizophrenic in Asian Diaspora Literature', in *Immigrant Subjectivities in Asian American and Diaspora Literatures* (New York, SUNY, 1998).

75   See Qun Wang, 'Double Consciousness and the Asian American Experience', *Race, Gender, and Class* 4.3 (1997).

76   Ling, *Between Worlds*.

77   Huntley, *Amy Tan*, 33, 73.

78   Huntley, *Amy Tan*, 54, 86, 128.

79   Tan quoted in Stanton, 'Breakfast', 12.

80   Tan quoted in Stanton, 'Breakfast', 7–8.

81   Chow, 'Women', 218.

Select bibliography

Works by Amy Tan

FICTION

The Joy Luck Club (London, Minerva, 1989).
The Kitchen God's Wife (London, Flamingo, 1991).
The Hundred Secret Senses (London, Flamingo, 1995).
The Bonesetter's Daughter (London, Flamingo, 2001).

CHILDREN'S FICTION

The Moon Lady (Aladdin, Hong Kong, 1992).
The Chinese Siamese Cat (Aladdin, Hong Kong, 1994).

FILM

The Joy Luck Club (1993; co-written by Amy Tan and Ronald Bass, and directed by Wayne Wang).

NON-FICTION

The Opposite of Fate (London, Flamingo, 2003), which includes 'The CliffsNotes Version of My Life' (7–38), 'Joy Luck and Hollywood' (176–204), 'My Love Affair with Vladimir Nabokov' (221–7), 'Mother Tongue' (271–9), 'The Language of Discretion' (280–90) and 'Required Reading and Other Dangerous Subjects' (299–323).

Criticism on Tan

BOOK

Huntley, E. D., *Amy Tan: A Critical Companion* (Westport, Connecticut, Greenwood Press, 1998).

JOURNALS

The World of Amy Tan, in Ben Bennani (ed.), *Paintbrush: A Journal of Multicultural Literature* 12 (Autumn 1995).

Amy Tan, Hitting Critical Mass: A Journal of Asian American Cultural Criticism 4.1 (Fall 1996).

WEBSITES AND OTHER ONLINE RESOURCES (Available March 2004)

'Academy of Achievement: Amy Tan':
   www.achievement.org/autodoc/page/tanobio-1

'Amy Tan':
   www.webenglishteacher.com/tan.html

'Amy Tan', '*The Joy Luck Club*', '*The Kitchen God's Wife*', '*The Hundred Secret Senses*', '*The Bonesetter's Daughter*' and '*The Opposite of Fate*':
   www.LitEncyc.com

'An Interview with Amy Tan':
   www.fireandwater.com/Authors/Interview.asp?interviewid=210

'Anniina's Amy Tan Page':
   www.luminarium.org/contemporary/amytan/

'Crystal's Amy Tan Page':
   http://members.tripod.com/%7ERoella/AmyTan/

Giles, Gretchen, 'Ghost Writer':
   www.metroactive.com/papers/sonoma/12.14.95/tan-9550.html

'The Salon Interview: The Spirit Within':
   www.salon.com/12nov1995/feature/tan.html

'Study Guide on *The Joy Luck Club*':
   www.metromagazine.com.au/metro/studyguides/files/
   The_Joy_Luck_Club.pdf

'Voices from the Gaps, Women Writers of Color: Amy Tan':
    http://voices.cla.umn.edu/newsite/authors/TANamy.htm
'Wired for Books: Audio Interview with Amy Tan':
    http://wiredforbooks.org/amytan/

ARTICLES, ESSAYS AND INTERVIEWS

Boldt, Chris, 'Why is the Moon Lady in Amy Tan's *The Joy Luck Club*
    Revealed to be a Man?' *Notes on Contemporary Literature* 24.4
    (September 1994), 9–10.

Braendlin, Bonnie, 'Mother/Daughter Dialog(ic)s in, around and about
    Amy Tan's *The Joy Luck Club*', in Nancy Owen Nelson (ed.),
    Private Voice, Public Lives: Women Speak on the Literary Life
    (Denton, Texas, North Texas University Press, 1995), 111–23.

Caesar, Judith, 'Patriarchy, Imperialism, and Knowledge in *The Kitchen
    God's Wife*', *North Dakota Quarterly* 62.4 (1994–95), 164–74.

Chan, Mimi, '"Listen, Mom, I'm a Banana": Mother and Daughter in
    Maxine Hong Kingston's *The Woman Warrior* and Amy Tan's *The
    Joy Luck Club*', in Mimi Chan and Roy Harris (eds.), *Asian Voices
    in English* (Hong Kong, Hong Kong University Press, 1991), 65–78.

Chen, Victoria, 'Chinese American Women, Language and Moving
    Subjectivity', *Women and Language* 18.1 (1995), 3–7.

Cheng, Sinkwan, 'Fantasizing the *Jouissance* of the Chinese Mother:
    The Joy Luck Club and Amy Tan's Quest for Stardom in the
    Market of Neo-Racism', *Savoir: Psychanalyse Et Analyse
    Culturelle* 3.1–2 (February 1997), 95–133.

Chow, Rey, 'Women in the Holocene: Ethnicity, Fantasy, and the Film *The
    Joy Luck Club*', in Carmen Luke (ed.), *Feminism and the Pedago-
    gies of Everyday Life* (New York, SUNY Press, 1995), 204–21.

Conceison, Claire A., 'Translating Collaboration: *The Joy Luck Club* and
    Intercultural Theatre', *The Drama Review* 39.3 (Fall 1995), 151–66.

Corrigan, Sue, 'It's your Funeral', *Mail on Sunday* (20 May 2001), 82.

Davis, Rocío G., 'Identity in Community in Ethnic Short Story Cycles:
    Amy Tan's *The Joy Luck Club*, Louise Erdrich's *Love Medicine*,
    Gloria Naylor's *The Women of Brewster Place*', in Julie Brown
    (ed.), *Ethnicity and the American Short Story* (New York,
    Garland Publishing, 1997), 3–23.

Davis, Rocío G., 'Wisdom (Un)heeded: Chinese Mothers and American
    Daughters in Amy Tan's *The Joy Luck Club*', *Cuadernos de*

Investigacion Filologica 19–20 (1993–94), 89–100.

Delicka, Magdalena, 'American Magic Realism: Crossing the Borders in Literatures of the Margins', *Journal of American Studies of Turkey* 6 (1997), 25–33.

Delucchi, Michael, 'Self and Identity Among Aging Immigrants in *The Joy Luck Club*', *Journal of Aging and Identity* 3.2 (1998), 59–66.

Dew, Robb Forman, 'Pangs of an Abandoned Child', *New York Times Book Review* (16 June 1991), 9.

Gately, Patricia, 'Ten Thousand Different Ways: Inventing Mothers, Inventing Hope', *Paintbrush: A Journal of Multicultural Literature* 12 (Autumn 1995), 51–5.

Green, Suzanne D., 'Thematic Deviance or Poetic License? The Filming of *The Joy Luck Club*', in Barbara Tepa LUniversity Pressack (ed.), *Vision/Re-Vision: Adapting Contemporary American Fiction by Women to Film* (Bowling Green, Ohio, Bowling Green State University Popular Press, 1996), 211–25.

Hamilton, Patricia L., '*Feng Shui*, Astrology and the Five Elements: Traditional Chinese Belief in Amy Tan's *The Joy Luck Club*', *MELUS* 24.2 (Summer 1999), 125–45.

Harrison, Patricia Marby, 'Genocide or Redemption? Asian American Autobiography and the Portrayal of Christianity in Amy Tan's *The Joy Luck Club* and Joy Kogawa's *Obasan*', *Christianity and Literature* 46.2 (Winter 1997), 145–68.

Hawley, John C., 'Assimilation and Resistance in Female Fiction of Immigration: Bharati Mukherjee, Amy Tan, and Christine Bell', in Leslie Bary, Janet Gold, Marketta Laurila, Anrulfo Ramírez, Joseph Ricapito and Jesús Torrecilla (eds.), *Rediscovering America 1492–1992: National, Cultural and Disciplinary Boundaries Re-examined* (Baton Rouge, Louisiana, Louisiana State University Press, 1992), 226–34.

Heung, Marina, 'Daughter-Text/Mother-Text: Matrilineage in Amy Tan's *Joy Luck Club*', *Feminist Studies* 19.3 (1993), 597–616.

Ho, Wendy, 'Swan-Feather Mothers and Coca-Cola Daughters: Teaching Amy Tan's *The Joy Luck Club*', in John R. Maitino and David R. Peck (eds.), *Teaching American Ethnic Literatures: Nineteen Essays* (Albuquerque, New Mexico University Press, 1996), 327–45.

Holt, Patricia, 'Between the Lines: Students Read a Lot into Amy Tan', *San Francisco Chronicle* (18 August 1996), 2.

Jaggi, Maya, 'Ghosts at my Shoulder', *Guardian Weekend* (3 March 2001), 29–33.

Jaggi, Maya, 'Of Mothers and Daughters', *Guardian* (10 July 1991), 19.

Kafka, Phillipa, 'Amy Tan, *The Kitchen God's Wife*: Chasing Away a Big Stink', *(Un)Doing the Missionary Position: Gender Asymmetry in Contemporary Asian American Women's Writing* (Westport, Connecticut, Greenwood Press, 1997), 17–50.

Kepner, Susan, 'The Amazing Adventures of Amy Tan', *San Francisco Focus* 36.5 (May 1989), 58–60, 160–2.

Lee, Hermione, 'Scattered Fragments of a Broken China', *Independent on Sunday* (14 July 1991), 26.

Li, David Leiwei, 'Genes, Generation, and Geospiritual (Be)longings', in *Imagining the Nation: Asian American Literature and Cultural Consent* (Stanford, Stanford University Press, 1998), 111–25.

Lowe, Lisa 'Heterogeneity, Hybridity, Multiplicity: Marking Asian American Differences', *Diaspora* 1.1 (Spring 1991), 24–44.

McAlister, Melanie, '(Mis)Reading *The Joy Luck Club*', *Asian America: Journal of Culture and the Arts* 1 (1992), 102–18.

Olson, Carol Booth and Pat Clark, 'Using Amy Tan's "The Moon Lady" to Teach Analytical Writing in the Multicultural Classroom', *Paintbrush: A Journal of Multicultural Literature* 12 (Autumn 1995), 85–99.

Rothstein, Mervyn, 'A New Novel by Amy Tan', *New York Times* (13 June 1991), C13, C18.

Schell, Orville, 'Your Mother is in Your Bones: *The Joy Luck Club*', *New York Times Book Review* (19 March 1989), 3, 28.

Schueller, Malini Johar, 'Theorizing Ethnicity and Subjectivity: Maxine Hong Kingston's *Tripmaster Monkey* and Amy Tan's *The Joy Luck Club*', *GENDERS* 15 (Winter 1992), 72–85.

Shear, Walter, 'Generational Difference and the Diaspora in *The Joy Luck Club*', *Critique: Studies in Contemporary Fiction* 34.3 (Spring 1993), 193–9.

Shen, Gloria, 'Born of a Stranger: Mother–Daughter Relationships and Storytelling in Amy Tan's *The Joy Luck Club*', in Anne E. Browne and Marjanne E. Goozé (eds.), *International Women's Writing: New Landscapes of Identity* (Westport, Connecticut, Greenwood Press, 1995), 233–44.

Smorada, Claudia Kovach, 'Side-Stepping Death: Ethnic Identity, Contradiction, and the Mother(land) in Amy Tan's Novels', *Fu Jen Studies* 24 (1991), 31–45.

SondrUniversity Press, Steven P., 'Hanyu at the Joy Luck Club', in

Mabel Lee and Hua Meng (eds.), *Cultural Dialogue and Misreading* (Sydney, Australia, Wild Peony, 1997), 400–8.

Souris, Stephen, '"Only Two Kinds of Daughters": Inter-Monologue Dialogicity in *The Joy Luck Club*', *MELUS* 19.2 (Summer 1994), 99–123.

Stanton, David, 'Breakfast with Amy Tan,' *Paintbrush: A Journal of Multicultural Literature* 12 (Autumn 1995), 5–19.

Streitfield, David, 'The "Luck" of Amy Tan', *Washington Post* (8 October 1989), F8–9.

Taylor, Annie 'The Difference a Day Made', *Guardian* (8 February 1996), 15.

Tibbetts, John C., 'A Delicate Balance: An Interview with Wayne Wang about *The Joy Luck Club*', *Film Quarterly* 2.1 (1994), 2–6.

Tseo, George K. Y., '*Joy Luck*: The Perils of Transcultural "Translation"', *Film Quarterly* 24.4 (1996), 338–43.

Ty, Eleanor, 'Exoticism Repositioned: Old and New World Pleasures in Wang's *The Joy Luck Club* and Lee's *Eat Drink Man Woman*', in Larry E. Smith and John Rieder (eds.), *Changing Representations of Minorities East and West* (Hawaii, Hawaii University Press, 1996), 59–74.

Wang, Dorothy, '*The Joy Luck Club*', *Newsweek* (17 April 1989), 68–9.

Wilcoxon, Hardy C., 'No Types of Ambiguity: Teaching Chinese American Texts in Hong Kong', in Julie Brown (ed.) *Ethnicity and the American Short Story* (New York, Garland Publishing, 1997), 141–54.

Wong, Sau-ling Cynthia, '"Sugar Sisterhood": The Amy Tan Phenomenon', in David Palumbo-Liu (ed.), *The Ethnic Canon: Histories, Institutions, and Interventions* (Minneapolis, Minnesota University Press, 1995), 174–210.

Xu, Ben, 'Memory and the Ethnic Self: Reading Amy Tan's *The Joy Luck Club*', in Amritjit Singh, Joseph T. Skerrett, Jr., Robert E. Hogan (eds.), *Memory, Narrative, and Identity: New Essays in Ethnic American Literatures* (Boston, Northeastern University Press, 1994), 261–77.

Xu, Wenying, 'A Womanist Production of Truths: The Use of Myths in Amy Tan', *Paintbrush: A Journal of Multicultural Literature* 12 (Autumn 1995), 56–66.

Yin, Xiao-huang, 'Multiple Voices and the "War of Words": Contemporary Chinese American Literature', *Chinese American Literature since the 1850s* (Urbana and Chicago, Illinois University Press, 2000), 231–53.

Young, Mary E., 'Sui Sin Far to Amy Tan', *Mules and Dragons: Popular Culture Images in the Selected Writings of African-American and Chinese-American Women Writers* (Westport, Connecticut, Greenwood Press, 1993), 109–31.

Yuan, Yuan, 'The Semiotics of China Narratives in the Contexts of Kingston and Tan', *Critique* 40.3 (Spring 1999), 292–303.

General works

Ahmad, Aijaz, *In Theory: Classes, Nations, Literature* (London, Verso, 1992).

Ancheta, Angelo N., *Race, Rights, and the Asian American Experience* (New Brunswick, New Jersey, Rutgers University Press, 1998).

Anderson, Benedict, *Imagined Communities: Reflections on the Origin and Spread of Nationalism* (London, Verso, 1983).

Barthes, Roland, *Mythologies*, trans. Annette Lavers (London, Vintage, 2000).

Barthes, Roland, *The Rustle of Language*, trans. Richard Howard (New York, Hill and Wang, 1986).

Bakhtin, M. M., *The Dialogic Imagination: Four Essays*, trans. Caryl Emerson and Michael Holquist (Austin, Texas University Press, 1981).

Bakhtin, M. M., *Rabelais and His World*, trans. Hélène Iswolsky (Bloomington, Indiana University Press, 1984).

Belsey, Catherine, *Critical Practice*, (London, Routledge, 1980).

Benjamin, Walter, *Illuminations*, ed. Hannah Arendt and trans. Harry Zohn (London: Fontana Press, 1973).

Bhabha, Homi (ed.), *Nation and Narration*, (London, Routledge, 1990).

Birch, Cyril and Donald Keene (eds.), *Anthology of Chinese Literature* (London, Penguin, 1965).

Bloom, Harold (ed.), *Asian-American Women Writers* (Philadelphia, Chelsea House Publishers, 1997).

Brown, Anne E. and Marjanne E. Goozé (eds.), *International Women's Writing: New Landscapes of Identity* (Westport, Connecticut, Greenwood Press, 1995).

Chan, Jeffery Paul, Frank Chin, Lawson Fusao Inada, and Shawn Wong (eds.), *The Big Aiiieeeee! An Anthology of Chinese American and Japanese American Literature* (New York, Meridian, 1991).

Chan, Sucheng, 'Asian Americans: Resisting Oppression, 1860s–

1920s', in Sucheng Chan, Douglas Henry Daniels, Mario T. García and Terry P. Wilson (eds.), *Peoples of Color in the American West* (Lexington, Massachusetts & Toronto, D. C. Heath Company, 1994), 367–76.

Chan, Sulia, 'CAMJ Intended to Set the Historical Record Straight', *Chinese American Forum* 3.4 (4 March 1988), 20–1.

Chang, Iris, *The Rape of Nanking: The Forgotten Holocaust of World War II* (New York, BasicBooks, 1997).

Cheung, King-kok (ed.), *An Interethnic Companion to Asian American Literature* (Cambridge, Cambridge University Press, 1997).

Cheung, King-Kok, 'The Woman Warrior versus The Chinaman Pacific: Must a Chinese American Critic Choose between Feminism and Heroism?', in Marianne Hirsch and Evelyn Fox Keller (eds.), *Conflicts in Feminism* (New York, Routledge, 1990), 234–51.

Chin, Frank, 'Come All Ye Asian American Writers of the Real and the Fake', in Jeffery Paul Chan, Frank Chin, Lawson Fusao Inada, and Shawn Wong (eds.), *The Big Aiiieeeee! An Anthology of Chinese American and Japanese American Literature* (New York, Meridian, 1991), 1–92.

Chin, Frank, 'Confessions of the Chinatown Cowboy', *Bulletin of Concerned Asian Scholars* 4.3 (1972), 58–70.

Chin, Frank, 'This is Not an Autobiography', *Genre* 18 (Summer 1985), 109–30.

Ching, Julia, *Chinese Religions* (London, Macmillan, 1993).

Chow, Esther Ngan-Ling, 'The Feminist Movement: Where are All the Asian American Women?', in Alison M. Jaggar and Paula S. Rothenberg (eds.), *Feminist Frameworks: Alternative Theoretical Accounts of the Relations between women and Men* (New York, McGraw-Hill, Inc., 1993), 212–19.

Chow, Rey, 'Violence in the Other Country: China as Crisis, Spectacle, and Woman', in Chandra Talpade Mohanty, Ann Russo and Lourdes Torres (eds.), *Third World Women and the Politics of Feminism* (Bloomington, Indiana University Press, 1991), 81–100.

Chow, Rey, 'Women in the Holocene: Ethnicity, Fantasy, and the Film *The Joy Luck Club*', in Carmen Luke (ed.), *Feminism and the Pedagogies of Everyday Life* (New York, SUNY Press, 1995), 204–21.

Chow, Rey, *Writing Diaspora: Tactics of Intervention in Contemporary Cultural Studies* (Bloomington, Indiana University Press, 1993).

Cooperman, Jeanette Batz, *The Broom Closet: Secret Meanings of Domesticity in Postfeminist Novels by Louise Erdrich, Mary*

Gordon, Toni Morrison, Marge Piercy, Jane Smiley and Amy Tan (New York, Peter Lang, 1999).

Davis, Rocío G., 'An Introduction to Asian American Literature in Europe', *Hitting Critical Mass: A Journal of Asian American Cultural Criticism* 4.1 (Fall 1996).

De Man, Paul, *Allegories of Reading: Figural Language in Rousseau, Nietzsche, Rilke, and Proust* (New Haven, Yale University Press, 1979).

De Man, Paul, *The Resistance to Theory* (Minneapolis, Minnesota University Press, 1986).

Eichenbaum, Boris, 'Introduction to the Formal Method', trans. I. R. Titunk, in Michael Rivkin and Julie Ryan (eds.), *Literary Theory: An Anthology* (Oxford, Blackwell, 1998), 8–16.

Eng, David L. and Alice Y. Hom (eds.), *Q & A: Queer in Asian America* (Philadelphia, Temple University Press, 1998).

Fairbank, John King, *The Great Chinese Revolution 1800–1985* (London, Pan, 1986).

Gerrard, Nicci and Sean French, 'Sexual Reading', *Observer Review* (27 September 1998).

Ghymn, Esther Mikyung, *Images of Asian American Women by Asian American Women Writers* (New York, Peter Lang, 1995).

Grice, Helena, Candida Hepworth, Maria Lauret and Martin Padget, *Beginning Ethnic American Literatures* (Manchester, Manchester University Press, 2001).

Guha, Ranajit (ed.), *A Subaltern Studies Reader 1986–1995* (Minneapolis, Minnesota University Press, 1997).

Hoppenstand, Gary 'Yellow Devil Doctors and Opium Dens: The Yellow Peril Stereotype in Mass Media Entertainment', in Jack Nachbar and Kevin Lause (eds.), *Popular Culture: An Introductory Text* (Bowling Green, Ohio, Popular, 1992), 277–91.

Huggan, Graham, *The Postcolonial Exotic: Marketing the Margins* (London, Routledge, 2001).

Hune, Shirley, Hyung-chan Kim, Stephen S. Fugita and Amy Ling (eds.), *Asian Americans: Comparative and Global Perspectives* (Pullman, Washington State University Press, 1991).

Jameson, Frederic, 'On Magic Realism in Film', *Critical Inquiry* 12.2 (Winter 1986), 301–25.

Kafka, Phillipa, *(Un)Doing the Missionary Position: Gender Asymmetry in Contemporary Asian American Women's Writing* (Westport, Connecticut, Greenwood Press, 1997).

Kim, Daniel Y., 'The Strange Love of Frank Chin', in David L. Eng and Alice Y. Hom (eds.), *Q & A: Queer in Asian America* (Philadelphia, Temple University Press, 1998), 270–303.

Kim, Elaine H., *Asian American Writers: An Introduction to the Writings and their Social Contexts* (Philadelphia, Texas University Press, 1982).

Kim, Elaine H., 'Defining Asian American Realities through Literature', *Cultural Critique* 6 (Spring 1987), 87–111.

Kim, Elaine H., '"Such Opposite Creatures": Men and Women in Asian American Literature', *Michigan Quarterly Review* 29 (1990), 68–93.

Kingston, Maxine Hong, 'Cultural Mis-readings by American Reviewers', in Guy Armirthanayagam (ed.), *Asian and Western Writers in Dialogue* (London, Macmillan, 1982), 55–65.

Landry, Donna and Gerald MacLean (eds.), *The Spivak Reader* (New York, Routledge, 1996).

Lee, Rachel C., *The Americans of Asian American Literature: Gendered Fictions of Nation and Transnation* (Princeton, New Jersey, Princeton University Press, 1999).

Li, David Leiwei, *Imagining the Nation: Asian American Literature and Cultural Consent* (Stanford, Stanford University Press, 1998).

Li, David Leiwei, 'The Naming of a Chinese American "I": Cross-Cultural Sign/ifications in *The Woman Warrior*', in *Criticism* 30.4 (Fall 1988), 497–515.

Lim, Shirley Geok-lin, 'Feminist and Ethnic Literary Theories in Asian American Literature', *Feminist Studies* 19.3 (Fall 1993), 571–95.

Lim, Shirley Geok-lin, 'Semiotics, Experience, and the Material Self: An Inquiry into the Subject of the Contemporary Asian Woman Writer', in Sidonie Smith and Julia Watson (eds.), *Women, Autobiography, Theory: A Reader* (Madison, Wisconsin, Wisconsin University Press, 1998), 441–52.

Lim, Shirley Geok-lin, 'Twelve Asian American Writers: In Search of Self-Definition', *MELUS* 13.1–2 (Spring–Summer 1986), 57–77.

Lim, Shirley Geok-lin and Amy Ling (eds.), *Reading the Literatures of Asian America* (Philadelphia, Temple University Press, 1992).

Ling, Amy, *Between Worlds: Women Writers of Chinese Ancestry* (New York, Pergamon Press, 1990).

Ling, Jinqi, *Narrating Nationalisms: Ideology and Form in Asian American Literature* (Oxford, Oxford University Press, 1998).

Liu, Tao Tao, 'Chinese Myths and Legends', in Carolyne Larrington (ed.), *The Feminist Companion to Mythology* (London, Pandora,

1992), 227–47.

Lowe, Lisa, *Critical Terrains: French and British Orientalisms* (Ithaca, Cornell University Press, 1991).

Lyotard, Jean-François, *The Postmodern Condition: A Report on Knowledge*, trans. Geoff Bennington and Brian Massumi (Manchester, Manchester University Press, 1984).

Ma, Sheng-mei, *Immigrant Subjectivities in Asian American and Diaspora Literatures* (New York, SUNY, 1998).

Mazumdar, Sucheta, 'Through Western Eyes: Discovering Chinese Women in America', in Clyde A. Milner II (ed.), *A New Significance: Re-envisioning the History of the American West* (Oxford, Oxford University Press, 1996), 158–68.

Miller, Stuart Creighton, *The Unwelcome Immigrant: The American Image of the Chinese, 1785–1882* (Berkeley, California University Press, 1969).

Mongia, Padmini (ed.), *Contemporary Postcolonial Theory: A Reader* (London, Arnold, 1996).

Okely, Judith and Helen Callaway (eds.), *Anthropology and Autobiography* (London, Routledge, 1992).

Said, Edward W., *Orientalism: Western Conceptions of the Orient* (London, Penguin, 1995).

Shapiro, Harry L., *Peking Man* (London, George Allen & Unwin Ltd., 1976).

Slemon, Stephen, 'Magic Realism as Post-Colonial Discourse', *Canadian Literature* 116 (1988), 9–24.

Spivak, Gayatri Chakravorty, 'Can the Subaltern Speak?', in Cary Nelson and Lawrence Grossberg (eds.), *Marxism and the Interpretation of Culture* (London, Macmillan, 1988), 271–313.

Spivak, Gayatri Chakravorty, *In Other Worlds: Essays in Cultural Politics* (London, Routledge, 1987).

Spivak, Gayatri Chakravorty, *Outside in the Teaching Machine* (London, Routledge, 1993).

Spivak, Gayatri Chakravorty and Sarah Harasym (ed.), *The Postcolonial Critic: Interviews, Strategies, Dialogues* (New York, Routledge, 1990).

Spivak, Gayatri Chakravorty, 'Poststructuralism, Marginality, Postcoloniality and Value', in Padmini Mongia (ed.), *Contemporary Postcolonial Theory: A Reader* (London, Arnold, 1996), 198–222.

TuSmith, Bonnie, *All My Relatives: Community in Contemporary Ethnic American Literatures* (Ann Arbor, Michigan University Press, 1993).

Wang, Qun, 'Asian American Short Stories: Dialogizing the Asian American Experience', in Julie Brown (ed.) *Ethnicity and the American Short Story* (New York, Garland Publishing, 1997), 115–23.

Wang, Qun, 'Double Consciousness and the Asian American Experience', *Race, Gender, and Class* 4.3 (1997), 88–94.

Wang, Veronica, 'Reality and Fantasy: The Chinese-American Woman's Quest for Identity', *MELUS* 12.3 (1985), 23–31.

Werner, E. T. C., *Myths and Legends of China* (London, Sinclair Browne Ltd., 1922).

Wong, Sau-Ling Cynthia, *Reading Asian American Literature: From Necessity to Extravagance* (Princeton, New Jersey, Princeton University Press, 1993).

Yamada, Mitsuye, 'Asian Pacific American Women and Feminism', in Cherríe Moraga and Gloria Anzaldúa (eds.), *This Bridge Called my Back: Writings by Radical Women of Color* (New York, Kitchen Table: Women of Color Press, 1981), 71–5.

Yamada, Mitsuye, 'Invisibility is an Unnatural Disaster: Reflections of an Asian American Woman', in Cherríe Moraga and Gloria Anzaldúa (eds.), *This Bridge Called my Back: Writings by Radical Women of Color* (New York, Kitchen Table: Women of Color Press, 1981), 35–40.

Yanagisako, Sylvia, 'Transforming Orientalism: Gender, Nationality, and Class in Asian American Studies', in Sylvia Yanagisako and Carol Delaney (eds.), *Naturalizing Power: Essays in Feminist Cultural Analysis* (New York, Routledge, 1995), 275–98.

Yin, Xiao-huang, *Chinese American Literature since the 1850s* (Urbana and Chicago, Illinois University Press, 2000).

Young, Mary E., *Mules and Dragons: Popular Culture Images in the Selected Writings of African-American and Chinese-American Women Writers* (Westport, Connecticut, Greenwood Press, 1993).

Yung, Judy, 'Unbinding the Feet, Unbinding their Lives: Chinese Immigrant Women in San Francisco, 1902–1931', in Shirley Hune, Hyung-chan Kim, Stephen S. Fugita and Amy Ling (eds.), *Asian Americans: Comparative and Global Perspectives* (Pullman, Washington State University Press, 1991), 68–85.

Zhou, Min and James V. Gatewood (eds.), *Contemporary Asian America: A Multidisciplinary Reader* (New York, New York University Press, 2000).

Žižek, Slavoj, 'Multiculturalism, Or, the Cultural Logic of Multinational Capitalism', *New Left Review* 225 (1997), 28–51.

Index

Note: 'n' after a page reference indicates the number of a note (or notes) on that page.